❝ Not a piece of architecture, as other buildings are, but the proud passions of an emperor's love wrought in living stones. **❞**

— Sir Edwin Arnold, English poet

D1542413

TAJ MAHAL
AN INCREDIBLE LOVE STORY

Author:	Rik Hoskin
Artist:	Aadil Khan
Colorist:	Ashwani Kashyap
Editors:	Shabari Choudhury and Sourav Dutta
Designer:	Vijay Sharma
Cover Artists:	Aadil Khan and Pradeep Sherawat

CAMPFIRE®

www.campfire.co.in

Mission Statement

To entertain and educate young minds by creating unique illustrated books
that recount stories of human values, arouse curiosity in the world around us,
and inspire with tales of great deeds of unforgettable people.

Published by Kalyani Navyug Media Pvt Ltd
101 C, Shiv House, Hari Nagar Ashram,
New Delhi 110014, India

ISBN: 978-93-81182-59-8

Printed in India

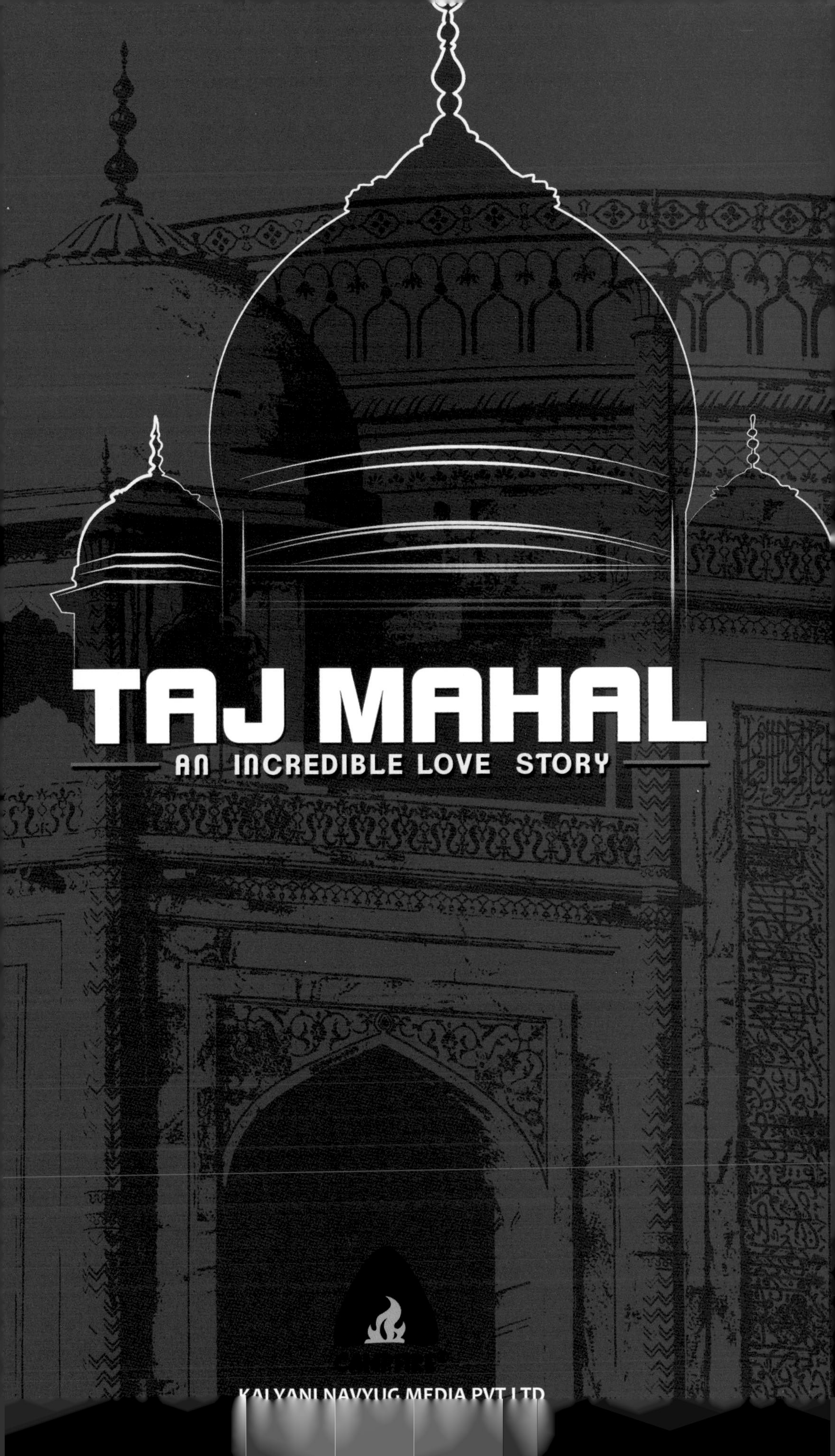

TAJ MAHAL

AN INCREDIBLE LOVE STORY

KALYANI NAVYUG MEDIA PVT LTD

Chapter 1 A Love Across Time

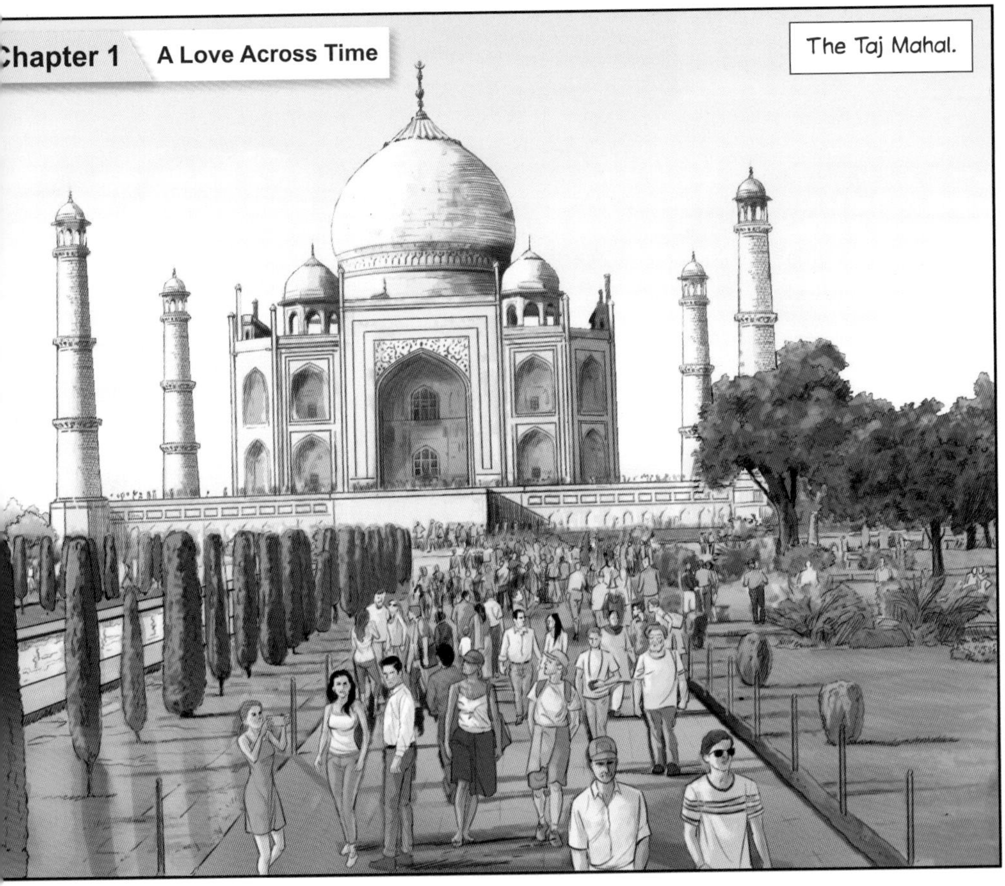
The Taj Mahal.

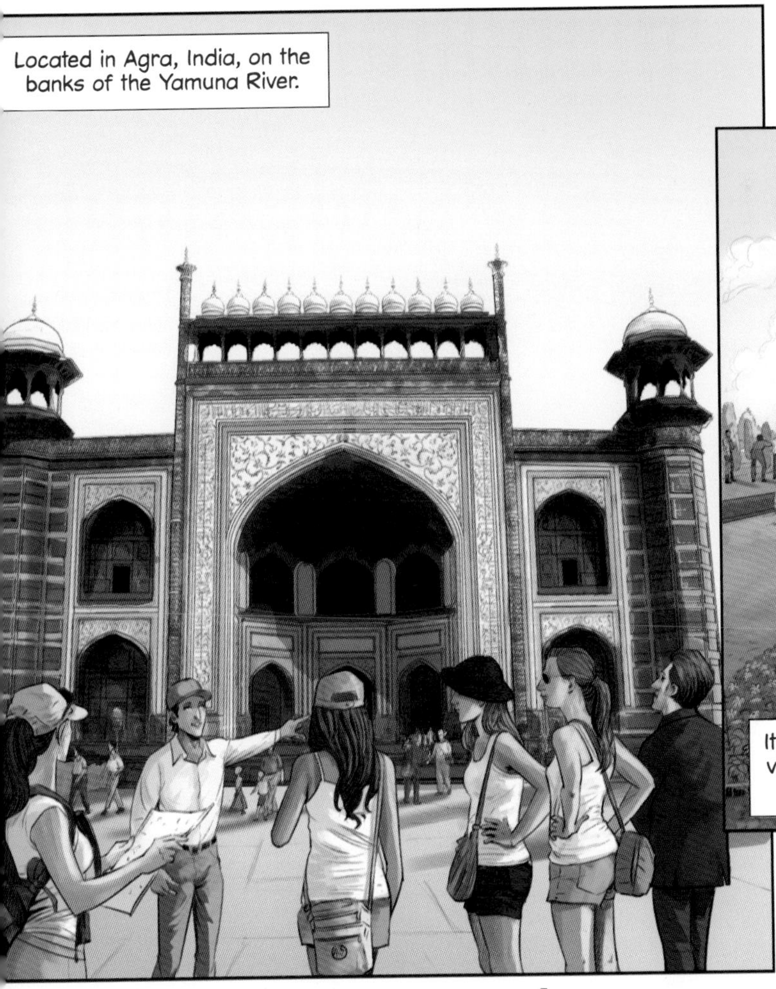
Located in Agra, India, on the banks of the Yamuna River.

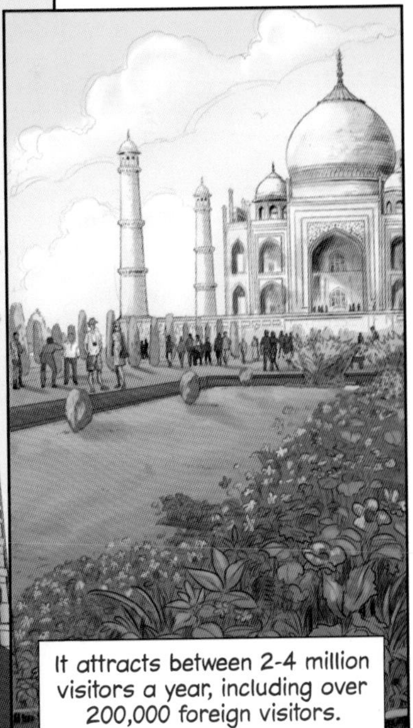
It attracts between 2-4 million visitors a year, including over 200,000 foreign visitors.

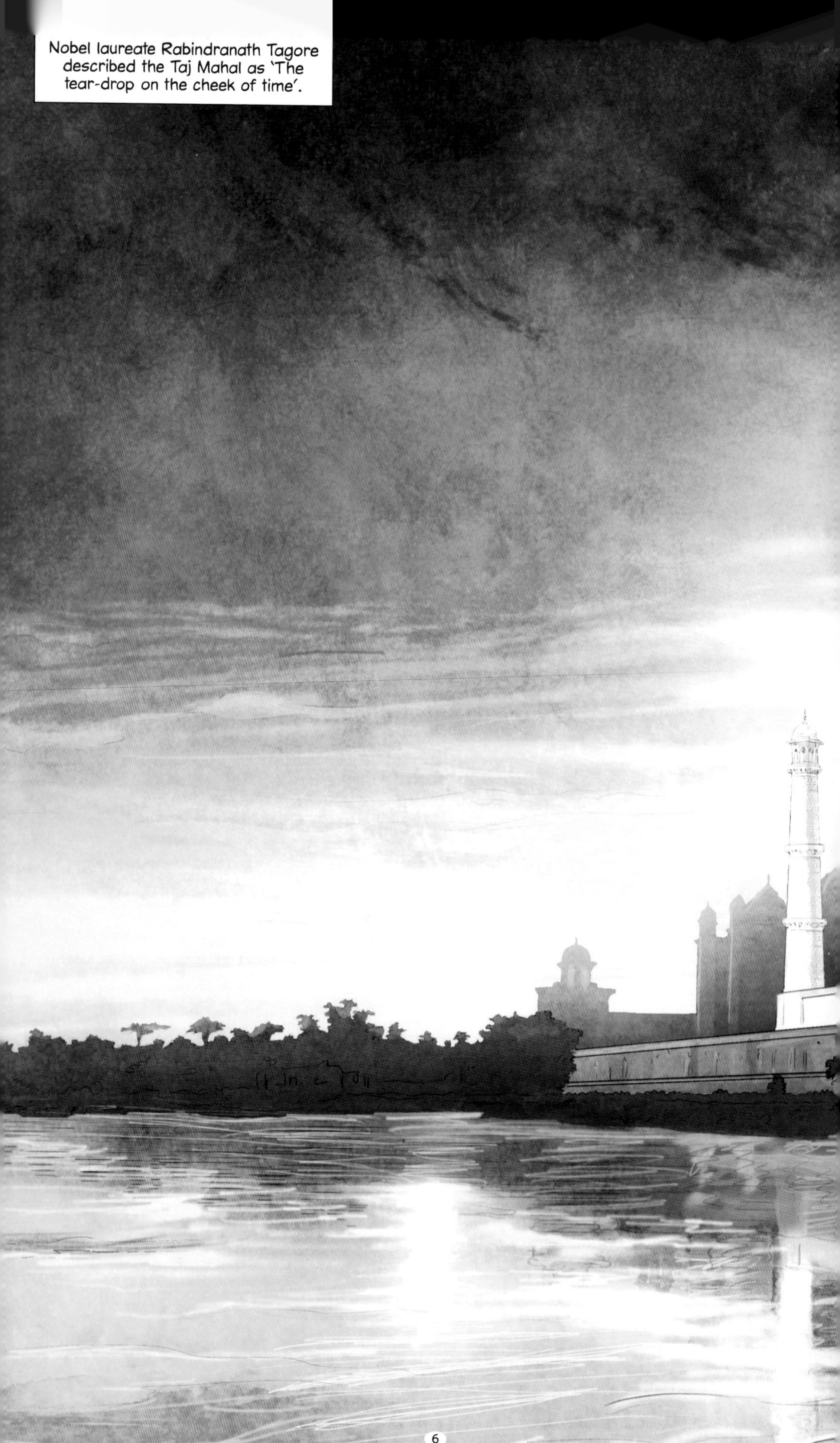
Nobel laureate Rabindranath Tagore described the Taj Mahal as 'The tear-drop on the cheek of time'.

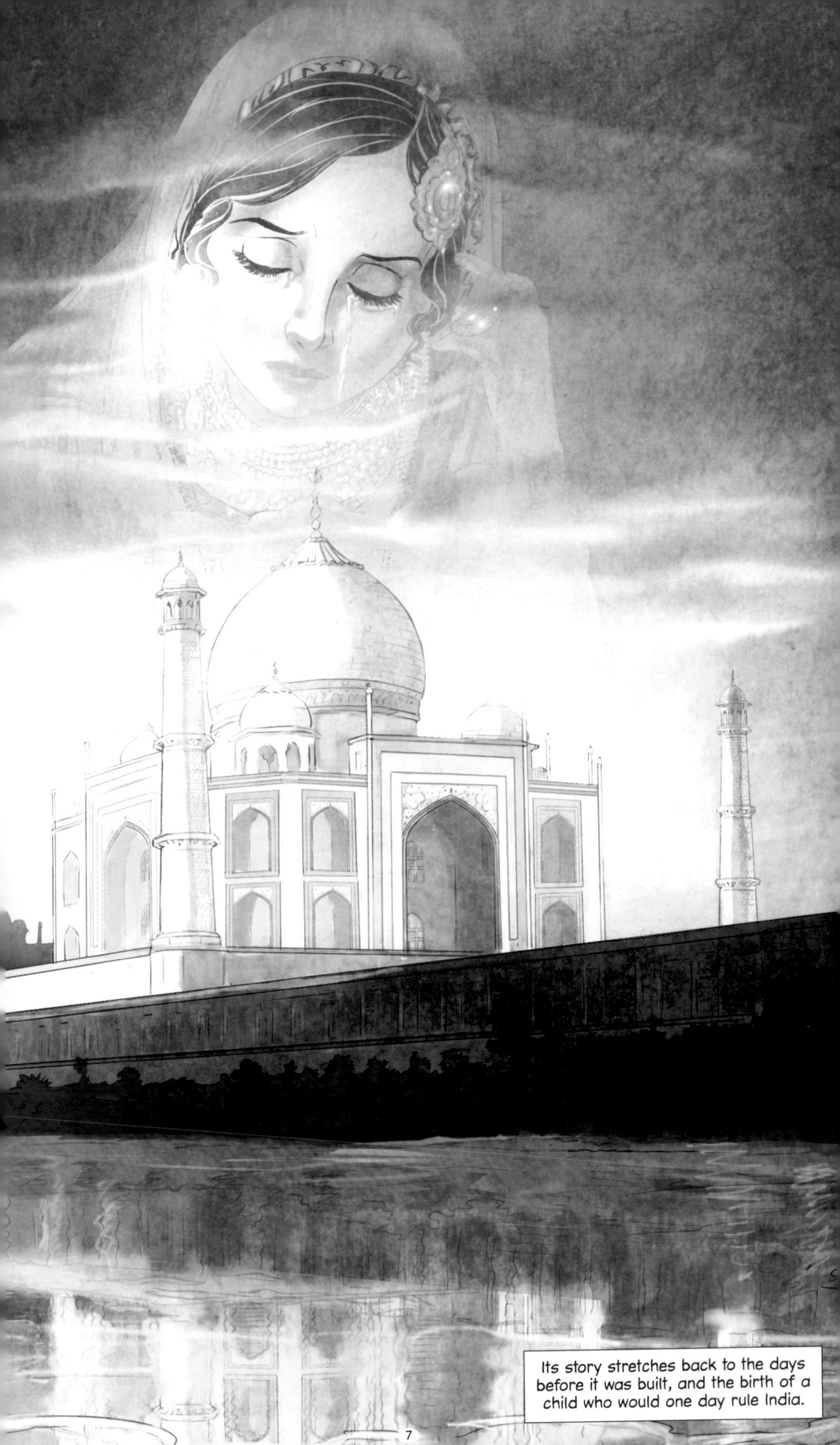
Its story stretches back to the days before it was built, and the birth of a child who would one day rule India.

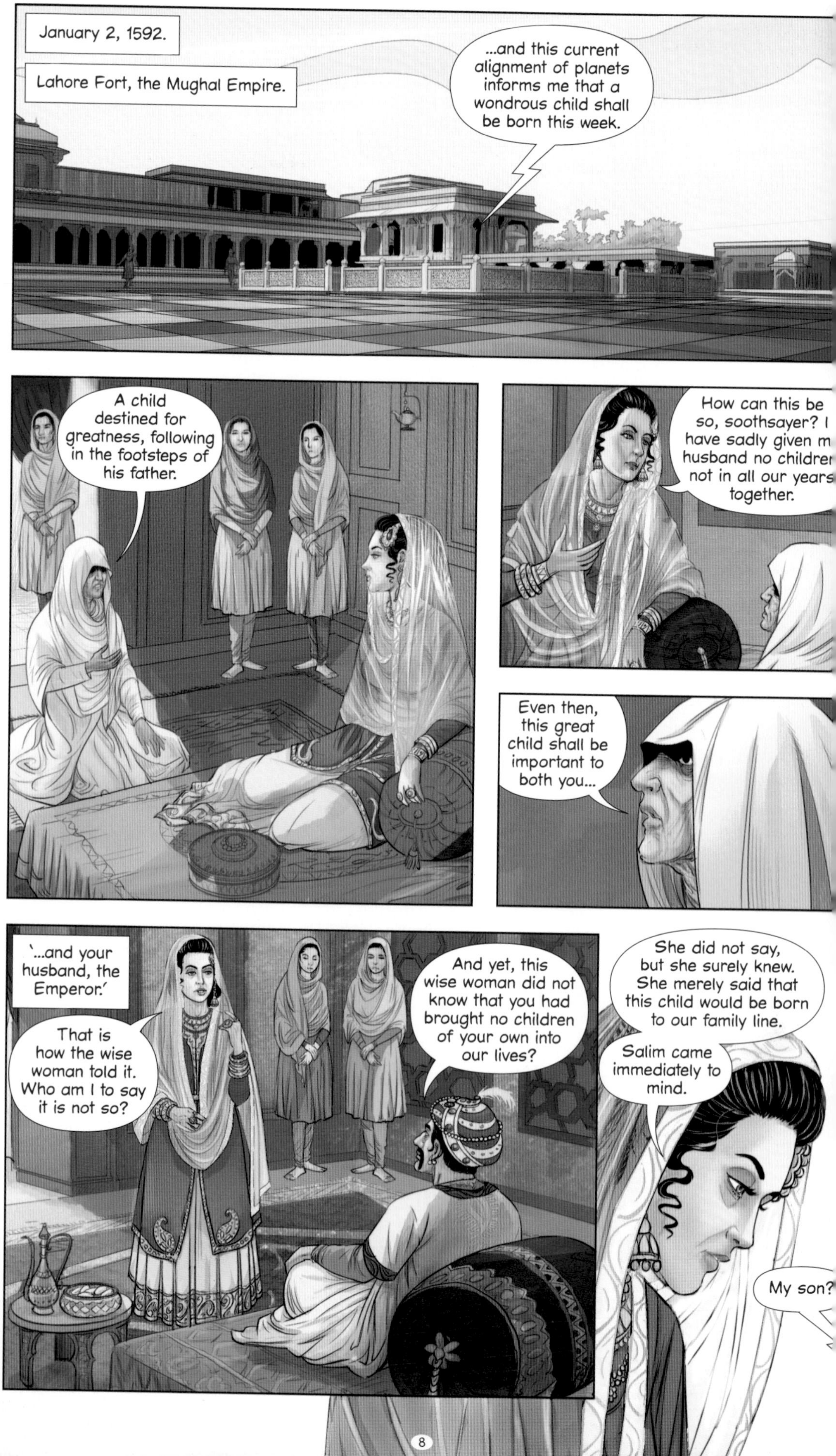
January 2, 1592.
Lahore Fort, the Mughal Empire.
...and this current alignment of planets informs me that a wondrous child shall be born this week.
A child destined for greatness, following in the footsteps of his father.
How can this be so, soothsayer? I have sadly given m husband no childre not in all our years together.
Even then, this great child shall be important to both you...
'...and your husband, the Emperor.'
That is how the wise woman told it. Who am I to say it is not so?
And yet, this wise woman did not know that you had brought no children of your own into our lives?
She did not say, but she surely knew. She merely said that this child would be born to our family line.
Salim came immediately to mind.
My son?

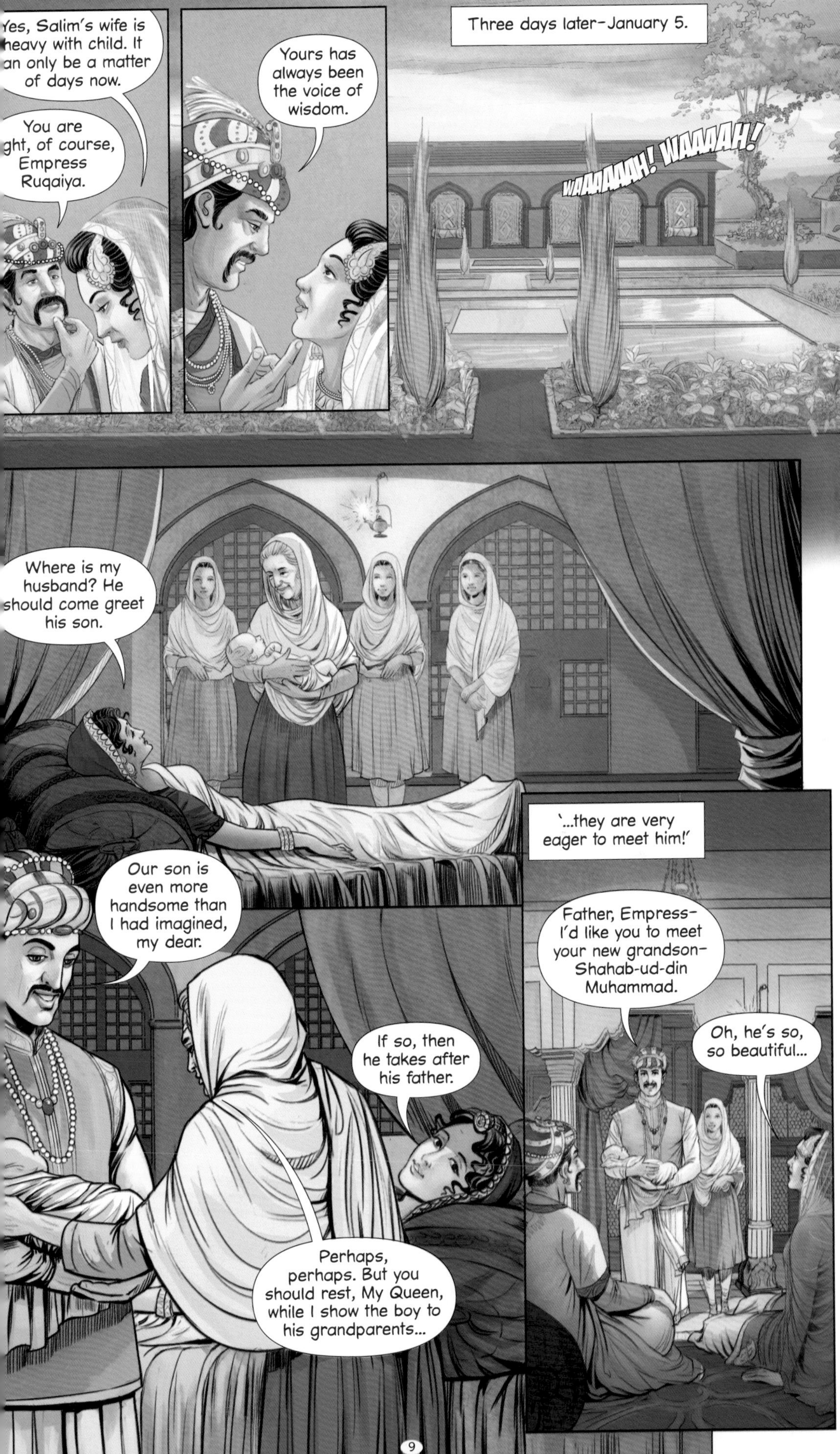

Yes, Salim's wife is heavy with child. It can only be a matter of days now.
You are right, of course, Empress Ruqaiya.
Yours has always been the voice of wisdom.
Three days later–January 5.
WAAAAAH! WAAAAH!
Where is my husband? He should come greet his son.
Our son is even more handsome than I had imagined, my dear.
If so, then he takes after his father.
Perhaps, perhaps. But you should rest, My Queen, while I show the boy to his grandparents...
'...they are very eager to meet him!'
Father, Empress– I'd like you to meet your new grandson– Shahab-ud-din Muhammad.
Oh, he's so, so beautiful...

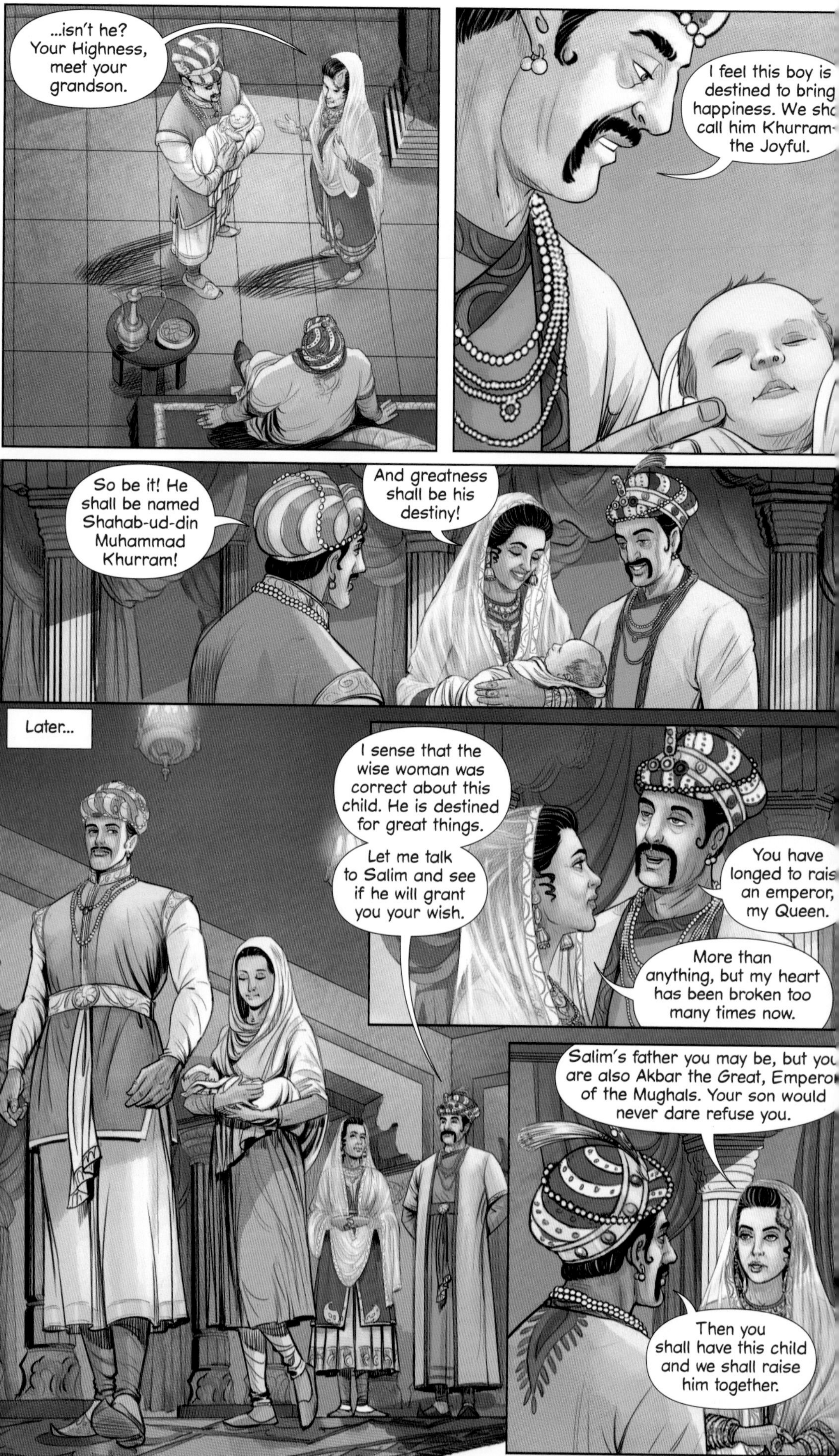
...isn't he? Your Highness, meet your grandson.
I feel this boy is destined to bring happiness. We sh call him Khurram- the Joyful.
So be it! He shall be named Shahab-ud-din Muhammad Khurram!
And greatness shall be his destiny!
Later...
I sense that the wise woman was correct about this child. He is destined for great things.
You have longed to rais an emperor, my Queen.
More than anything, but my heart has been broken too many times now.
Let me talk to Salim and see if he will grant you your wish.
Salim's father you may be, but yo are also Akbar the Great, Empero of the Mughals. Your son would never dare refuse you.
Then you shall have this child and we shall raise him together.

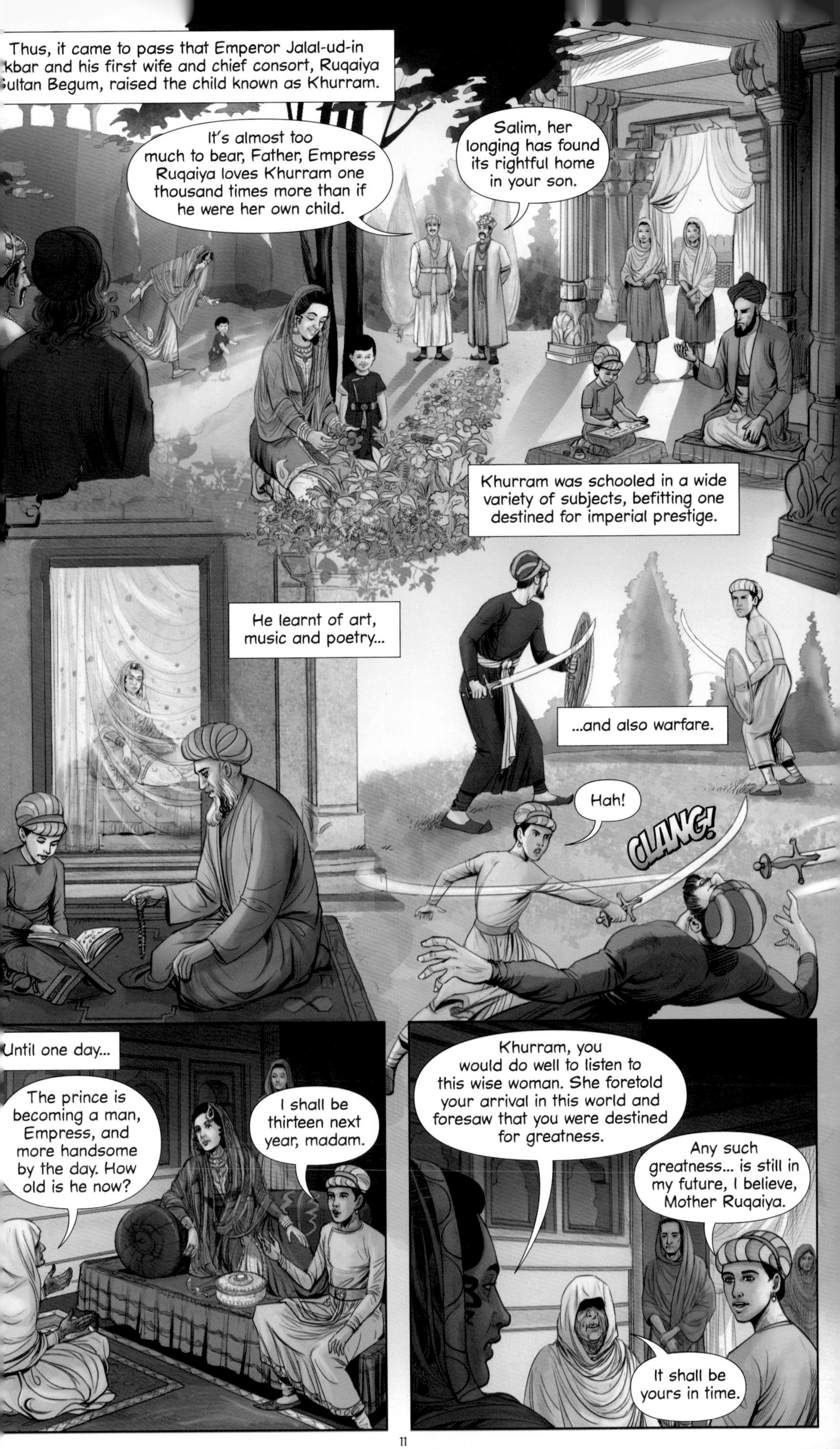

Thus, it came to pass that Emperor Jalal-ud-in kbar and his first wife and chief consort, Ruqaiya ultan Begum, raised the child known as Khurram.
It's almost too much to bear, Father, Empress Ruqaiya loves Khurram one thousand times more than if he were her own child.
Salim, her longing has found its rightful home in your son.
Khurram was schooled in a wide variety of subjects, befitting one destined for imperial prestige.
He learnt of art, music and poetry...
...and also warfare.
Hah!
CLANG!
Until one day...
The prince is becoming a man, Empress, and more handsome by the day. How old is he now?
I shall be thirteen next year, madam.
Khurram, you would do well to listen to this wise woman. She foretold your arrival in this world and foresaw that you were destined for greatness.
Any such greatness... is still in my future, I believe, Mother Ruqaiya.
It shall be yours in time.

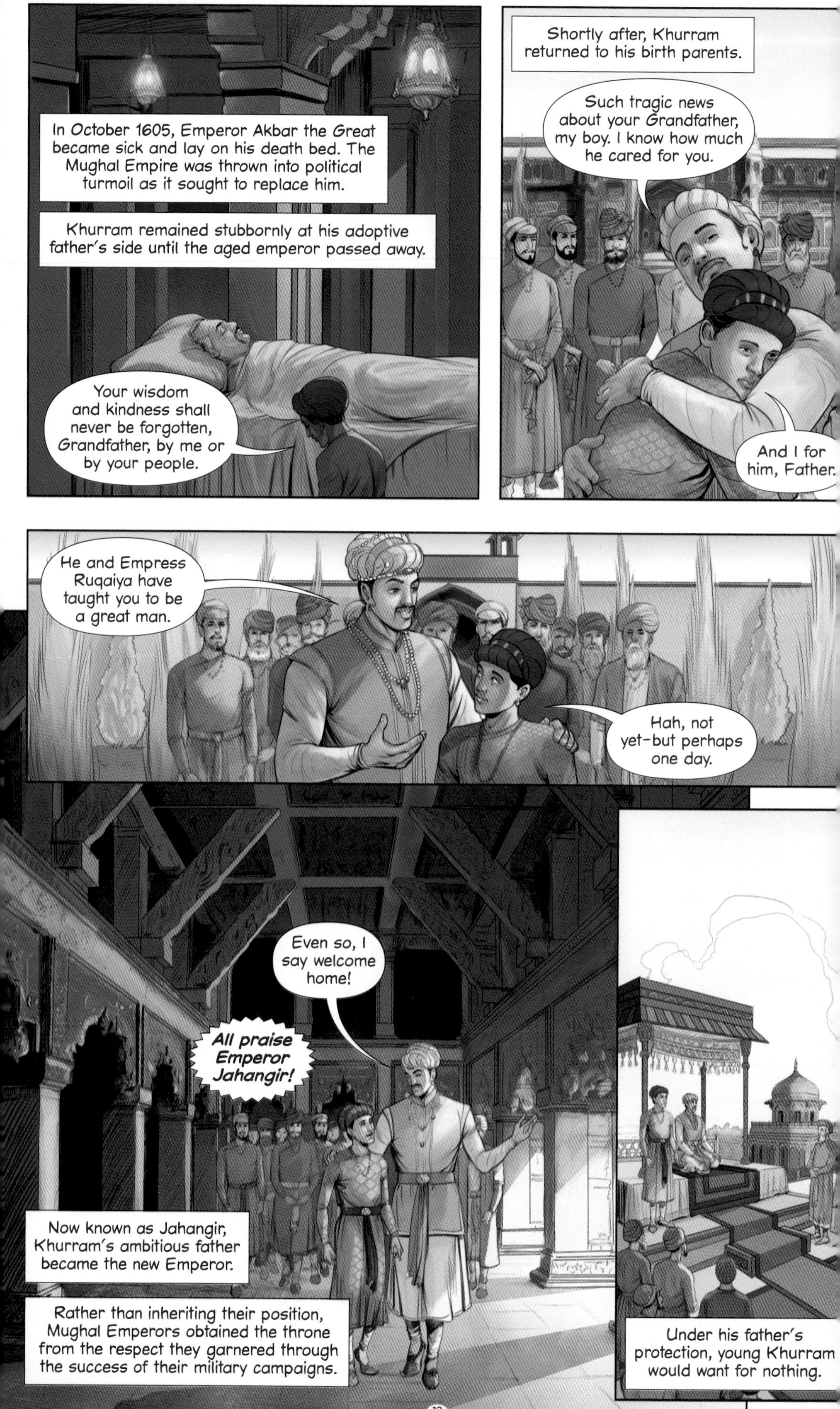
In October 1605, Emperor Akbar the Great became sick and lay on his death bed. The Mughal Empire was thrown into political turmoil as it sought to replace him.
Khurram remained stubbornly at his adoptive father's side until the aged emperor passed away.
Your wisdom and kindness shall never be forgotten, Grandfather, by me or by your people.
Shortly after, Khurram returned to his birth parents.
Such tragic news about your Grandfather, my boy. I know how much he cared for you.
And I for him, Father.
He and Empress Ruqaiya have taught you to be a great man.
Hah, not yet–but perhaps one day.
Even so, I say welcome home!
All praise Emperor Jahangir!
Now known as Jahangir, Khurram's ambitious father became the new Emperor.
Rather than inheriting their position, Mughal Emperors obtained the throne from the respect they garnered through the success of their military campaigns.
Under his father's protection, young Khurram would want for nothing.

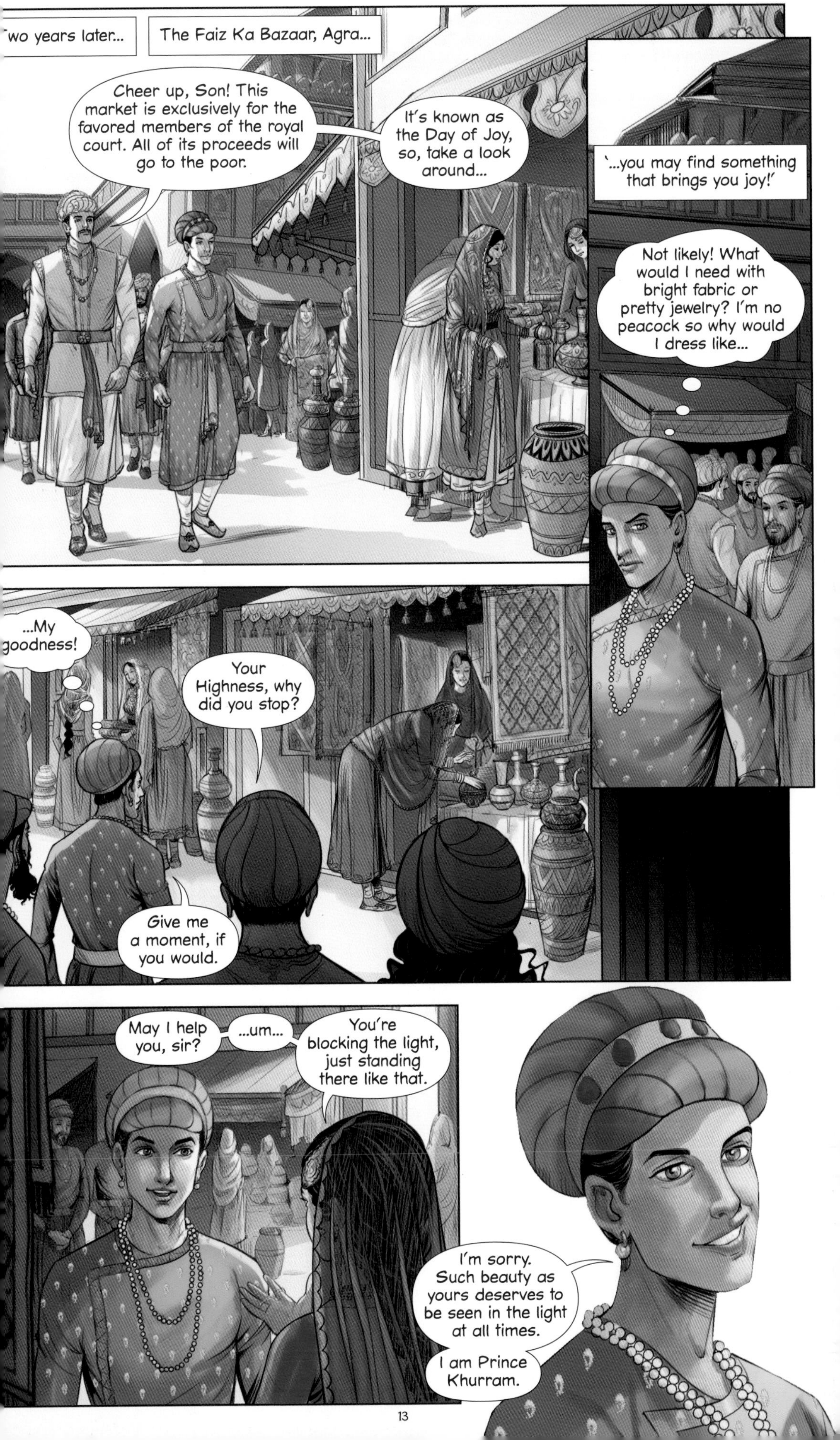

wo years later...
The Faiz Ka Bazaar, Agra...
Cheer up, Son! This market is exclusively for the favored members of the royal court. All of its proceeds will go to the poor.
It's known as the Day of Joy, so, take a look around...
'...you may find something that brings you joy!'
Not likely! What would I need with bright fabric or pretty jewelry? I'm no peacock so why would I dress like...
...My goodness!
Your Highness, why did you stop?
Give me a moment, if you would.
May I help you, sir?
...um...
You're blocking the light, just standing there like that.
I'm sorry. Such beauty as yours deserves to be seen in the light at all times.
I am Prince Khurram.

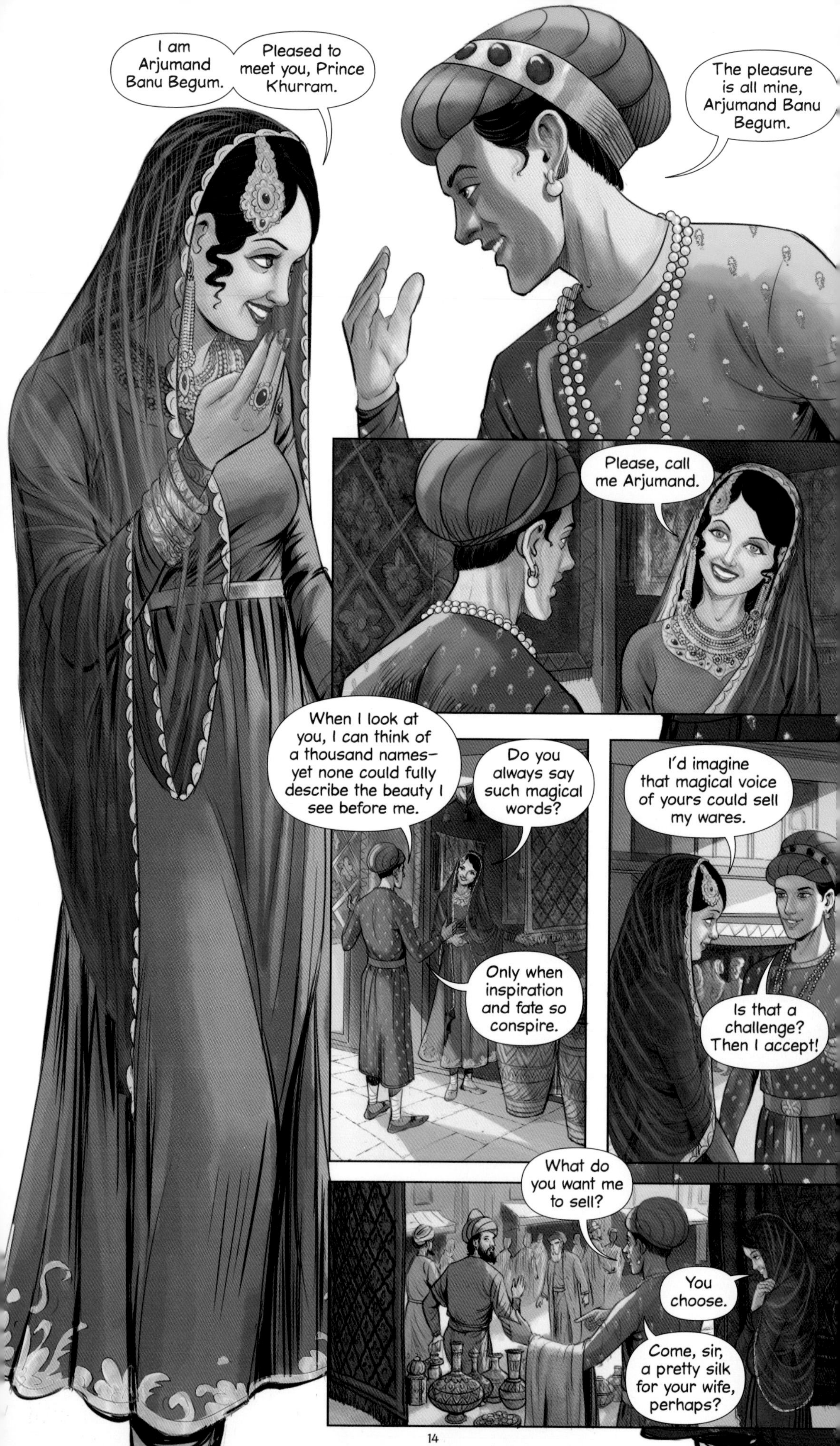

I am Arjumand Banu Begum.
Pleased to meet you, Prince Khurram.
The pleasure is all mine, Arjumand Banu Begum.
Please, call me Arjumand.
When I look at you, I can think of a thousand names— yet none could fully describe the beauty I see before me.
Do you always say such magical words?
Only when inspiration and fate so conspire.
I'd imagine that magical voice of yours could sell my wares.
Is that a challenge? Then I accept!
What do you want me to sell?
You choose.
Come, sir, a pretty silk for your wife, perhaps?

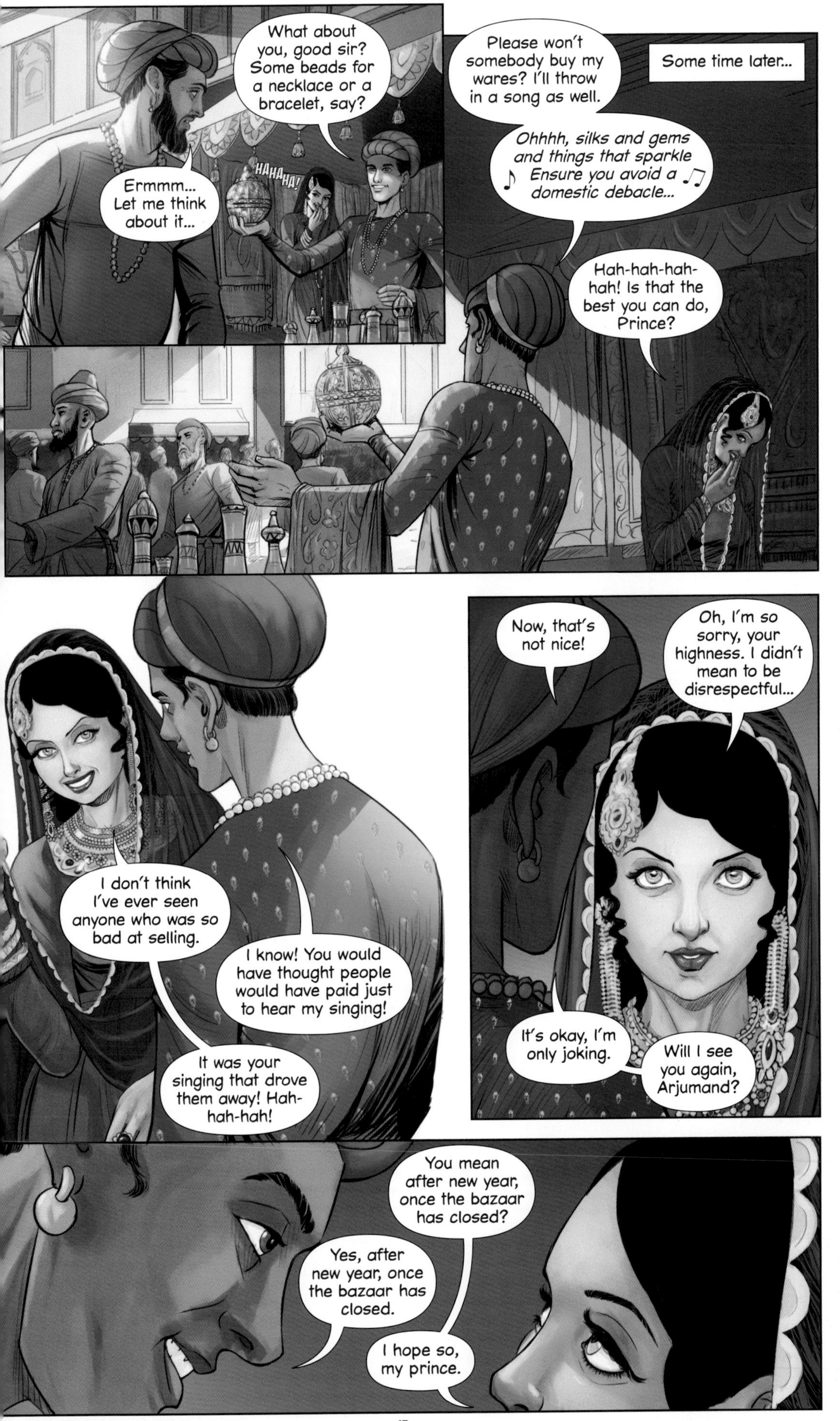
What about you, good sir? Some beads for a necklace or a bracelet, say?
Ermmm... Let me think about it...
HAHAHA!
Please won't somebody buy my wares? I'll throw in a song as well.
Some time later...
Ohhhh, silks and gems and things that sparkle ♪ Ensure you avoid a domestic debacle... ♫
Hah-hah-hah-hah! Is that the best you can do, Prince?
I don't think I've ever seen anyone who was so bad at selling.
I know! You would have thought people would have paid just to hear my singing!
It was your singing that drove them away! Hah-hah-hah!
Now, that's not nice!
Oh, I'm so sorry, your highness. I didn't mean to be disrespectful...
It's okay, I'm only joking.
Will I see you again, Arjumand?
You mean after new year, once the bazaar has closed?
Yes, after new year, once the bazaar has closed.
I hope so, my prince.

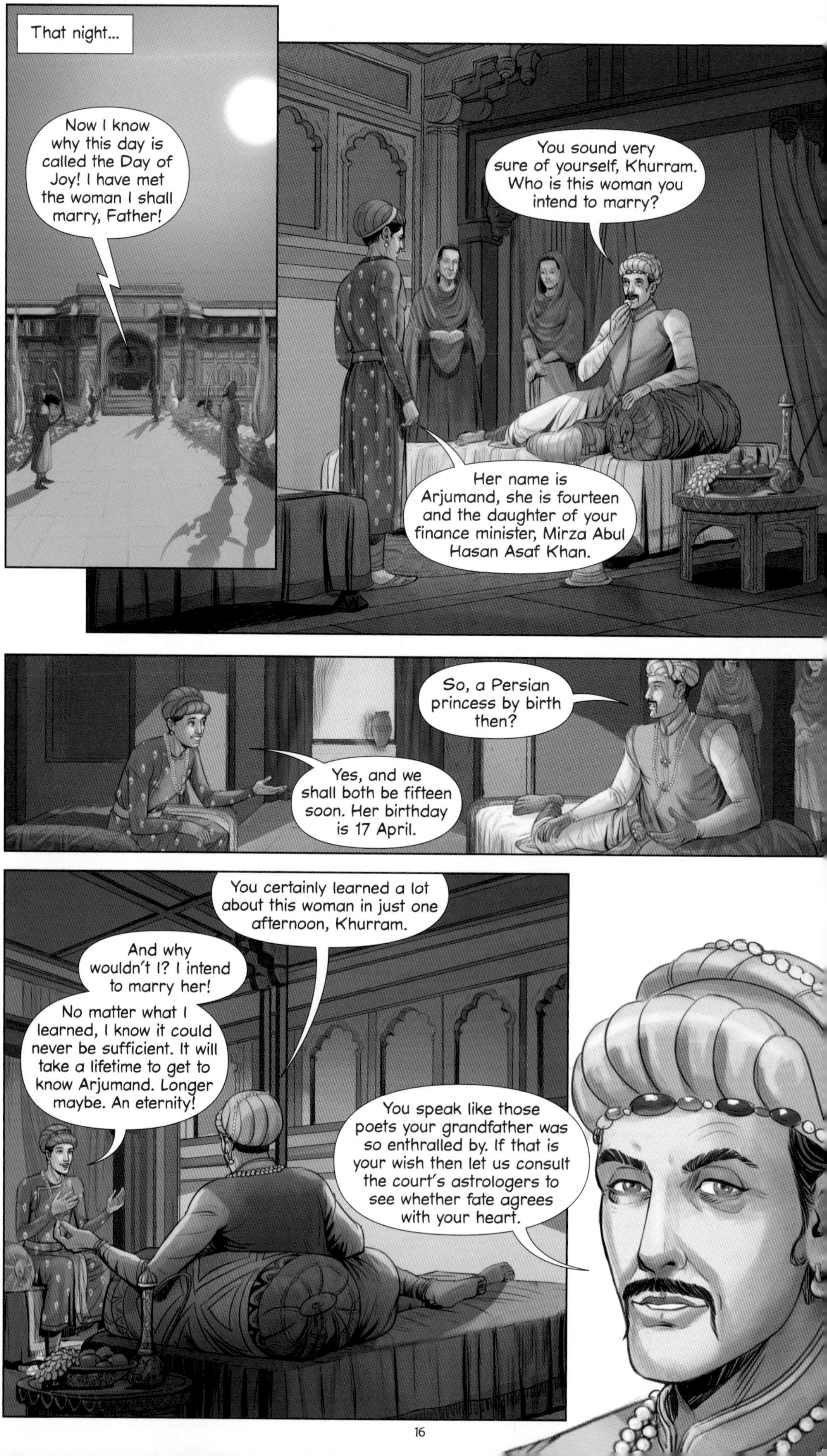

That night...
Now I know why this day is called the Day of Joy! I have met the woman I shall marry, Father!
You sound very sure of yourself, Khurram. Who is this woman you intend to marry?
Her name is Arjumand, she is fourteen and the daughter of your finance minister, Mirza Abul Hasan Asaf Khan.
So, a Persian princess by birth then?
Yes, and we shall both be fifteen soon. Her birthday is 17 April.
You certainly learned a lot about this woman in just one afternoon, Khurram.
And why wouldn't I? I intend to marry her!
No matter what I learned, I know it could never be sufficient. It will take a lifetime to get to know Arjumand. Longer maybe. An eternity!
You speak like those poets your grandfather was so enthralled by. If that is your wish then let us consult the court's astrologers to see whether fate agrees with your heart.

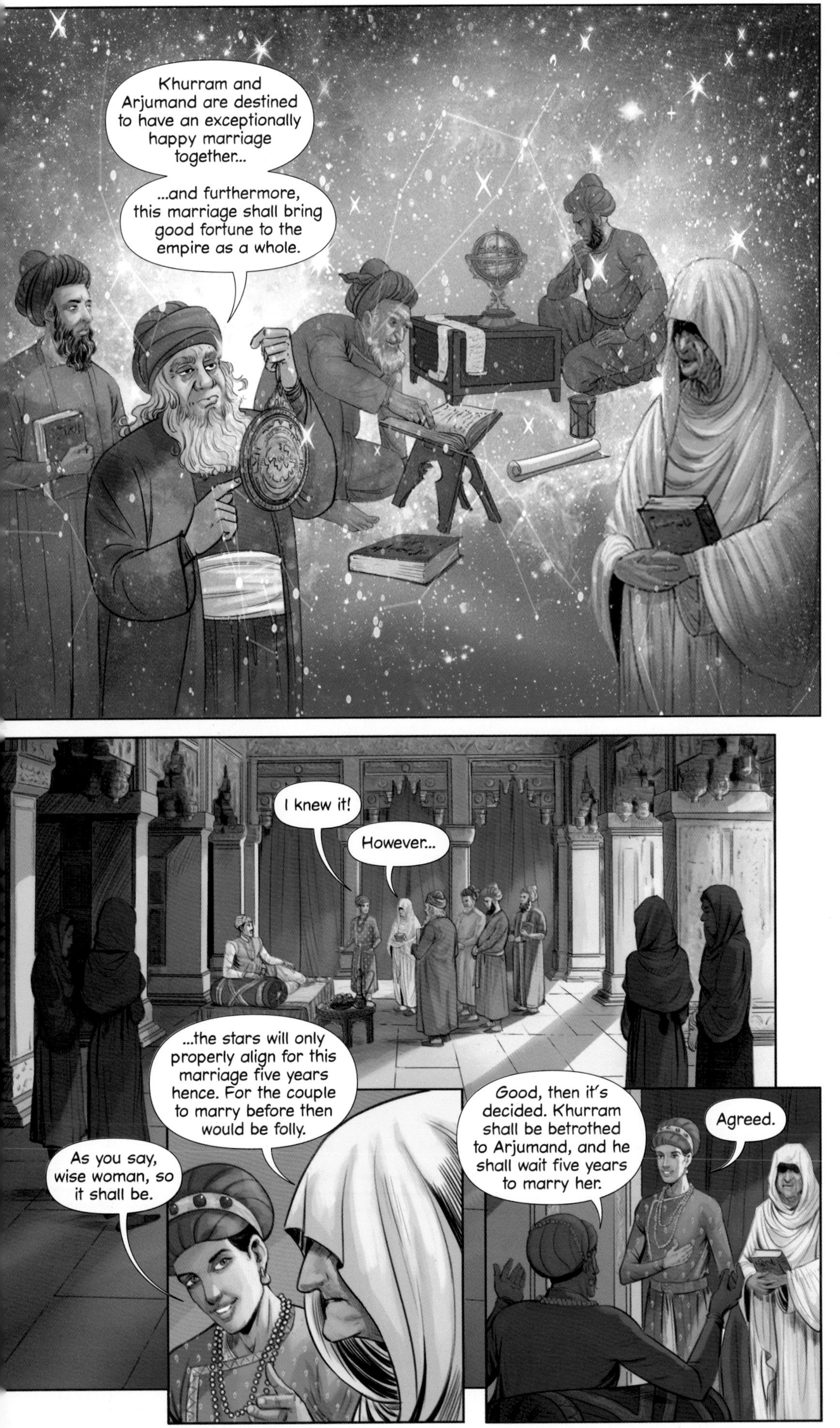

Khurram and Arjumand are destined to have an exceptionally happy marriage together...
...and furthermore, this marriage shall bring good fortune to the empire as a whole.
I knew it!
However...
...the stars will only properly align for this marriage five years hence. For the couple to marry before then would be folly.
As you say, wise woman, so it shall be.
Good, then it's decided. Khurram shall be betrothed to Arjumand, and he shall wait five years to marry her.
Agreed.

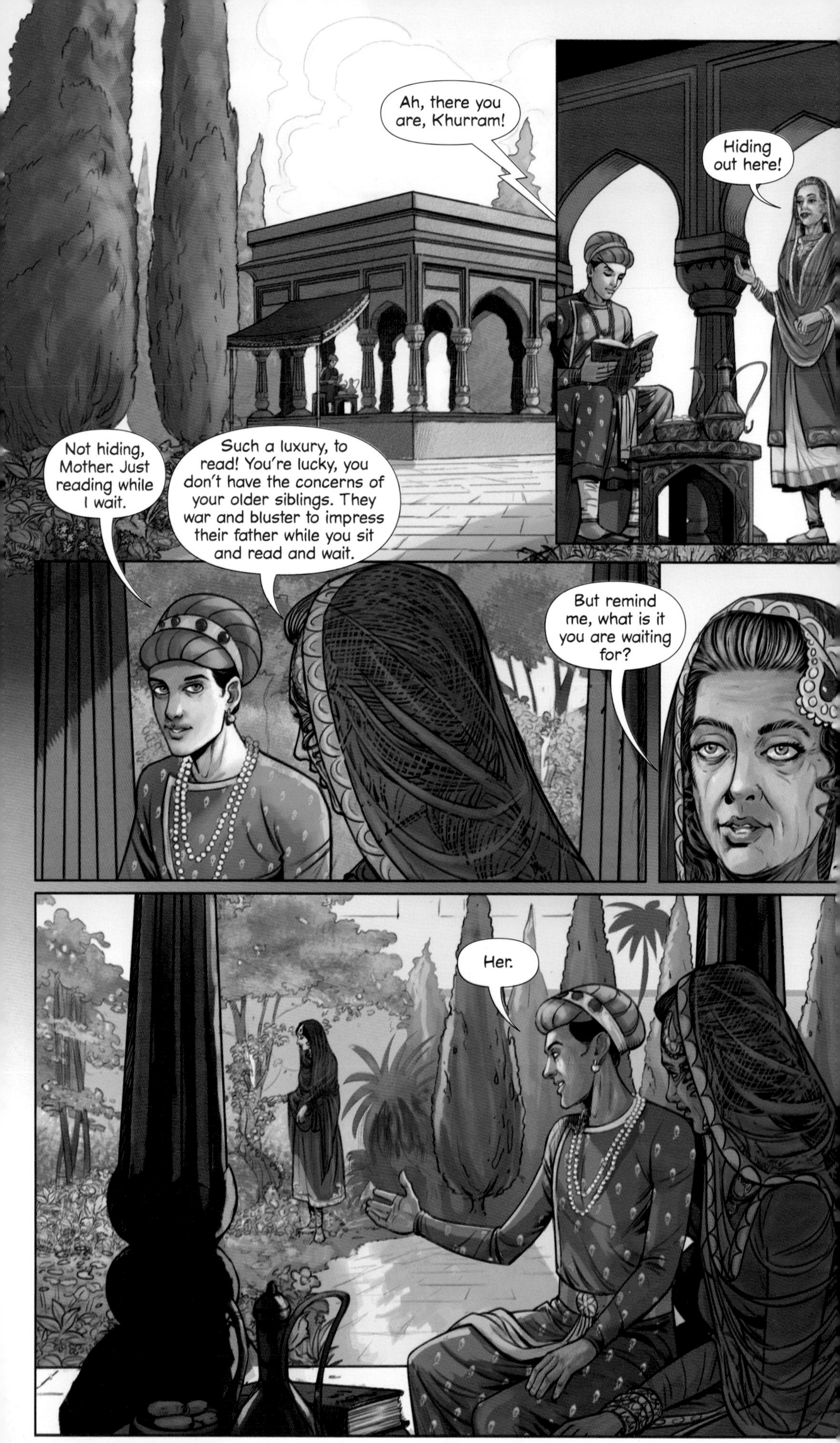
Ah, there you are, Khurram!
Hiding out here!
Not hiding, Mother. Just reading while I wait.
Such a luxury, to read! You're lucky, you don't have the concerns of your older siblings. They war and bluster to impress their father while you sit and read and wait.
But remind me, what is it you are waiting for?
Her.

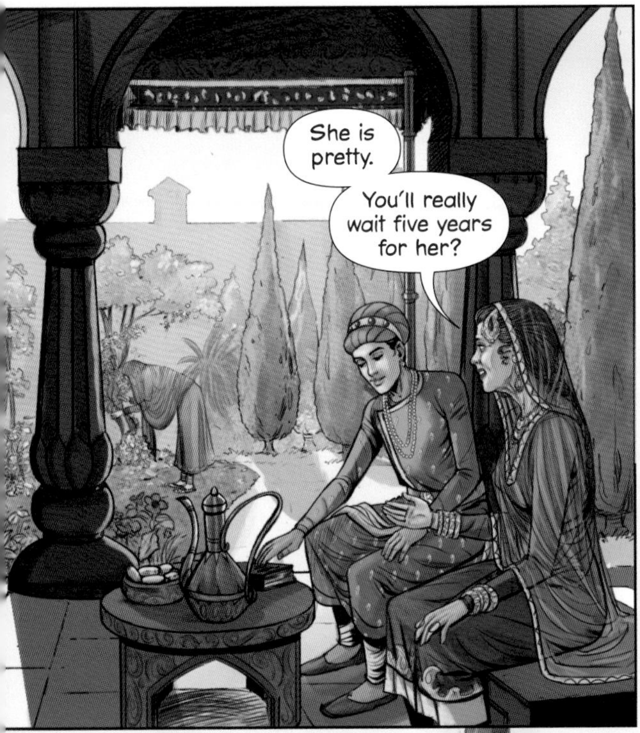
She is pretty.
You'll really wait five years for her?

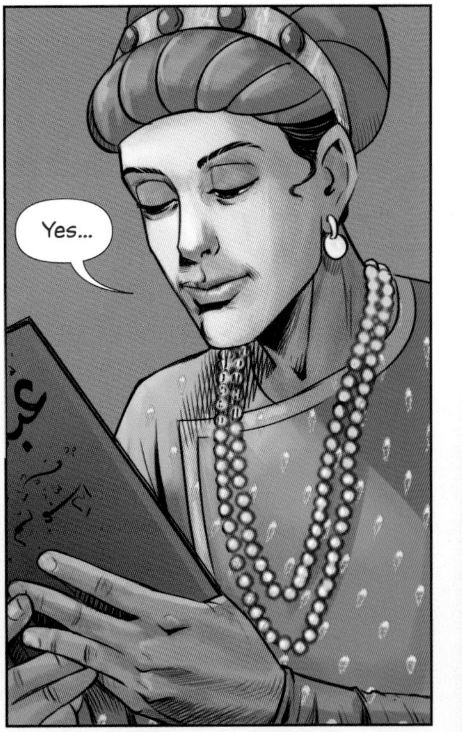
Yes...

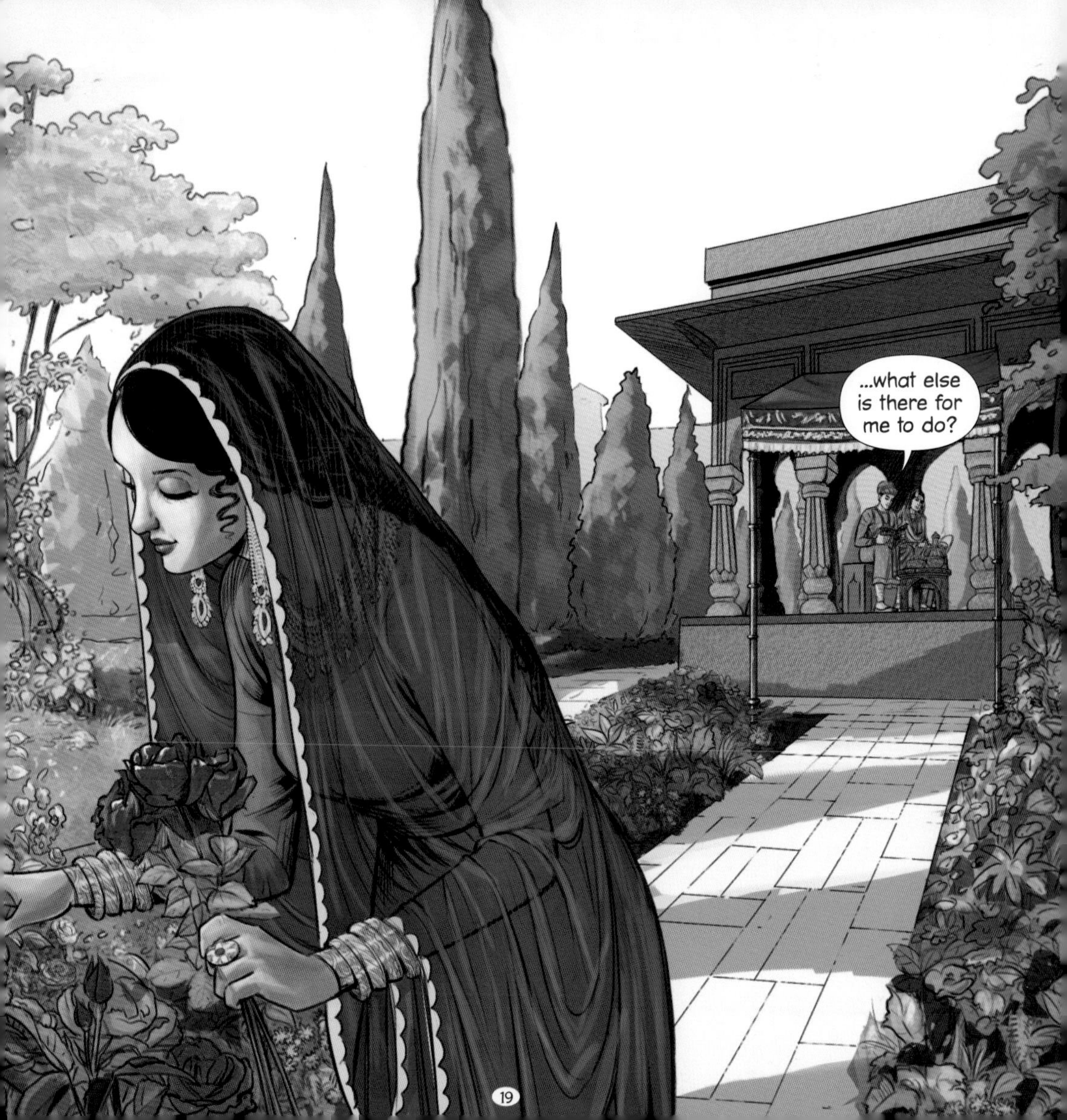
...what else is there for me to do?

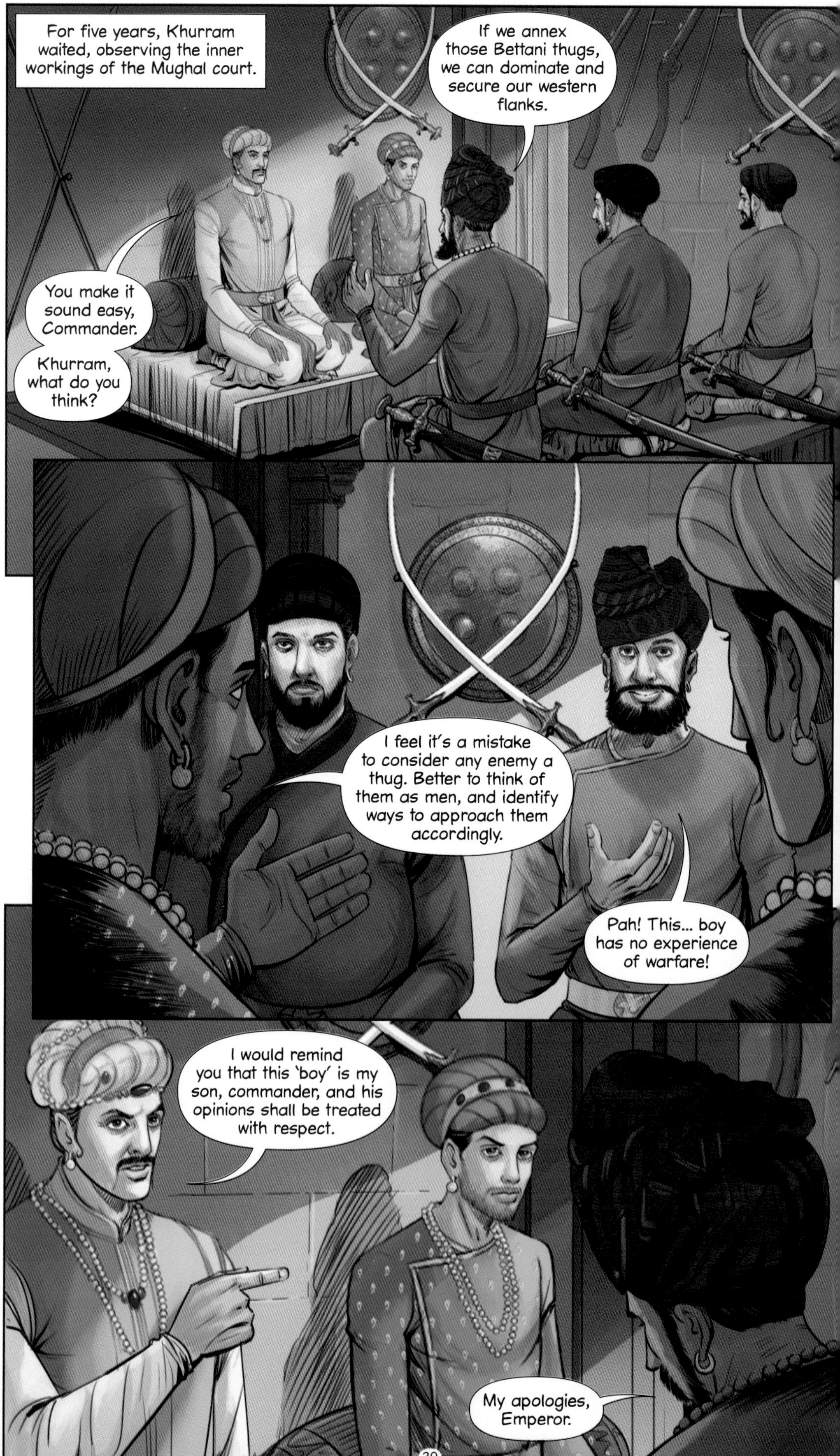

For five years, Khurram waited, observing the inner workings of the Mughal court.
If we annex those Bettani thugs, we can dominate and secure our western flanks.
You make it sound easy, Commander.
Khurram, what do you think?
I feel it's a mistake to consider any enemy a thug. Better to think of them as men, and identify ways to approach them accordingly.
Pah! This... boy has no experience of warfare!
I would remind you that this 'boy' is my son, commander, and his opinions shall be treated with respect.
My apologies, Emperor.

Shortly...

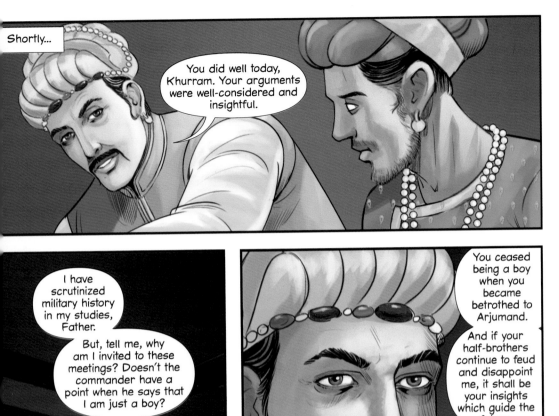

You did well today, Khurram. Your arguments were well-considered and insightful.

I have scrutinized military history in my studies, Father.

But, tell me, why am I invited to these meetings? Doesn't the commander have a point when he says that I am just a boy?

You ceased being a boy when you became betrothed to Arjumand.

And if your half-brothers continue to feud and disappoint me, it shall be your insights which guide the future.

'Feuds and disappointments he calls them...'

'My oldest brother, Khusrav, staged a failed rebellion against him when grandfather died, and was blinded and imprisoned for his transgression.'

'While father's second son, Parviz, presides over Deccan from Burhanpur at father's indulgence, far enough away to cause no trouble, but rumored to lack a strong hand.'

Feuds and disappointments... maybe he is right.

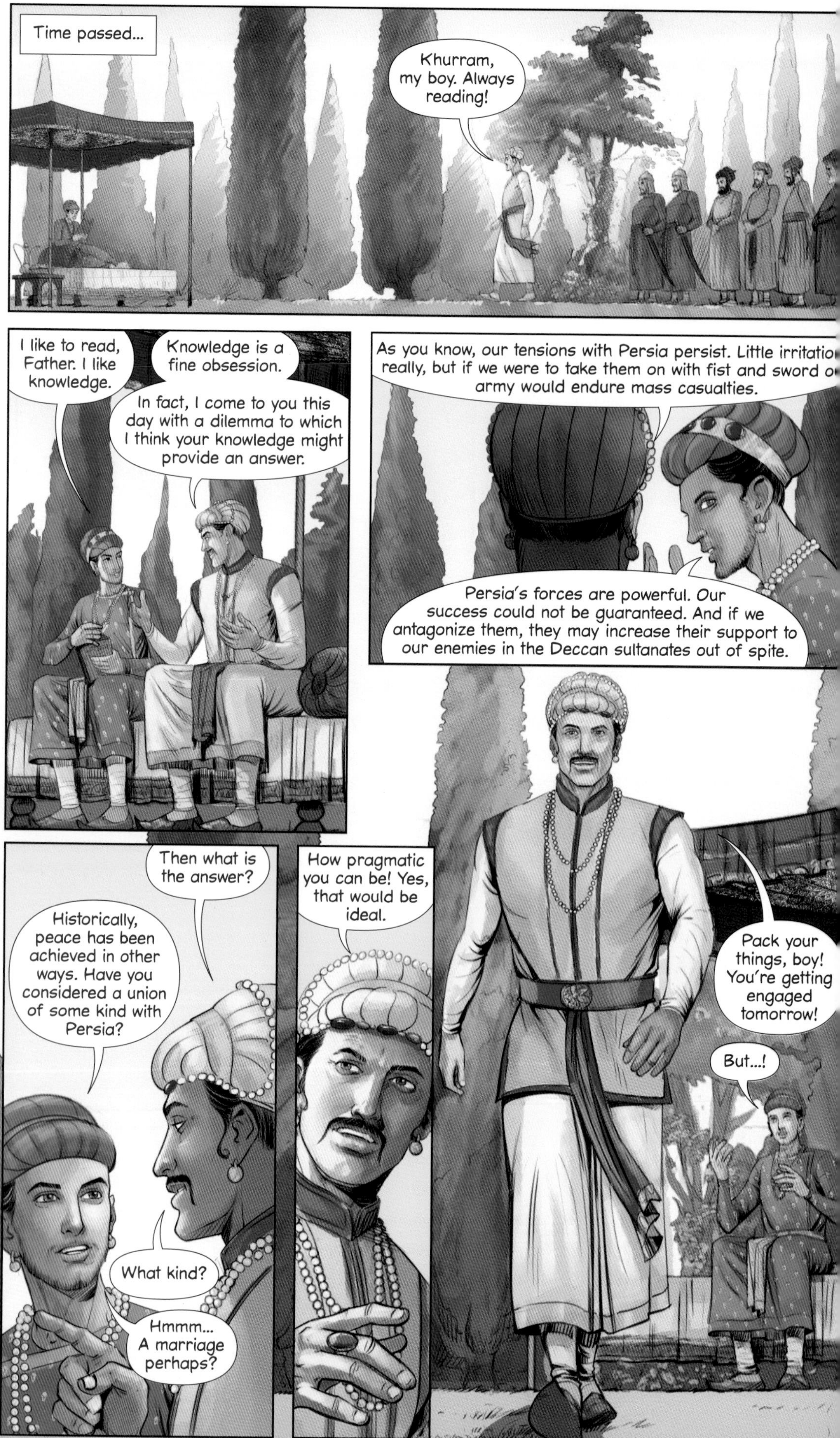

Time passed...
Khurram, my boy. Always reading!
I like to read, Father. I like knowledge.
Knowledge is a fine obsession.
In fact, I come to you this day with a dilemma to which I think your knowledge might provide an answer.
As you know, our tensions with Persia persist. Little irritatio really, but if we were to take them on with fist and sword o army would endure mass casualties.
Persia's forces are powerful. Our success could not be guaranteed. And if we antagonize them, they may increase their support to our enemies in the Deccan sultanates out of spite.
Then what is the answer?
Historically, peace has been achieved in other ways. Have you considered a union of some kind with Persia?
What kind?
Hmmm... A marriage perhaps?
How pragmatic you can be! Yes, that would be ideal.
Pack your things, boy! You're getting engaged tomorrow!
But...!

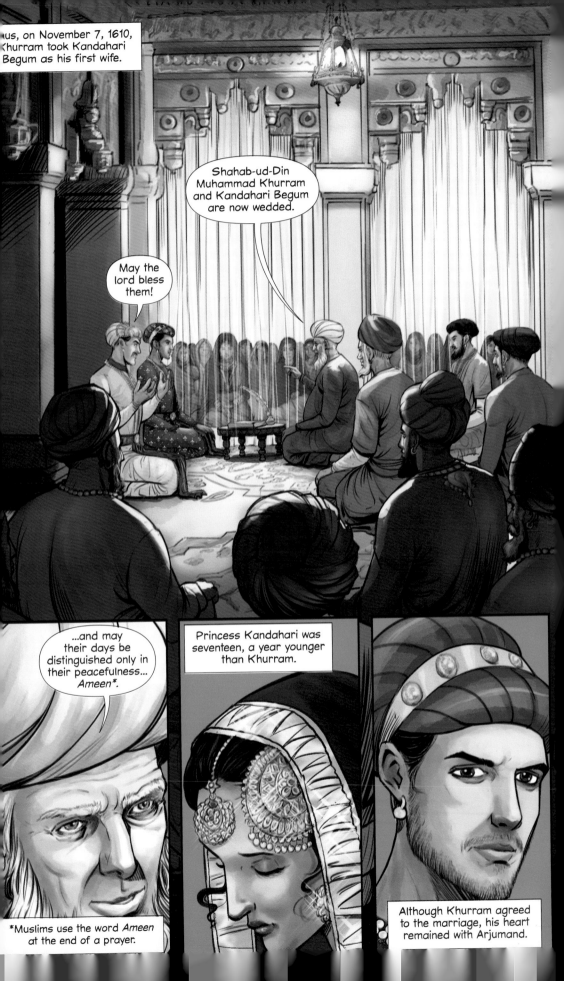

Thus, on November 7, 1610, Khurram took Kandahari Begum as his first wife.

Shahab-ud-Din Muhammad Khurram and Kandahari Begum are now wedded.

May the lord bless them!

...and may their days be distinguished only in their peacefulness... *Ameen*.

*Muslims use the word *Ameen* at the end of a prayer.

Princess Kandahari was seventeen, a year younger than Khurram.

Although Khurram agreed to the marriage, his heart remained with Arjumand.

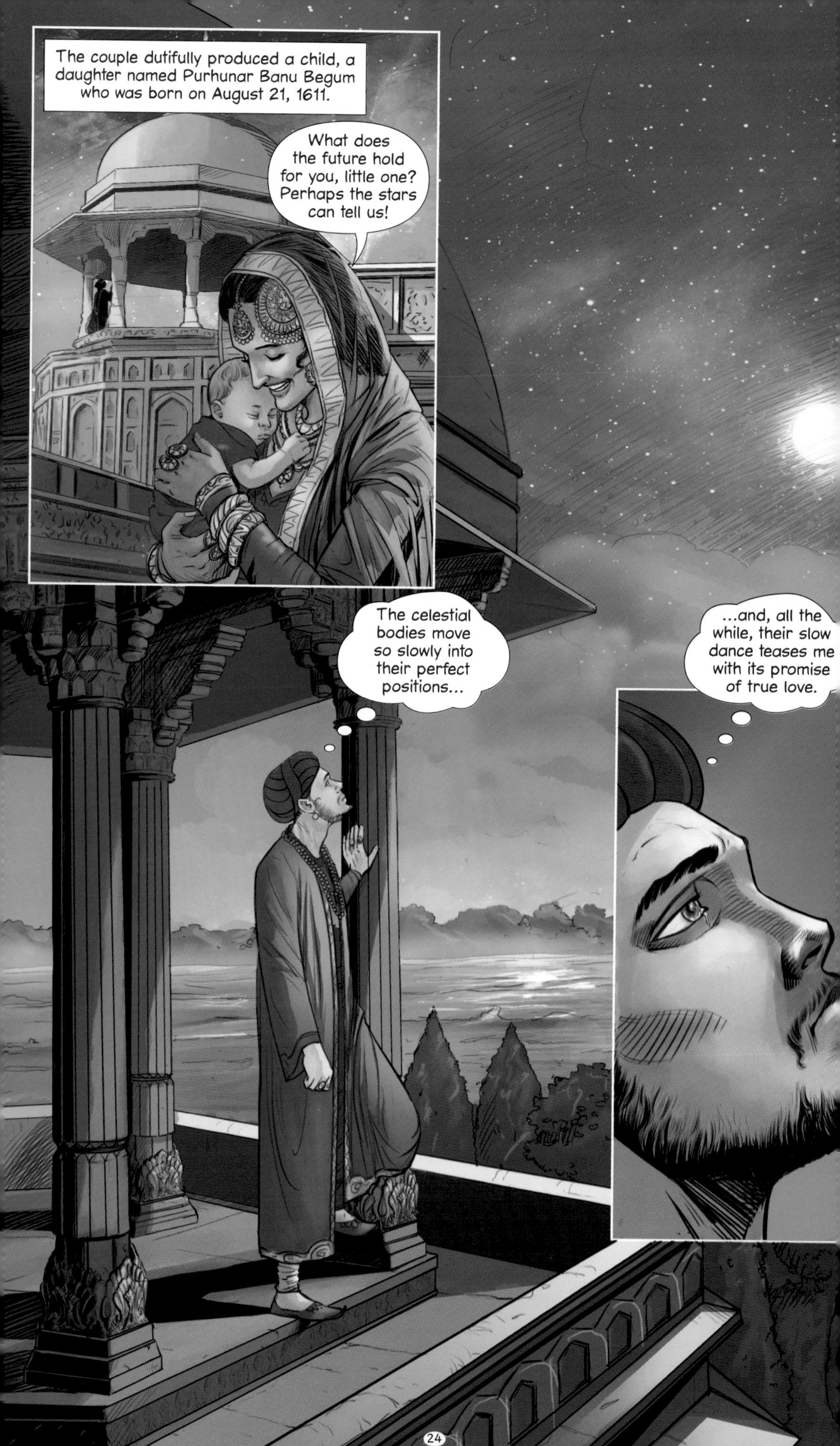
The couple dutifully produced a child, a daughter named Purhunar Banu Begum who was born on August 21, 1611.
What does the future hold for you, little one? Perhaps the stars can tell us!
The celestial bodies move so slowly into their perfect positions...
...and, all the while, their slow dance teases me with its promise of true love.

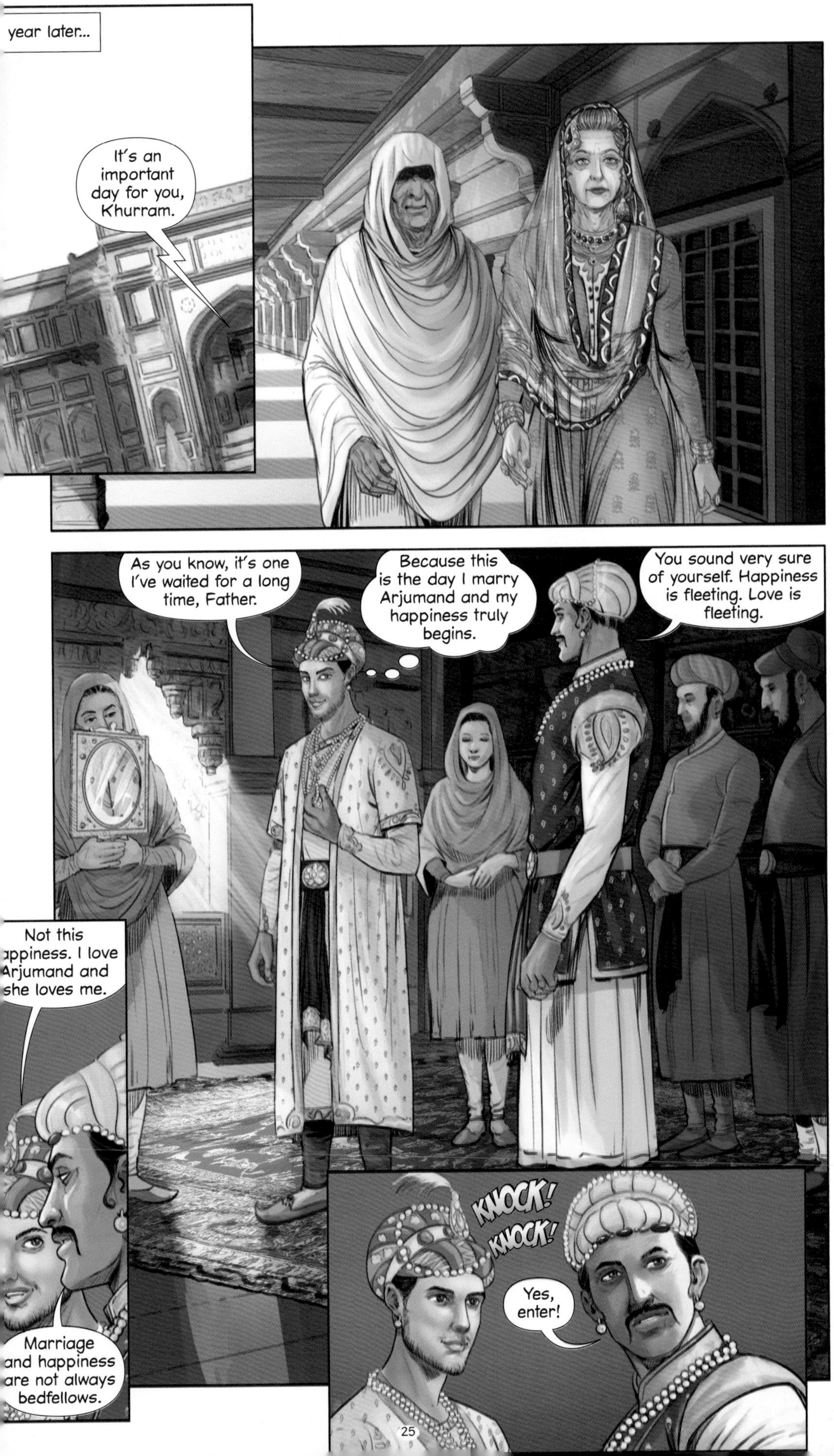

year later...
It's an important day for you, Khurram.
As you know, it's one I've waited for a long time, Father.
Because this is the day I marry Arjumand and my happiness truly begins.
You sound very sure of yourself. Happiness is fleeting. Love is fleeting.
Not this appiness. I love Arjumand and she loves me.
Marriage and happiness are not always bedfellows.
KNOCK! KNOCK!
Yes, enter!

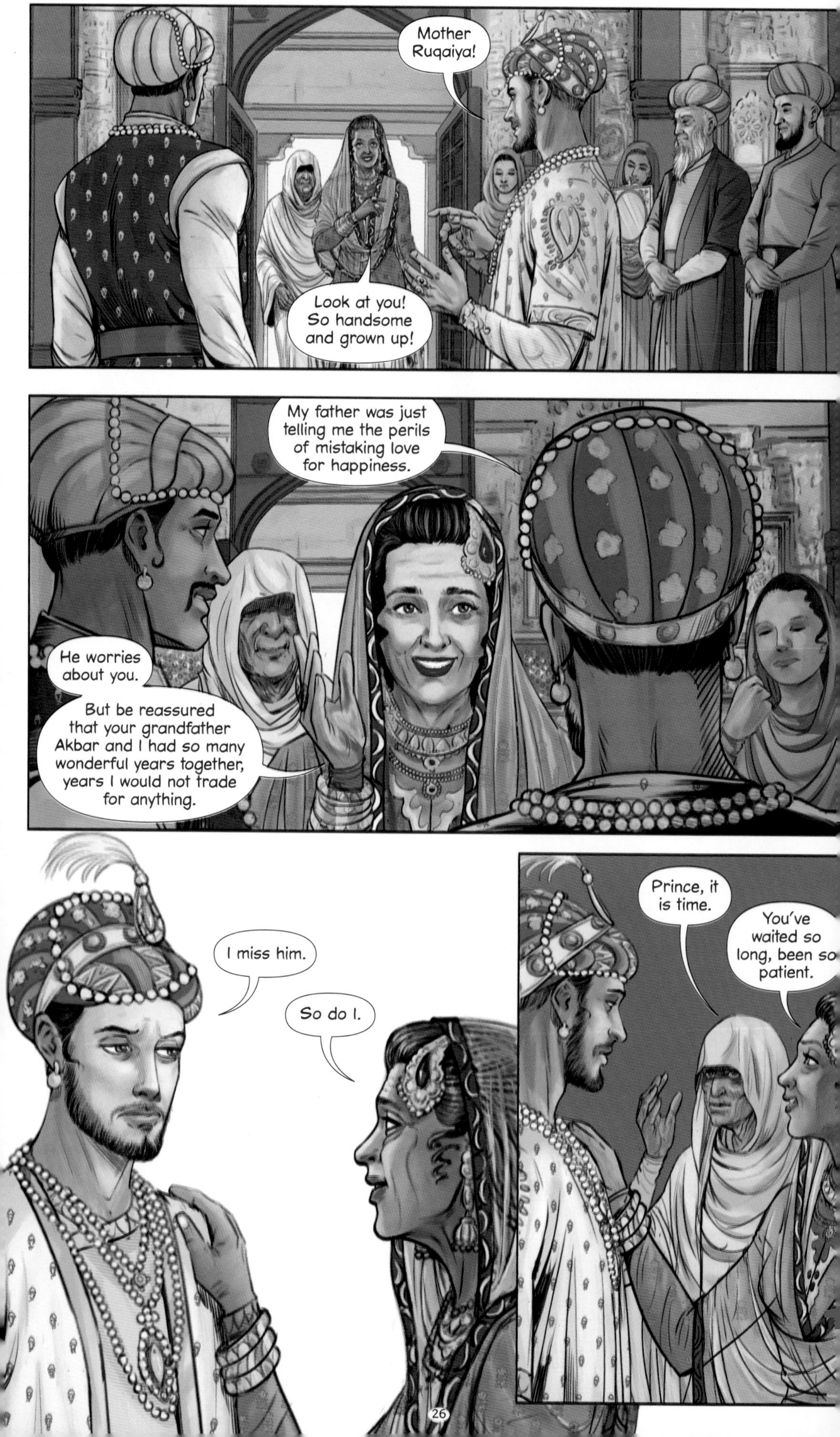
Mother Ruqaiya!
Look at you! So handsome and grown up!
My father was just telling me the perils of mistaking love for happiness.
He worries about you.
But be reassured that your grandfather Akbar and I had so many wonderful years together, years I would not trade for anything.
I miss him.
So do I.
Prince, it is time.
You've waited so long, been so patient.

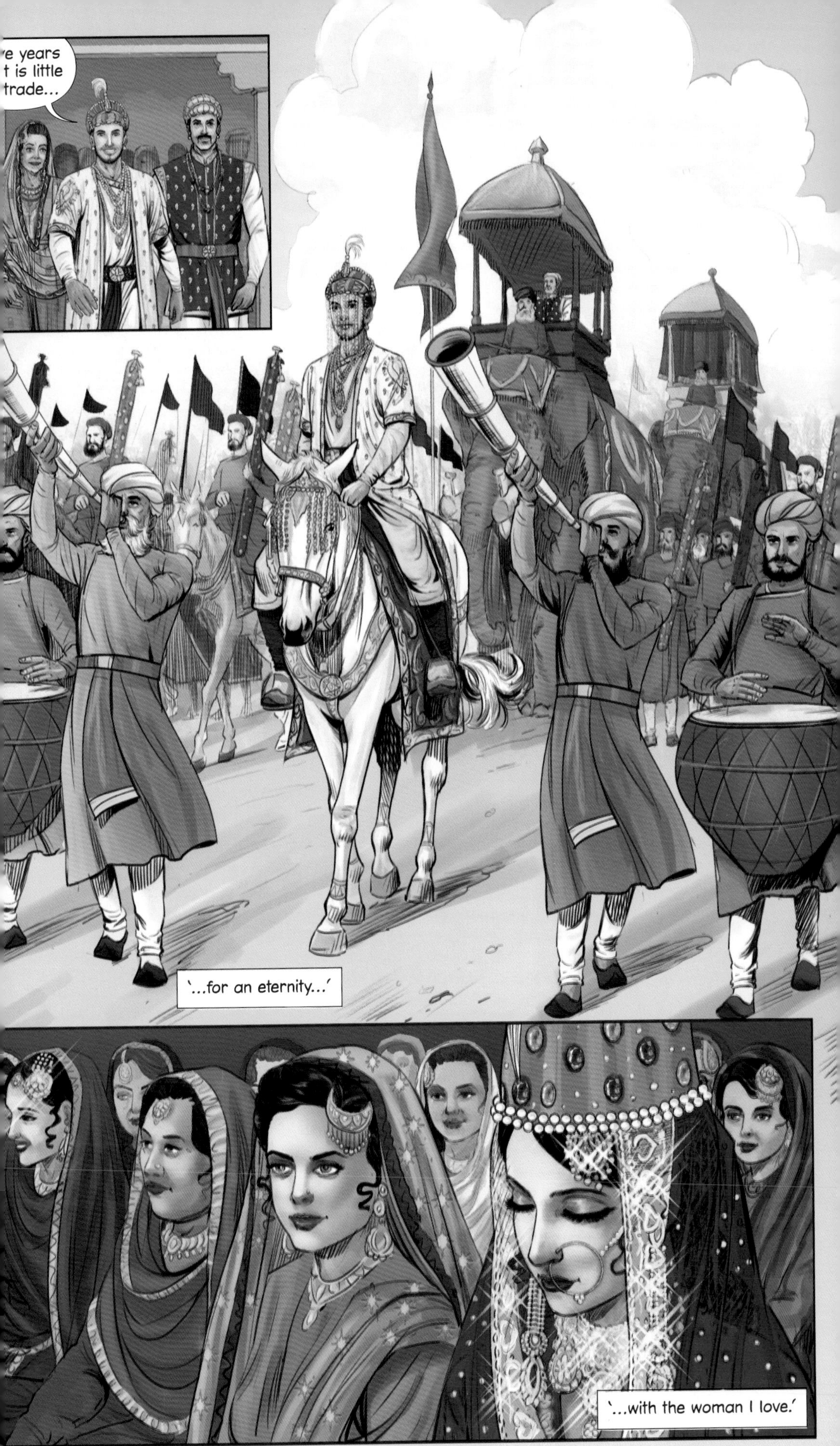
'e years
t is little
trade...
'...for an eternity...'
'...with the woman I love.'

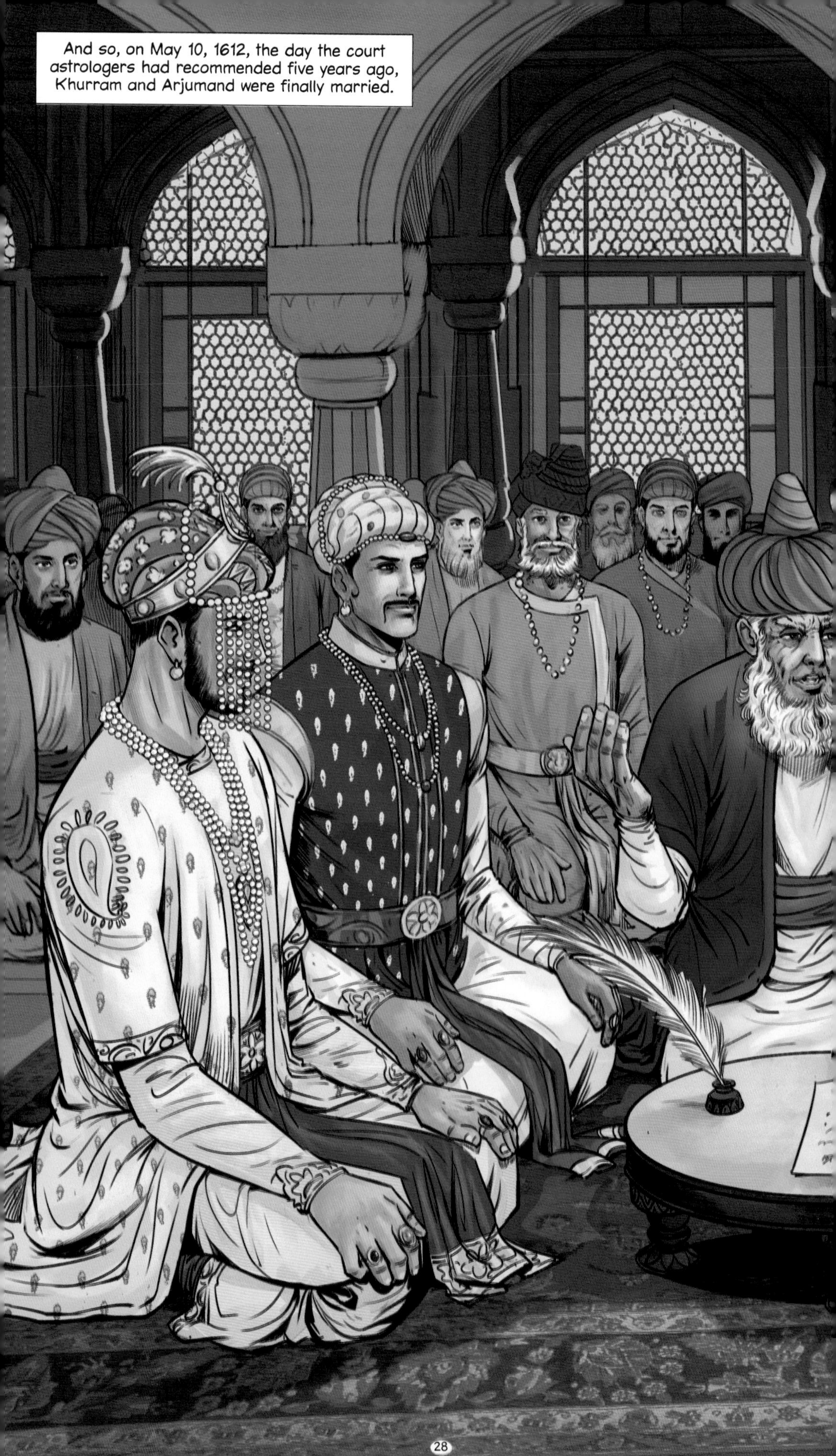
And so, on May 10, 1612, the day the court astrologers had recommended five years ago, Khurram and Arjumand were finally married.

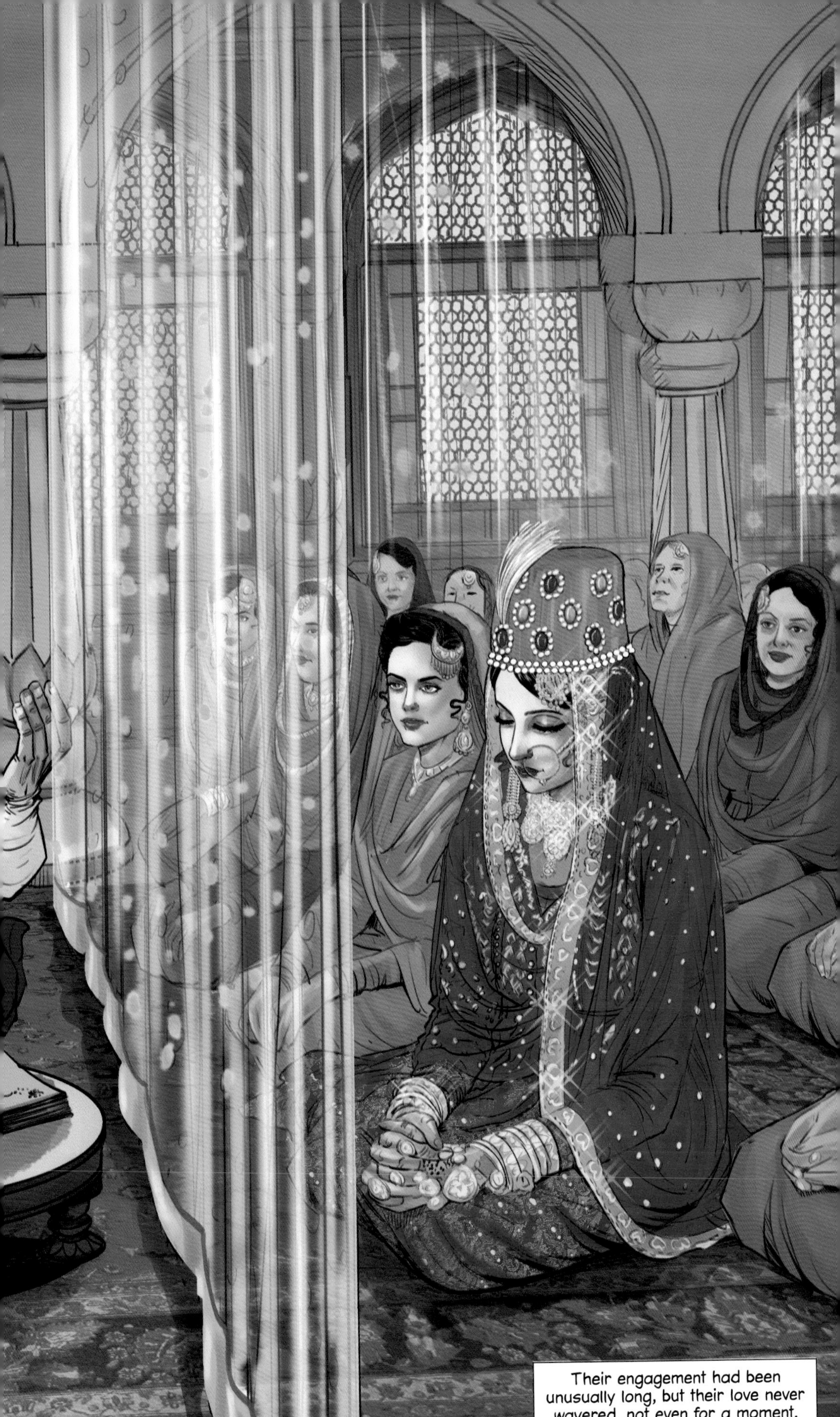
Their engagement had been unusually long, but their love never wavered, not even for a moment.

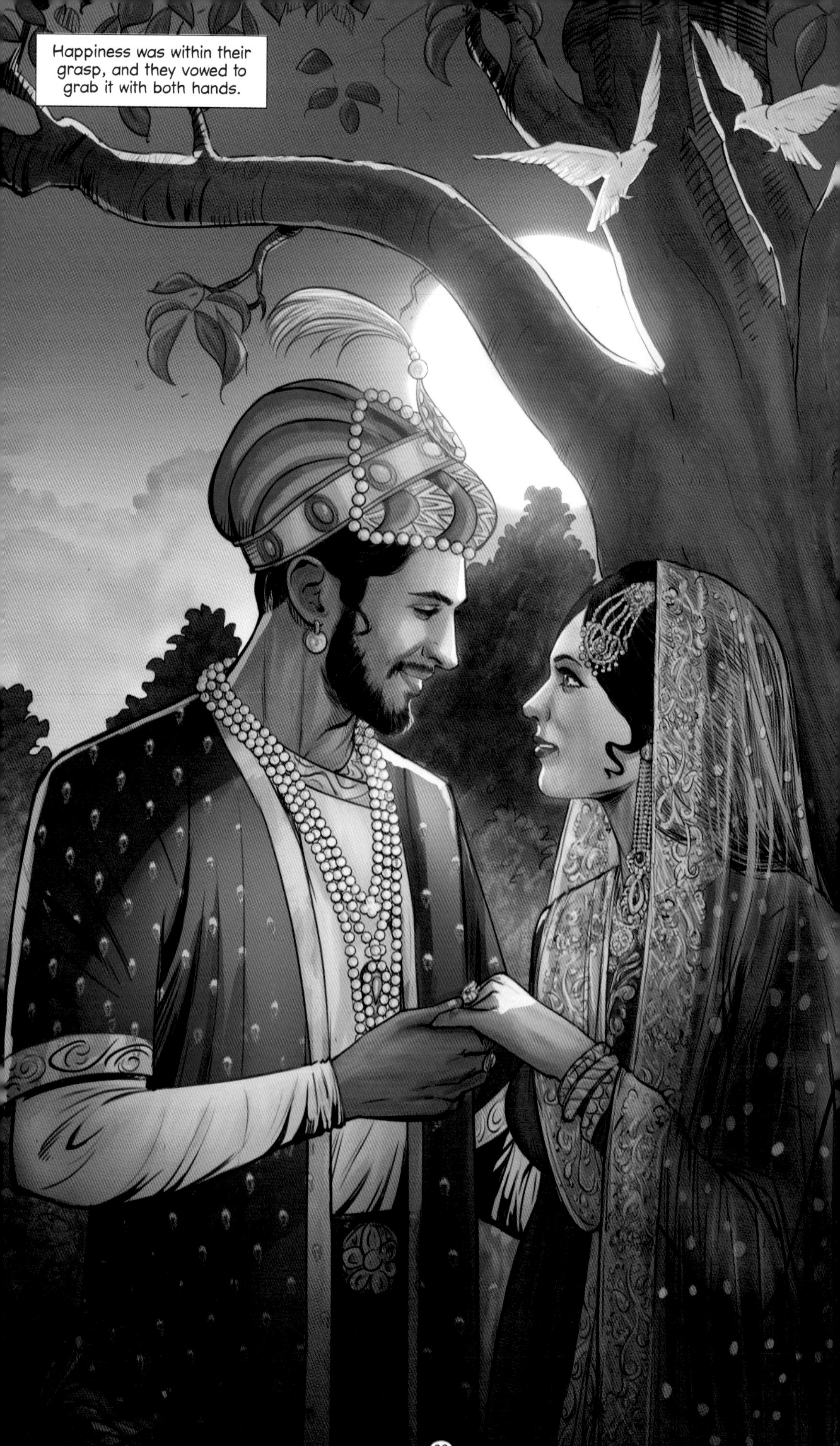
Happiness was within their grasp, and they vowed to grab it with both hands.

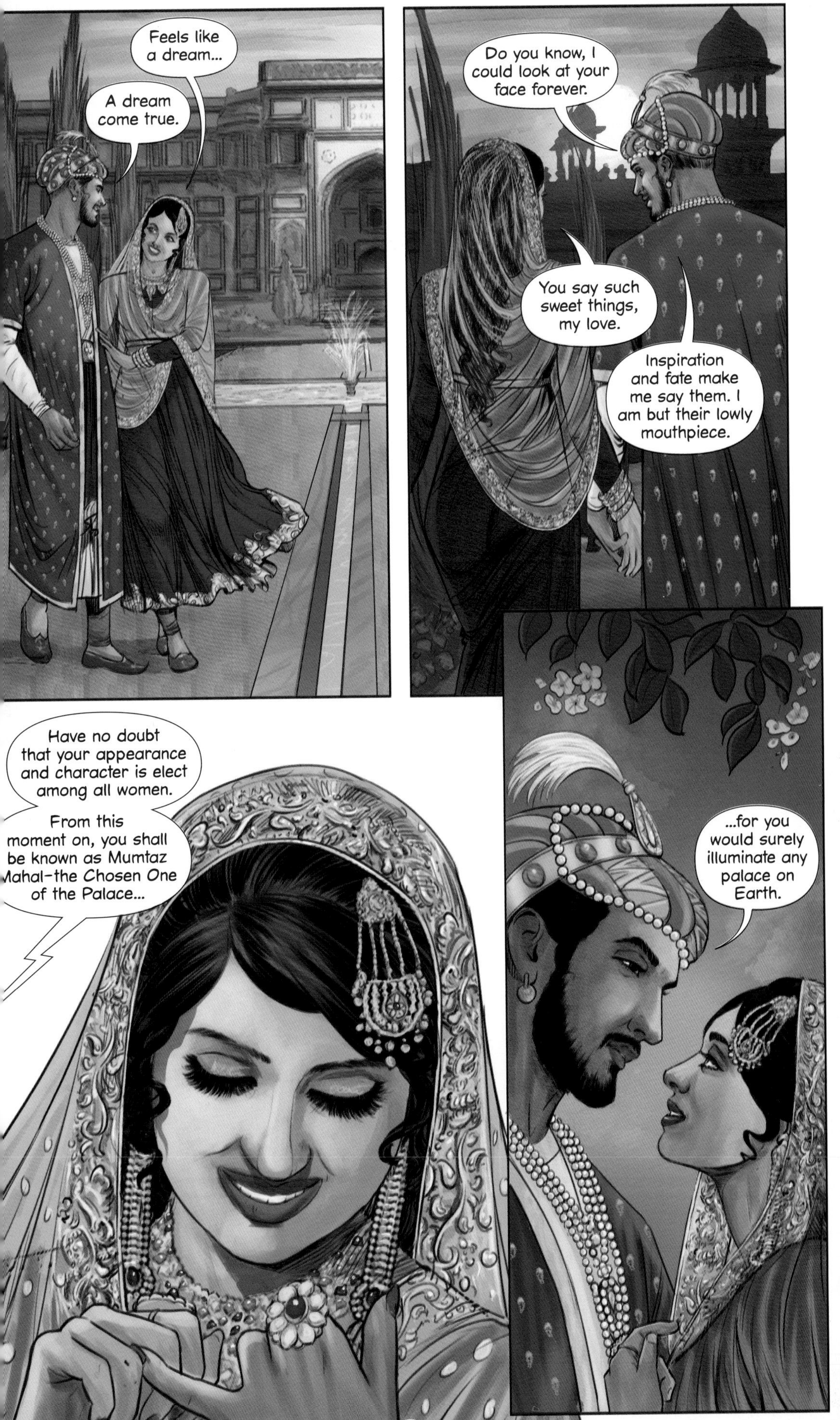

Feels like a dream...
A dream come true.
Do you know, I could look at your face forever.
You say such sweet things, my love.
Inspiration and fate make me say them. I am but their lowly mouthpiece.
Have no doubt that your appearance and character is elect among all women.
From this moment on, you shall be known as Mumtaz Mahal–the Chosen One of the Palace...
...for you would surely illuminate any palace on Earth.

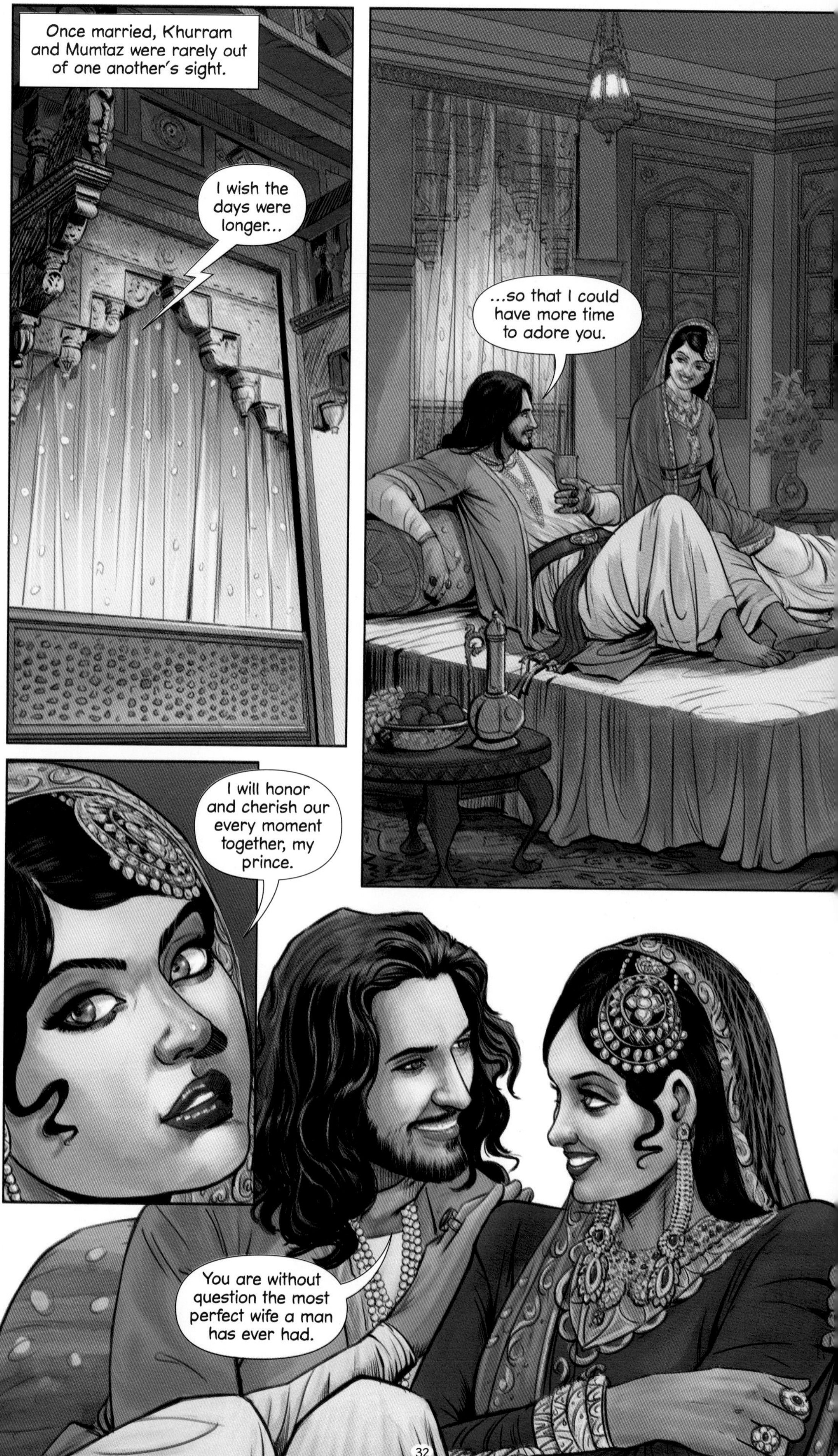
Once married, Khurram and Mumtaz were rarely out of one another's sight.
I wish the days were longer...
...so that I could have more time to adore you.
I will honor and cherish our every moment together, my prince.
You are without question the most perfect wife a man has ever had.

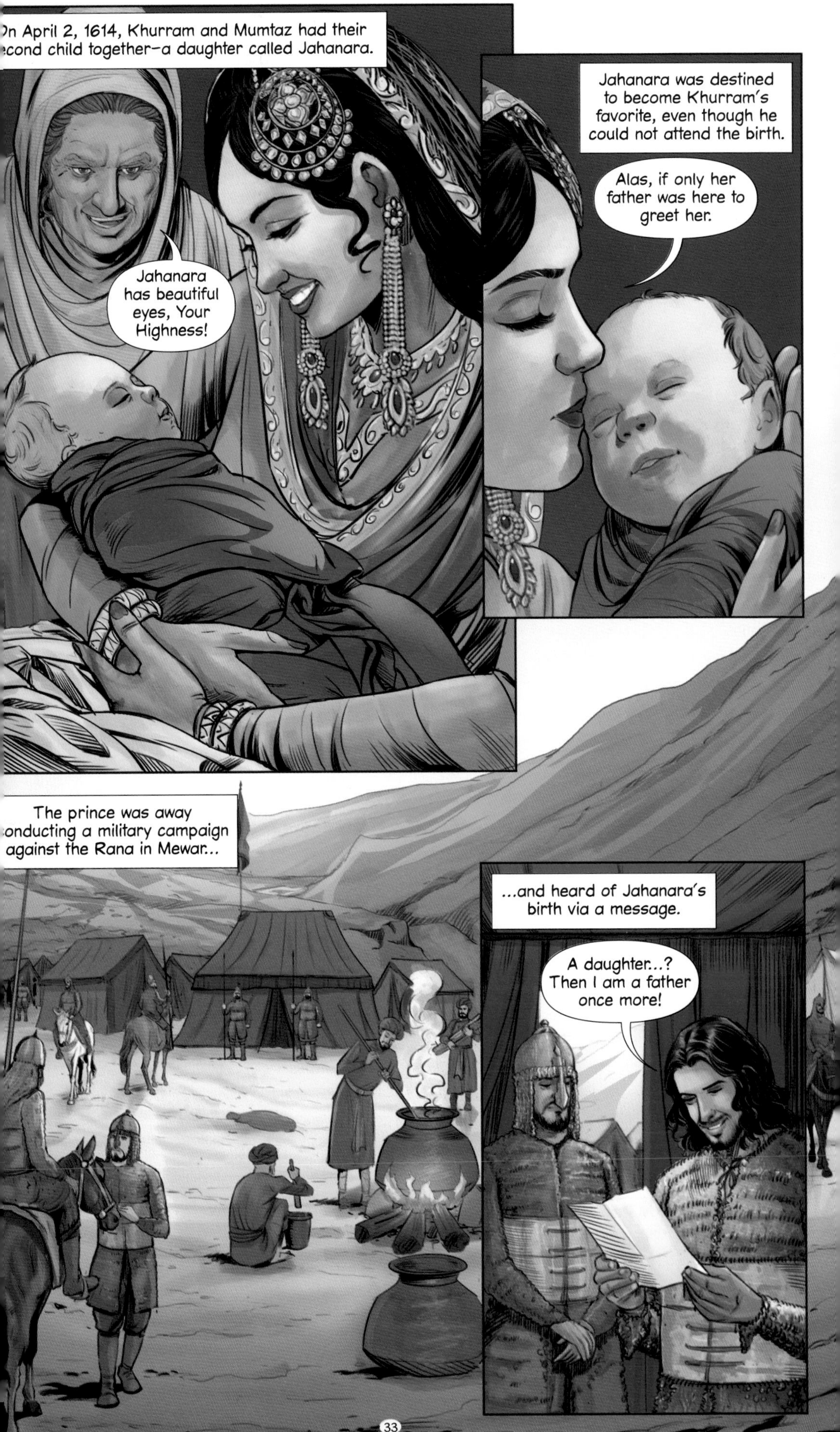

On April 2, 1614, Khurram and Mumtaz had their second child together–a daughter called Jahanara.
Jahanara has beautiful eyes, Your Highness!
Jahanara was destined to become Khurram's favorite, even though he could not attend the birth.
Alas, if only her father was here to greet her.
The prince was away conducting a military campaign against the Rana in Mewar...
...and heard of Jahanara's birth via a message.
A daughter...? Then I am a father once more!

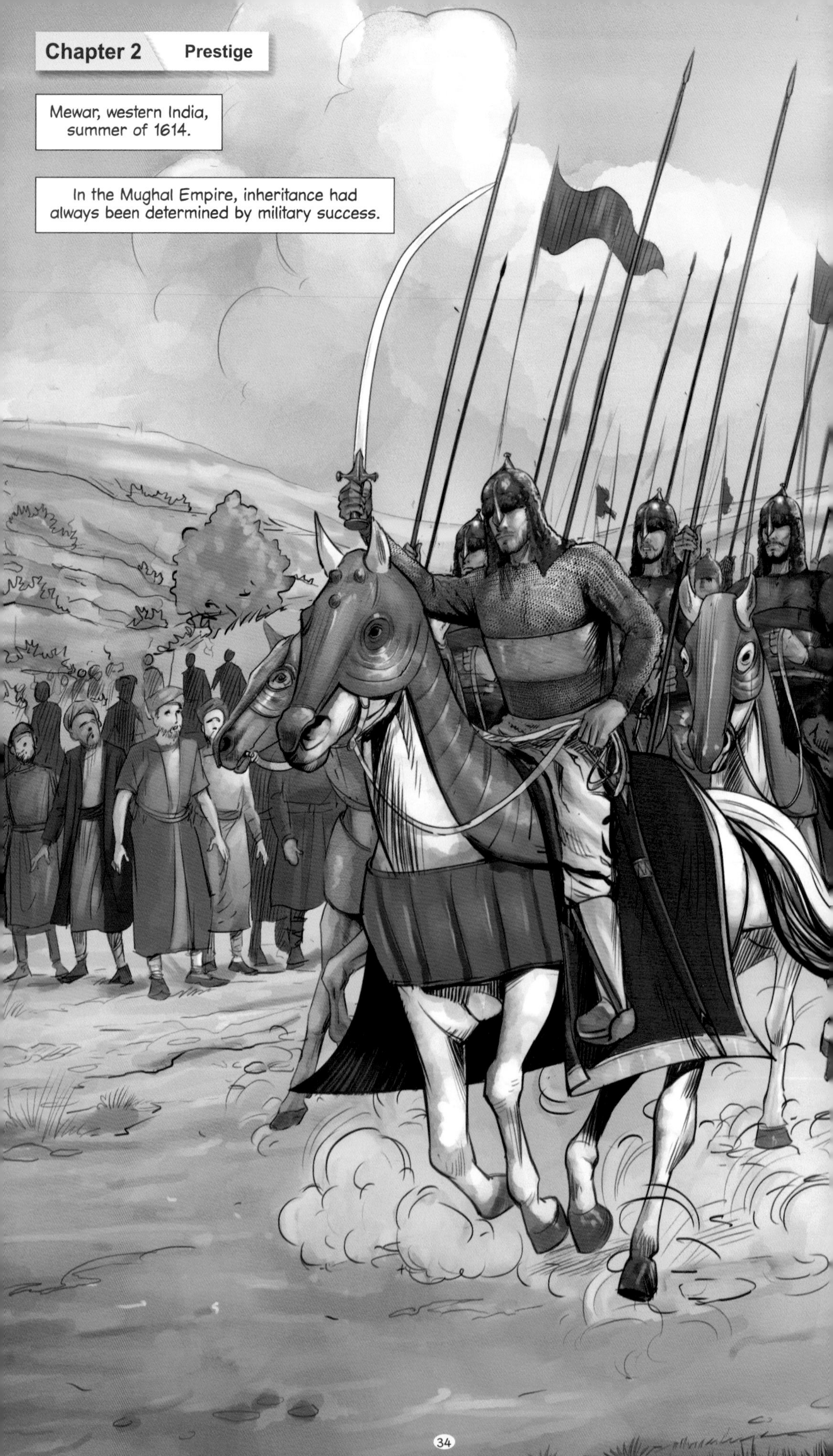
Chapter 2 Prestige
Mewar, western India, summer of 1614.
In the Mughal Empire, inheritance had always been determined by military success.

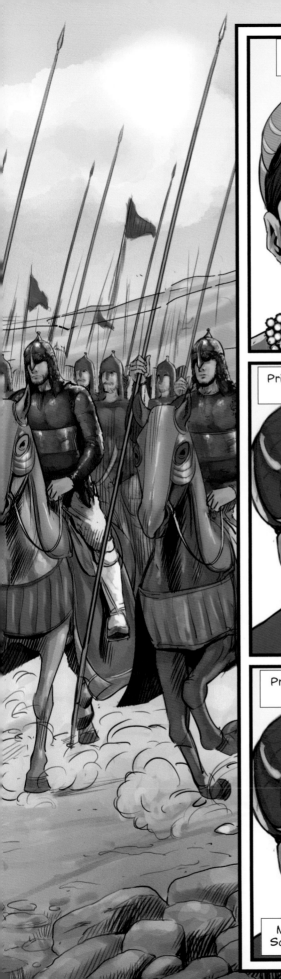

Prince Khusrav, first born son of Emperor Jahangir, born August 16, 1587.

Mother: Manbhawati Bai, first wife of Emperor Jahangir.

Prince Parviz, second son of Emperor Jahangir, born October 2, 1589.

Mother: Sahib-i-Jamal Begum, sixth wife of Emperor Jahangir.

Prince Khurram, third son of Emperor Jahangir, born January 5, 1592.

Mother: Taj Bibi Bilqis Makani Begum Sahiba, third wife of Emperor Jahangir.

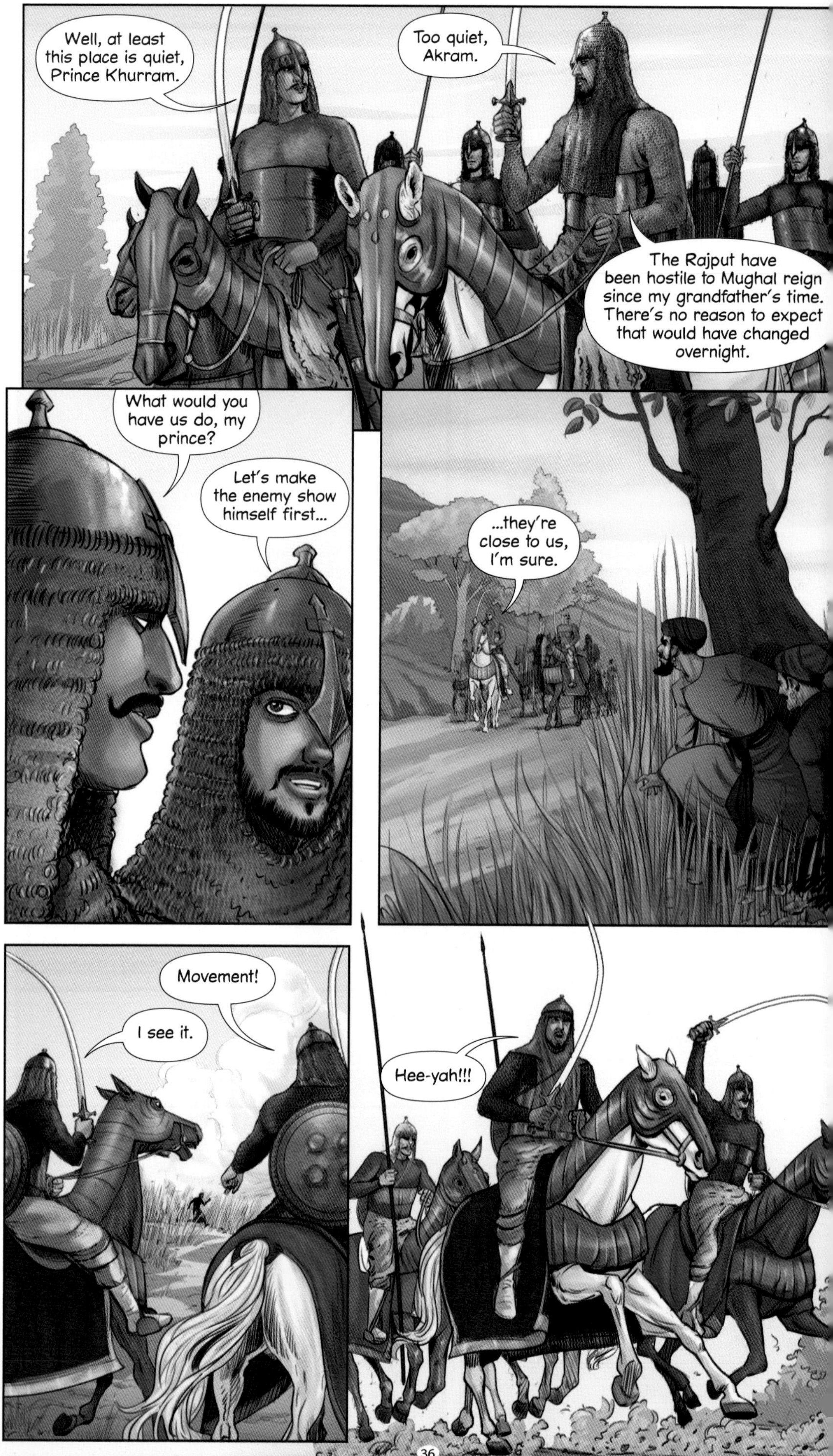
Well, at least this place is quiet, Prince Khurram.
Too quiet, Akram.
The Rajput have been hostile to Mughal reign since my grandfather's time. There's no reason to expect that would have changed overnight.
What would you have us do, my prince?
Let's make the enemy show himself first...
...they're close to us, I'm sure.
Movement!
I see it.
Hee-yah!!!

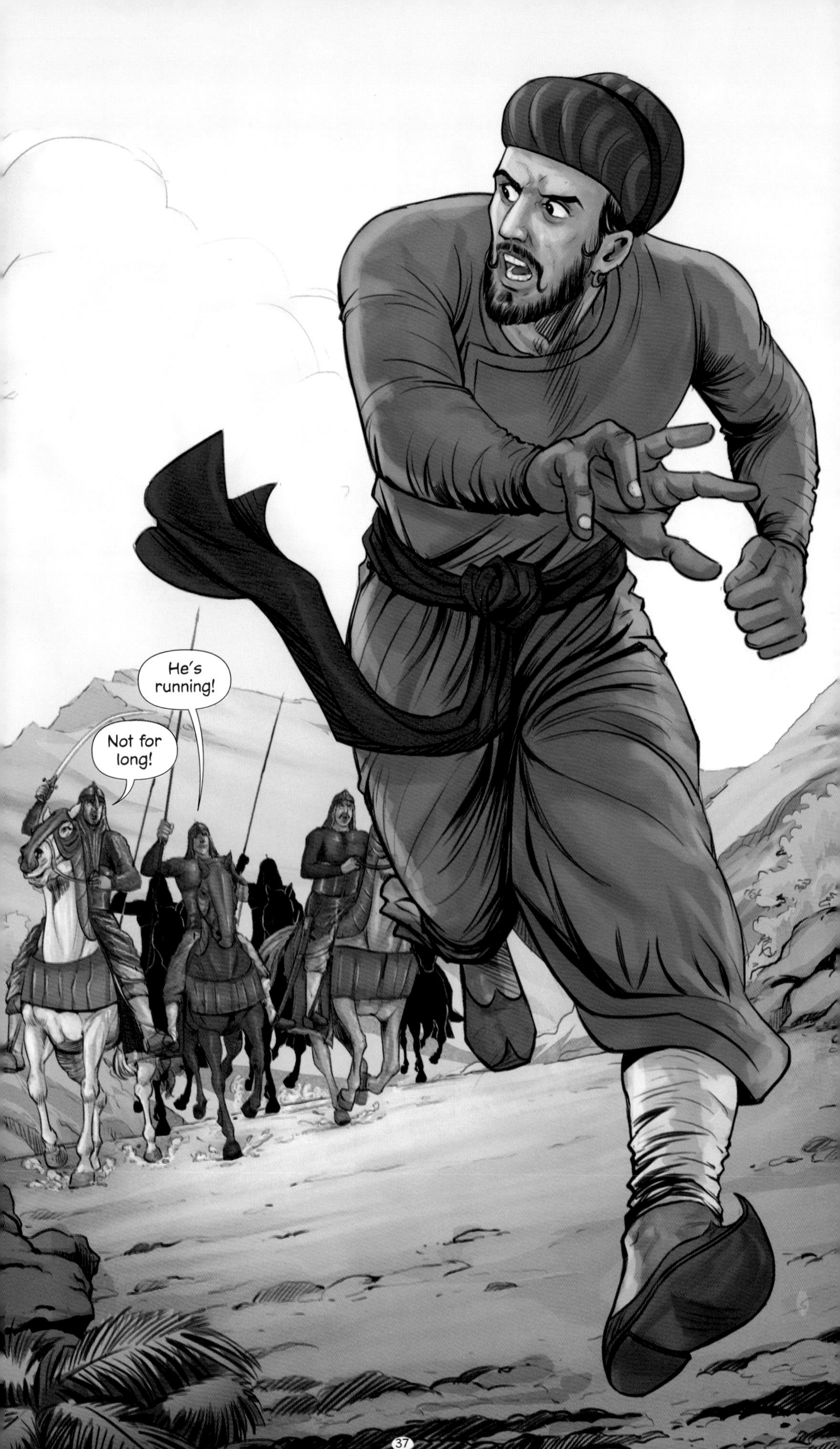
He's running!
Not for long!

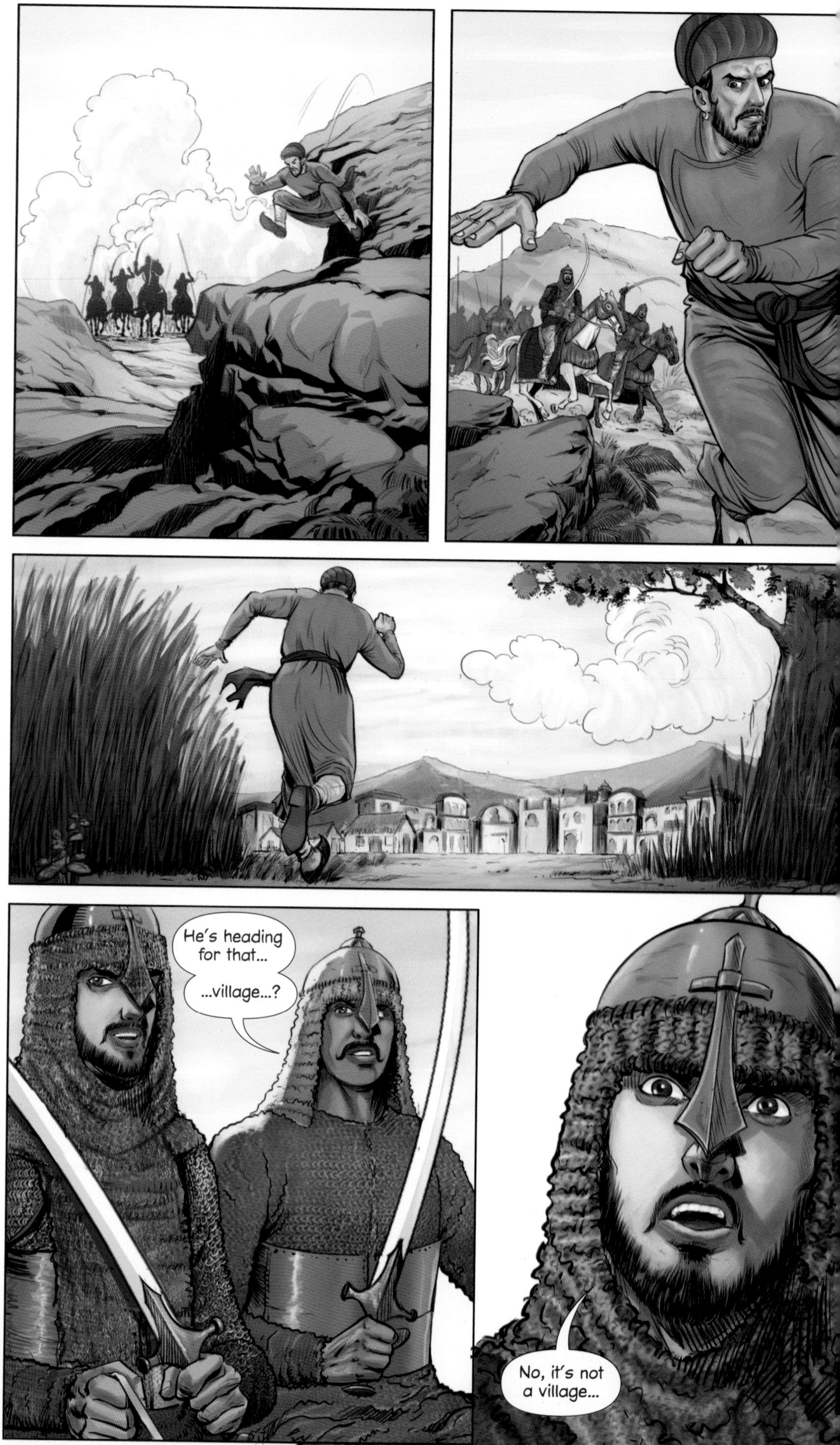
He's heading for that...
...village...?
No, it's not a village...

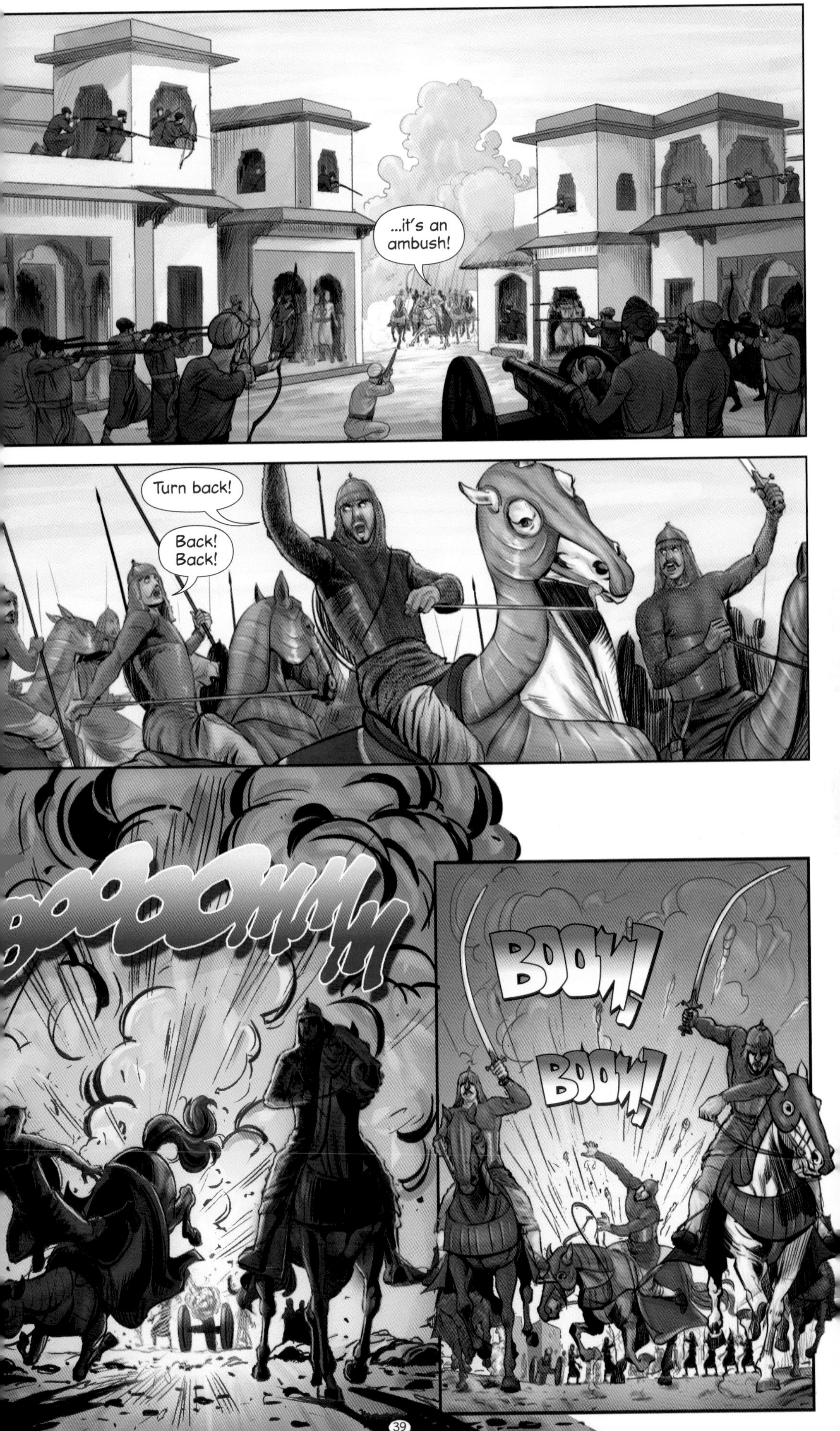

...it's an ambush!
Turn back!
Back! Back!
BOOOOMMM
BOOM!
BOOM!

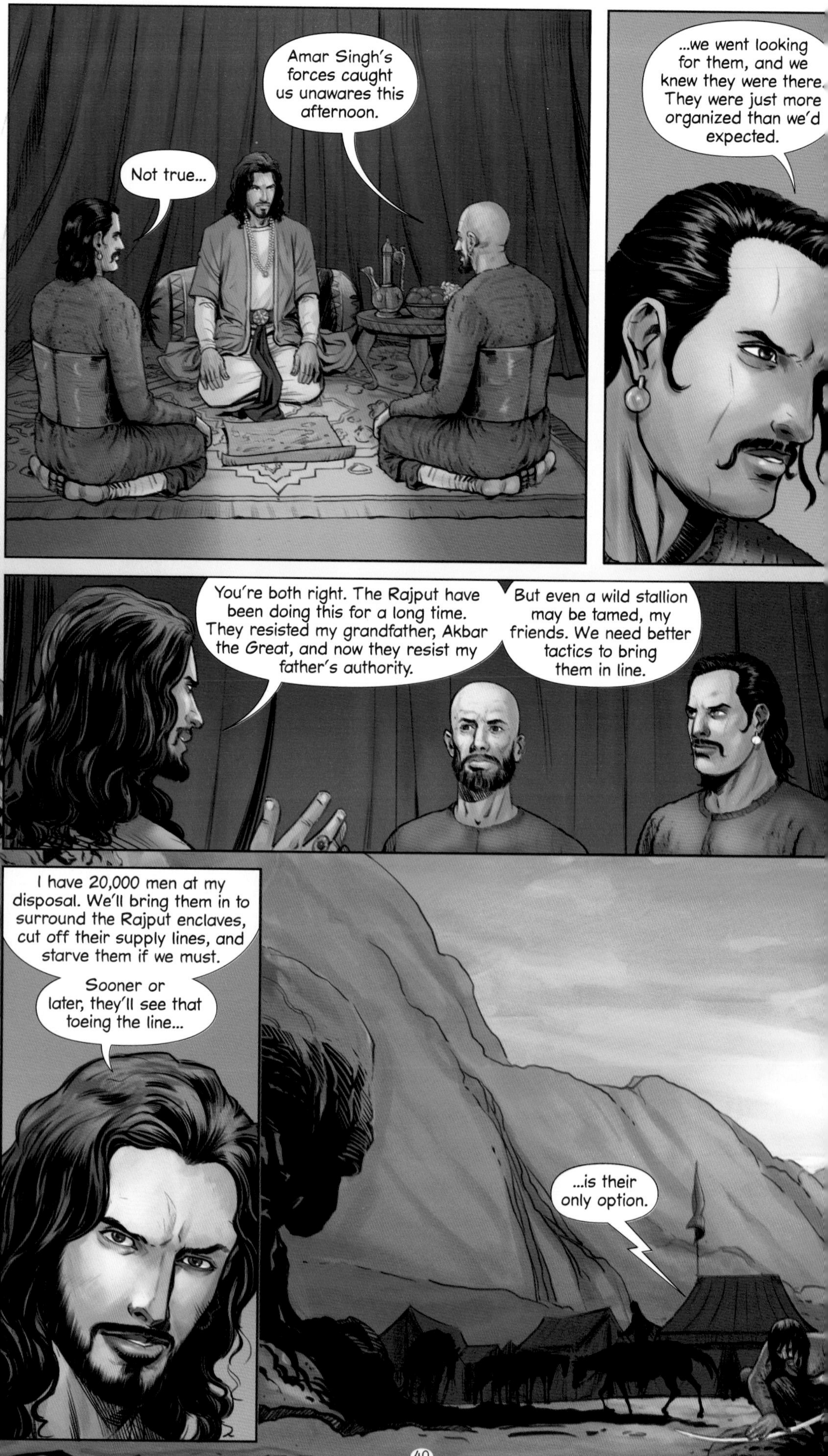
Amar Singh's forces caught us unawares this afternoon.
Not true...
...we went looking for them, and we knew they were there. They were just more organized than we'd expected.
You're both right. The Rajput have been doing this for a long time. They resisted my grandfather, Akbar the Great, and now they resist my father's authority.
But even a wild stallion may be tamed, my friends. We need better tactics to bring them in line.
I have 20,000 men at my disposal. We'll bring them in to surround the Rajput enclaves, cut off their supply lines, and starve them if we must.
Sooner or later, they'll see that toeing the line...
...is their only option.

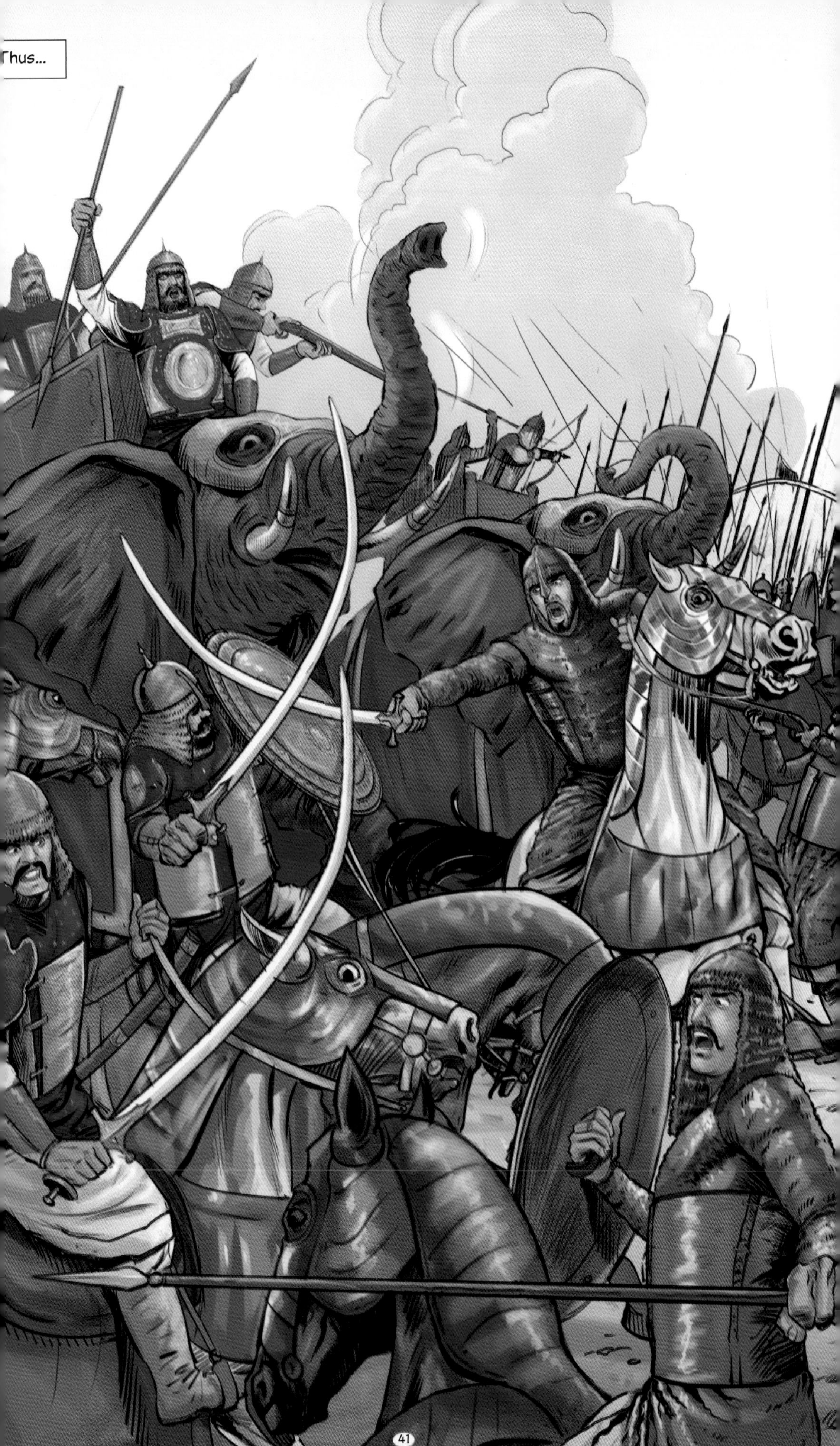

Thus...

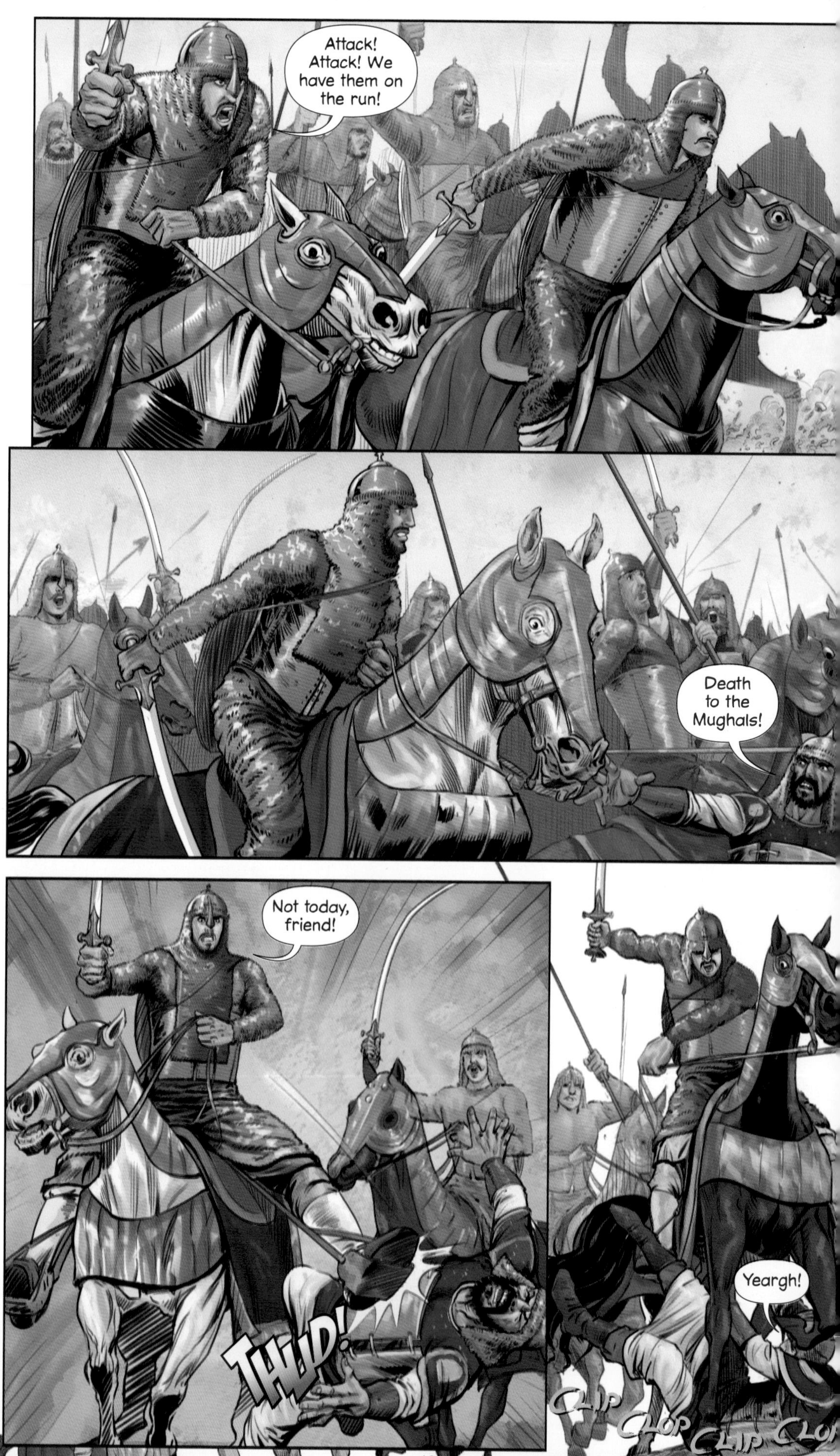

Attack! Attack! We have them on the run!
Death to the Mughals!
Not today, friend!
THUD!
Yeargh!
CLIP CLOP CLIP CLOP

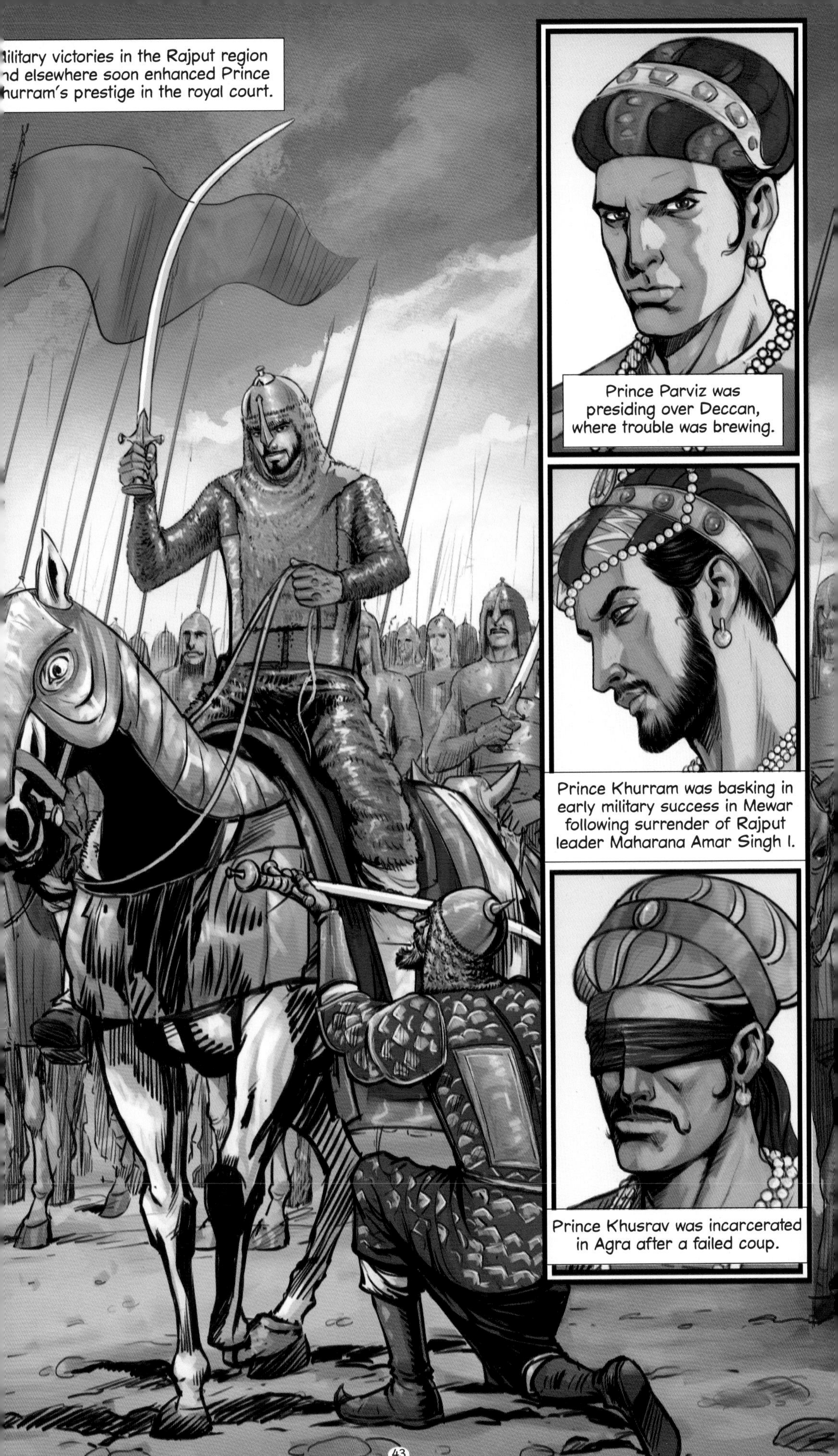
ilitary victories in the Rajput region
nd elsewhere soon enhanced Prince
hurram's prestige in the royal court.
Prince Parviz was presiding over Deccan, where trouble was brewing.
Prince Khurram was basking in early military success in Mewar following surrender of Rajput leader Maharana Amar Singh I.
Prince Khusrav was incarcerated in Agra after a failed coup.

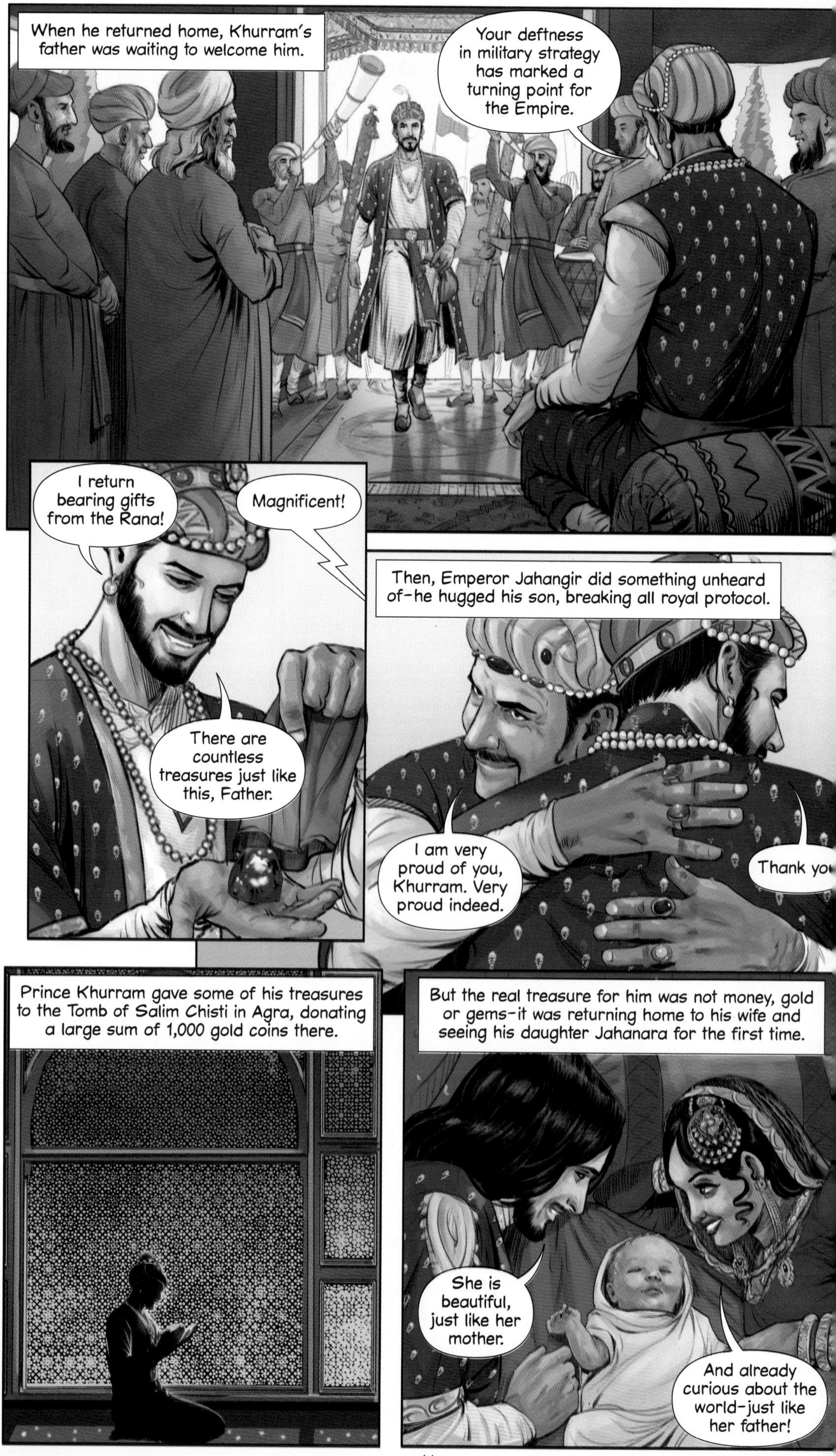

When he returned home, Khurram's father was waiting to welcome him.
Your deftness in military strategy has marked a turning point for the Empire.
I return bearing gifts from the Rana!
Magnificent!
There are countless treasures just like this, Father.
Then, Emperor Jahangir did something unheard of–he hugged his son, breaking all royal protocol.
I am very proud of you, Khurram. Very proud indeed.
Thank yo
Prince Khurram gave some of his treasures to the Tomb of Salim Chisti in Agra, donating a large sum of 1,000 gold coins there.
But the real treasure for him was not money, gold or gems–it was returning home to his wife and seeing his daughter Jahanara for the first time.
She is beautiful, just like her mother.
And already curious about the world–just like her father!

Early 1617.

Following Khurram's success in Mewar, he was assigned to deal with restlessness in the Deccan region on the Mughal Empire's southern border.

This region belongs to your brother Prince Parviz, does it not?

Yes, his seat of power is here in Burhanpur...

...but there have been tensions between the Mughals and the Faruqis here dating back to Miran Bahadur Khan's clashes with my grandfather, two decades ago. Now, that upstart Malik Ambar is stoking those tensions again.

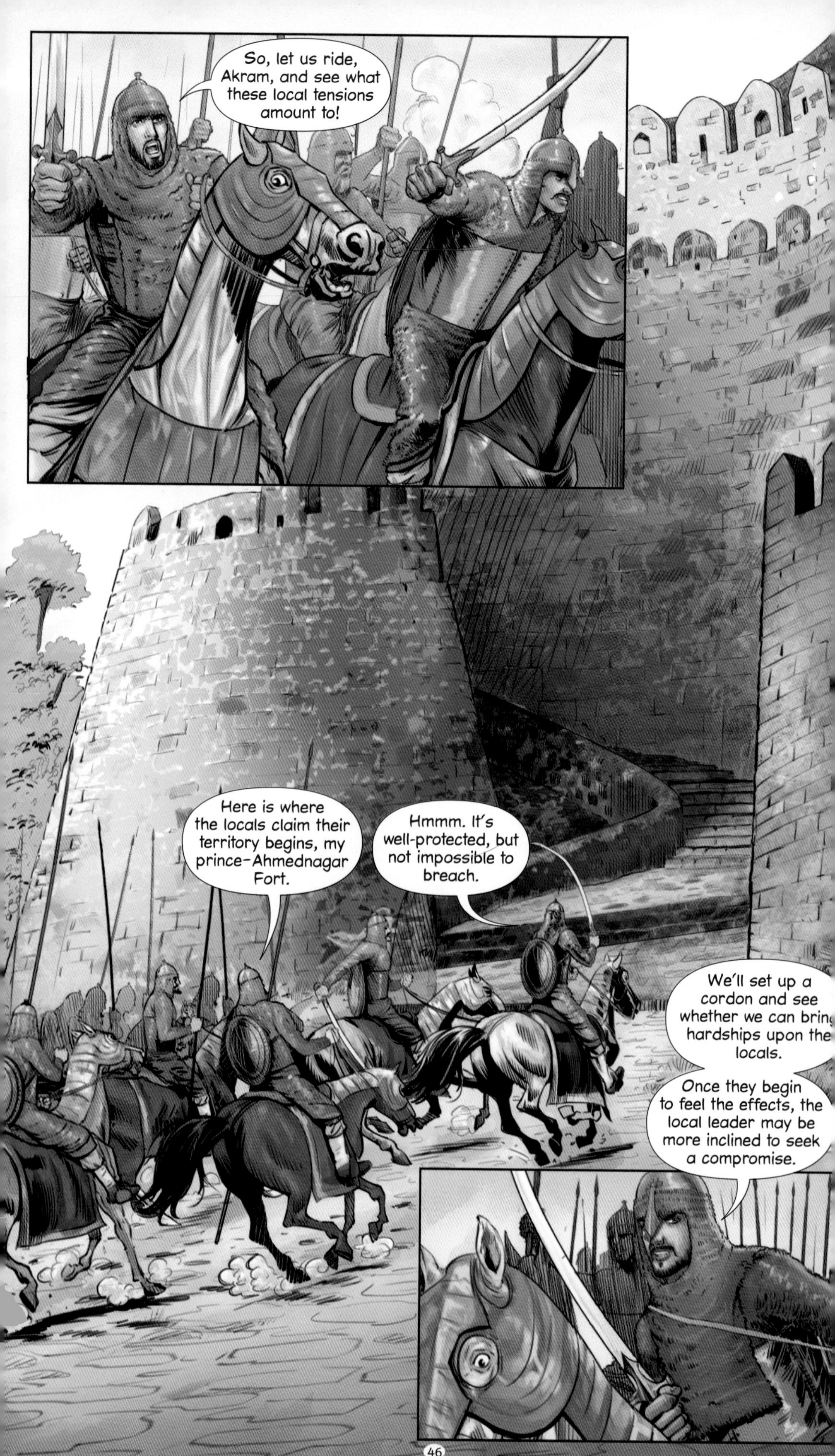
So, let us ride, Akram, and see what these local tensions amount to!
Here is where the locals claim their territory begins, my prince–Ahmednagar Fort.
Hmmm. It's well-protected, but not impossible to breach.
We'll set up a cordon and see whether we can brin hardships upon the locals.
Once they begin to feel the effects, the local leader may be more inclined to seek a compromise.

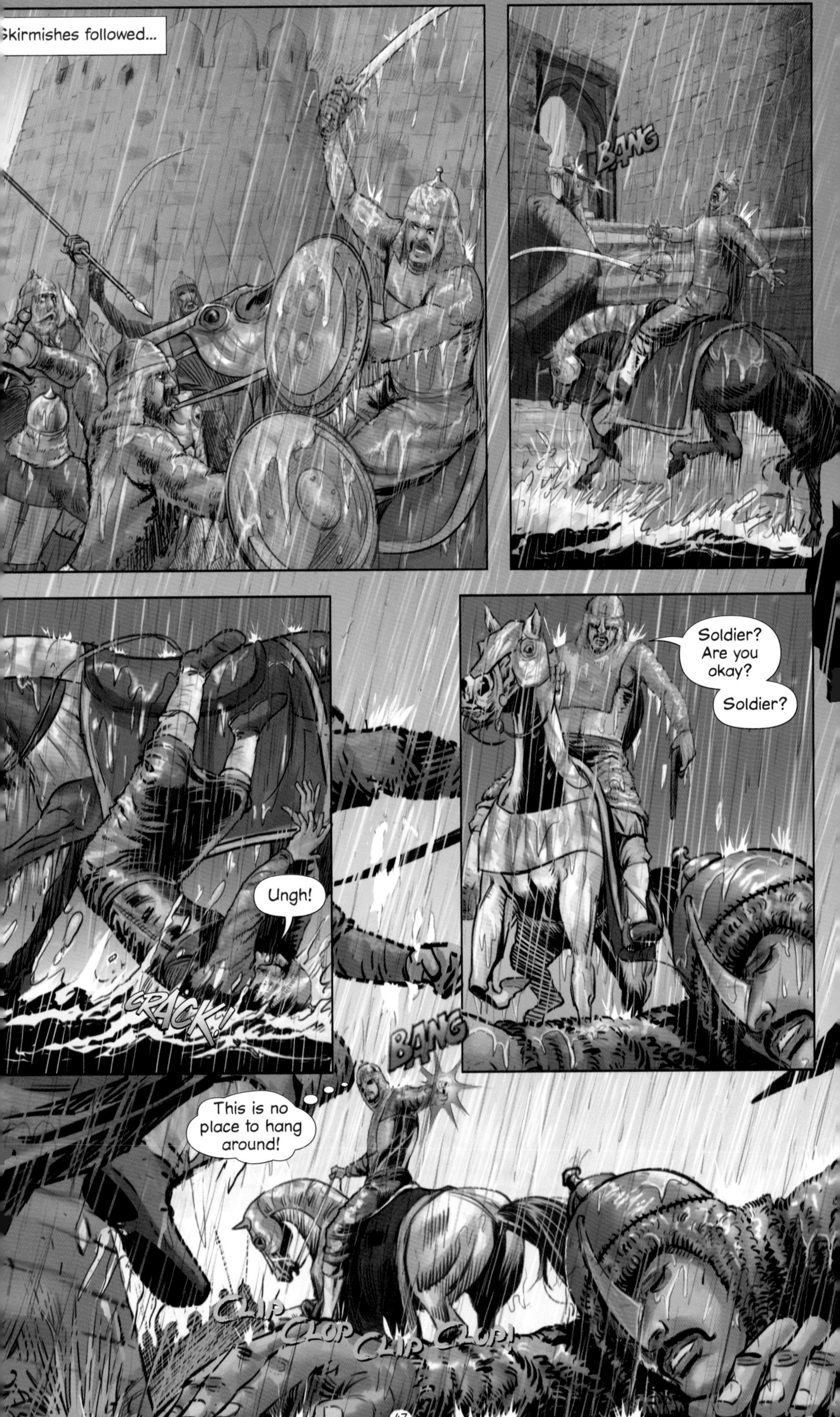
Skirmishes followed...
BANG
CRACK!
Ungh!
Soldier? Are you okay?
Soldier?
BANG
This is no place to hang around!
CLIP CLOP CLIP CLOP!

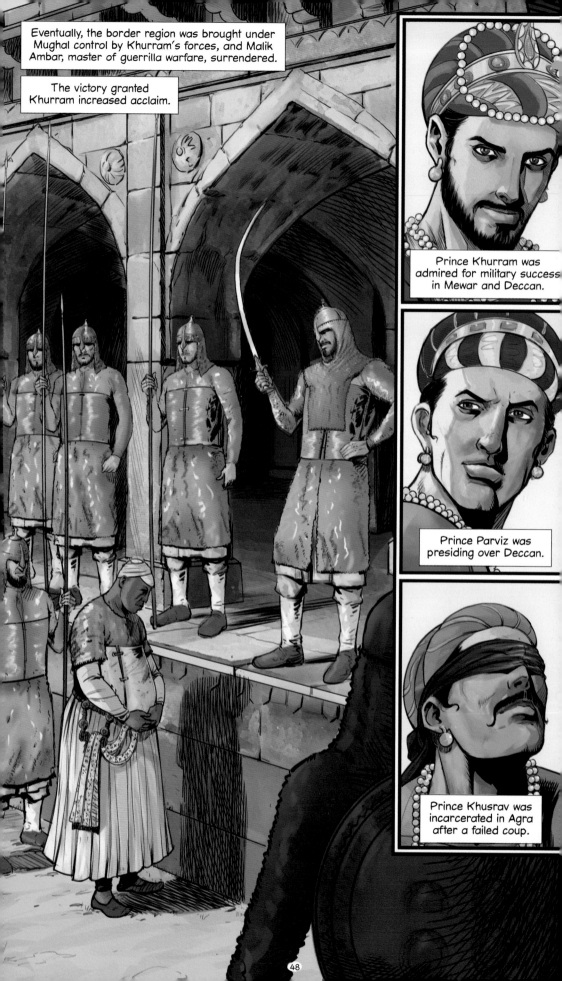

Eventually, the border region was brought under Mughal control by Khurram's forces, and Malik Ambar, master of guerrilla warfare, surrendered.

The victory granted Khurram increased acclaim.

Prince Khurram was admired for military success in Mewar and Deccan.

Prince Parviz was presiding over Deccan.

Prince Khusrav was incarcerated in Agra after a failed coup.

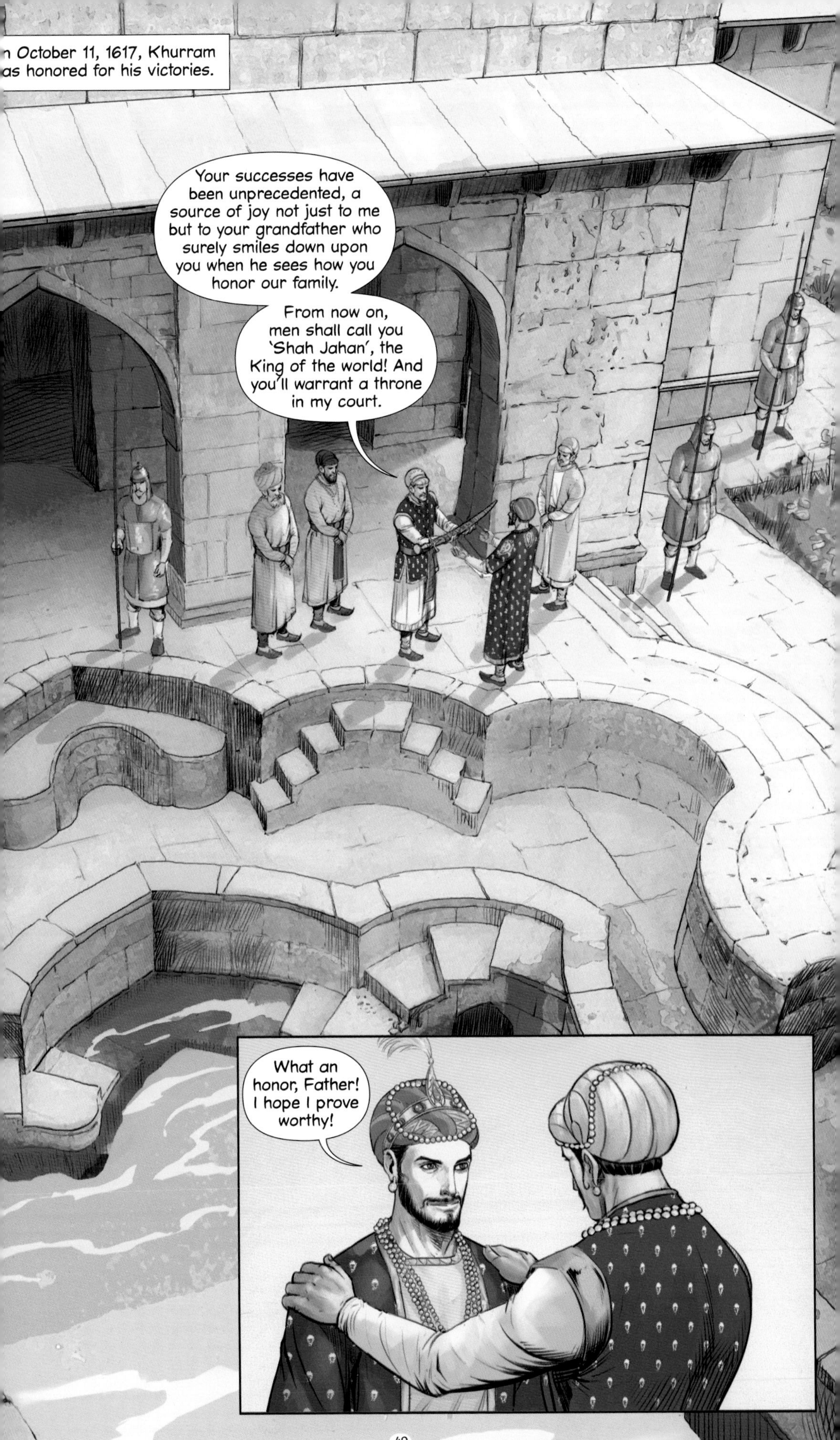
n October 11, 1617, Khurram as honored for his victories.
Your successes have been unprecedented, a source of joy not just to me but to your grandfather who surely smiles down upon you when he sees how you honor our family.
From now on, men shall call you 'Shah Jahan', the King of the world! And you'll warrant a throne in my court.
What an honor, Father! I hope I prove worthy!

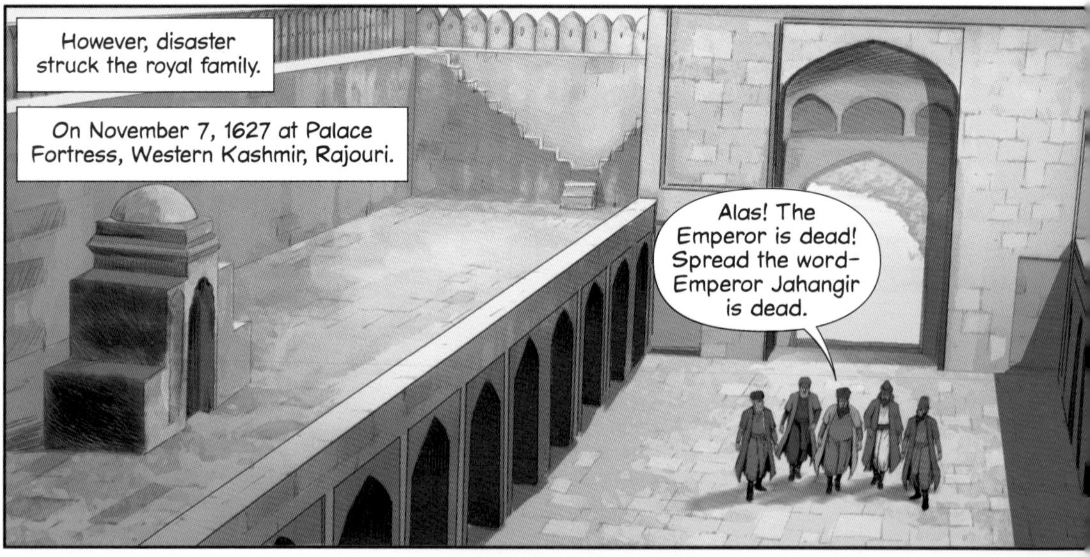
However, disaster struck the royal family.
On November 7, 1627 at Palace Fortress, Western Kashmir, Rajouri.
Alas! The Emperor is dead! Spread the word– Emperor Jahangir is dead.

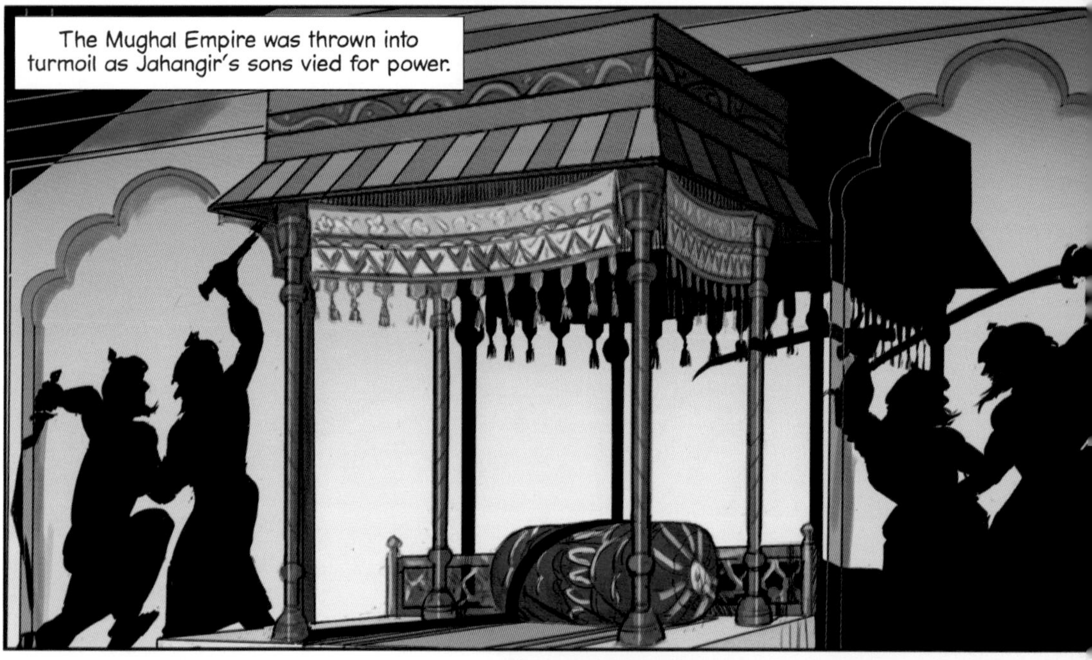
The Mughal Empire was thrown into turmoil as Jahangir's sons vied for power.

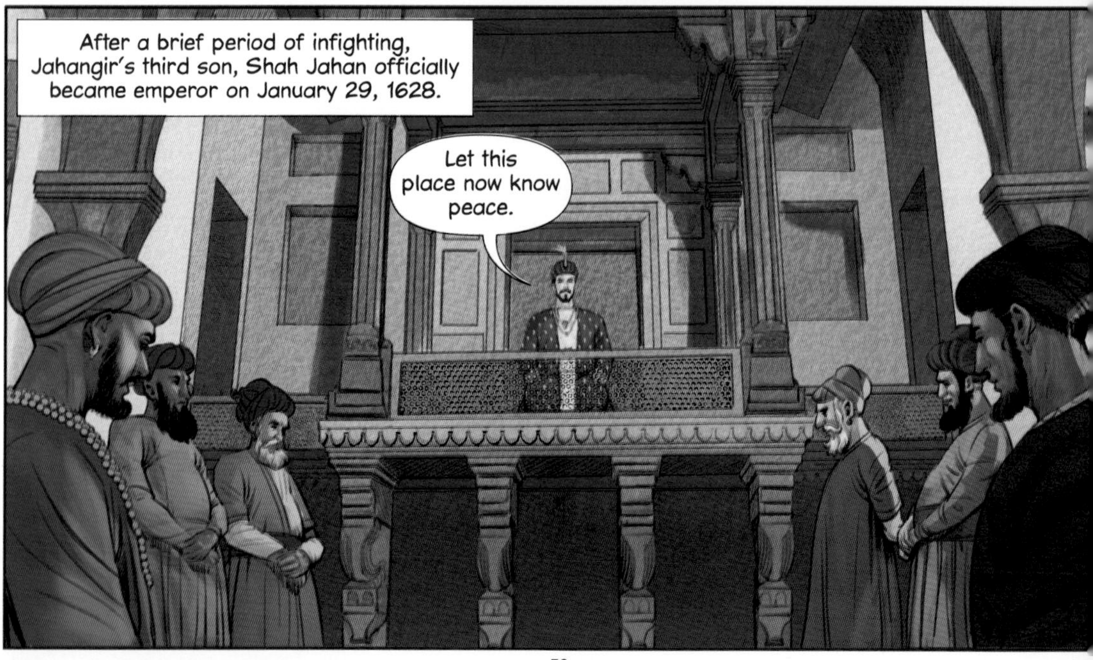
After a brief period of infighting, Jahangir's third son, Shah Jahan officially became emperor on January 29, 1628.
Let this place now know peace.

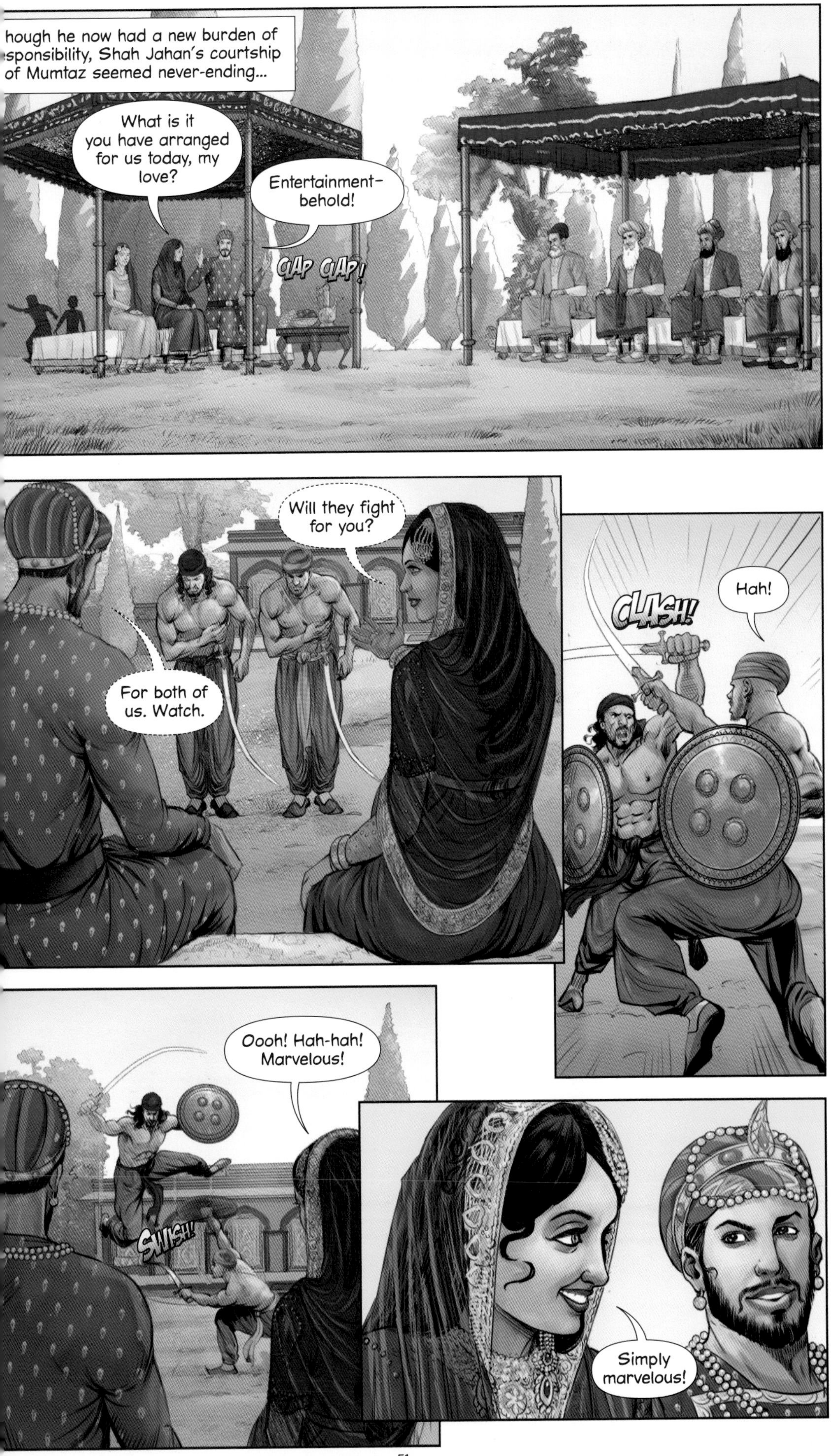
hough he now had a new burden of
sponsibility, Shah Jahan's courtship
of Mumtaz seemed never-ending...
What is it you have arranged for us today, my love?
Entertainment– behold!
CLAP CLAP!
Will they fight for you?
For both of us. Watch.
CLASH!
Hah!
Oooh! Hah-hah! Marvelous!
SWISH!
Simply marvelous!

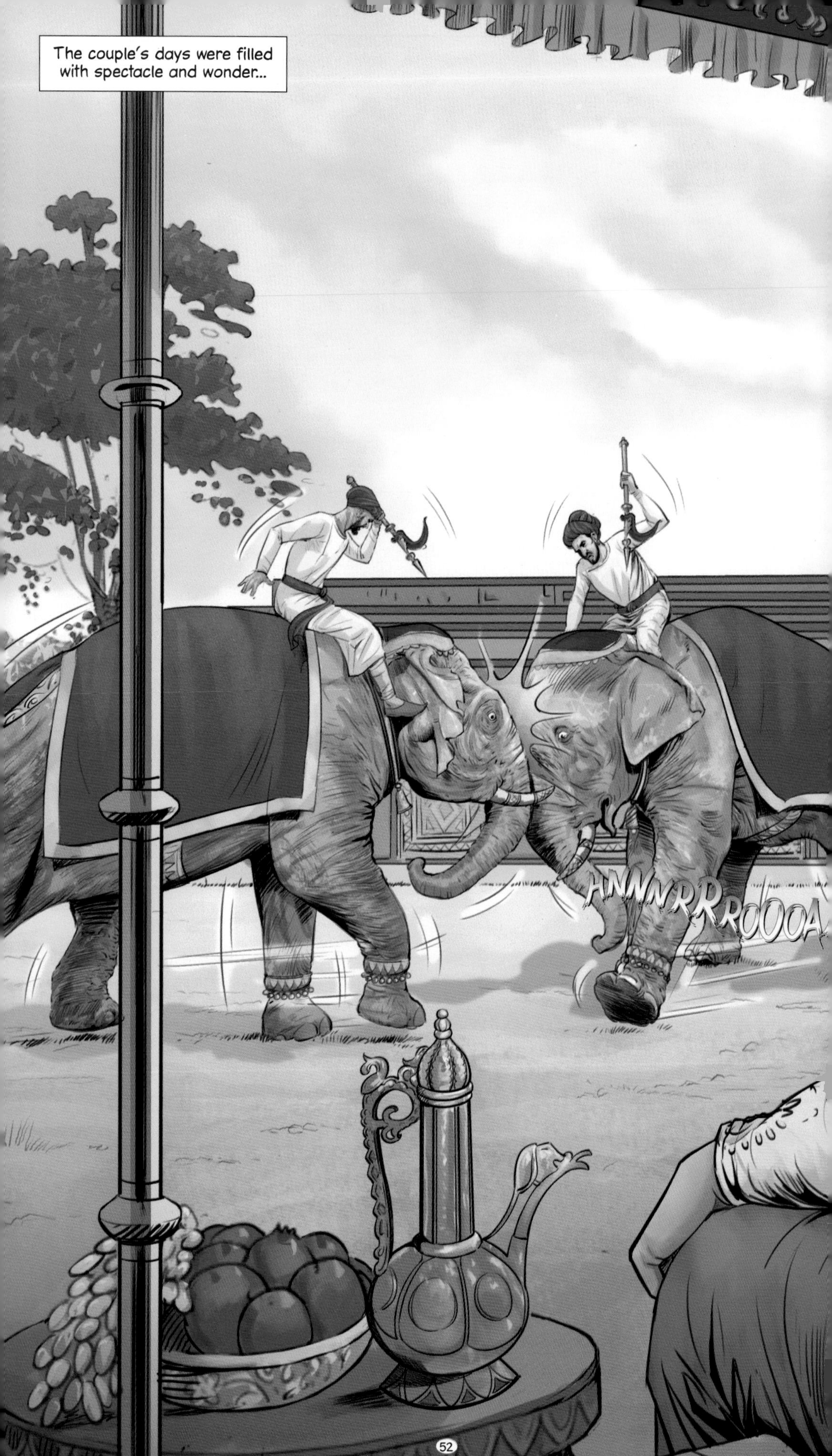
The couple's days were filled with spectacle and wonder...
HNNNRRROOOA

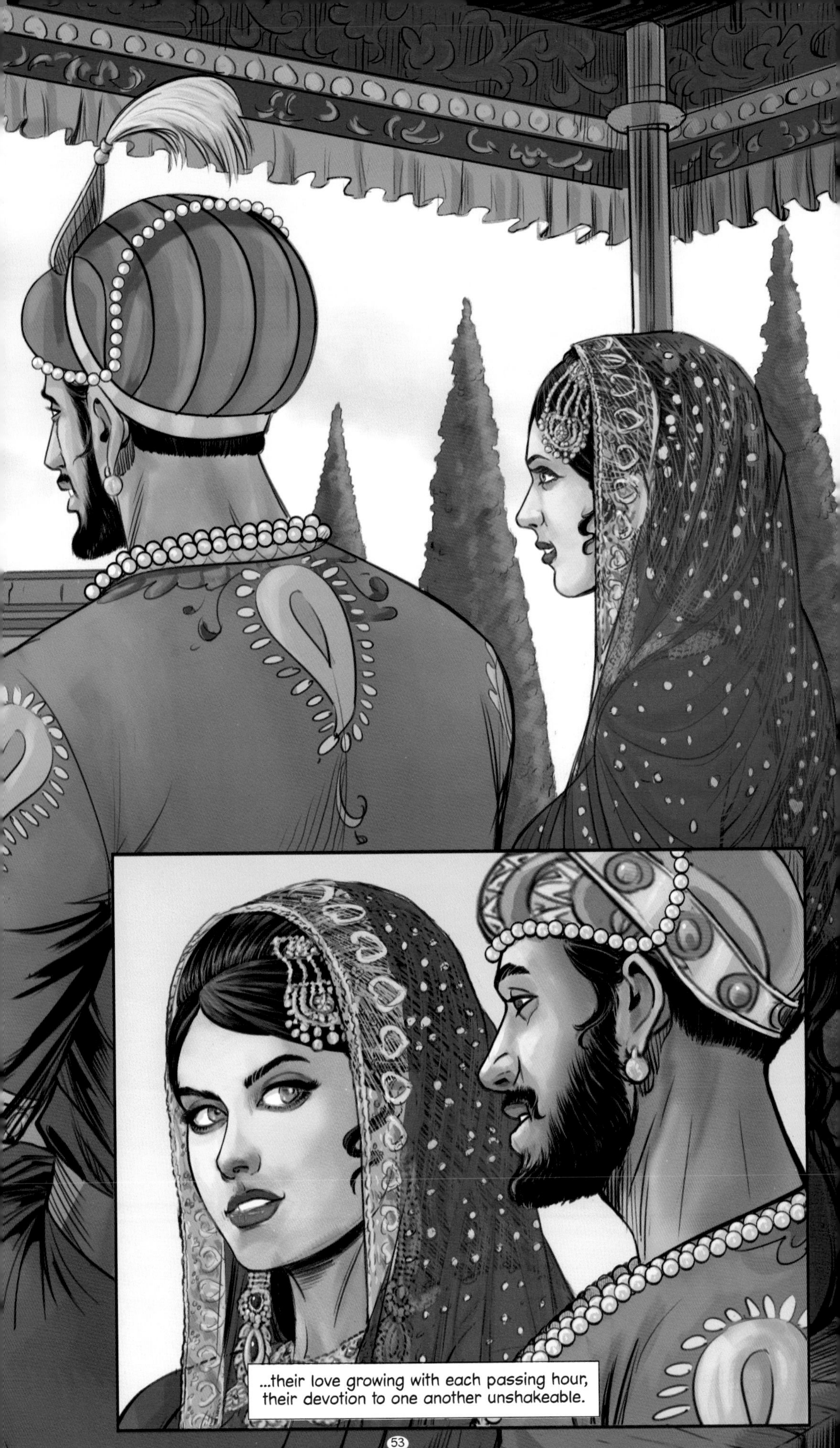
...their love growing with each passing hour, their devotion to one another unshakeable.

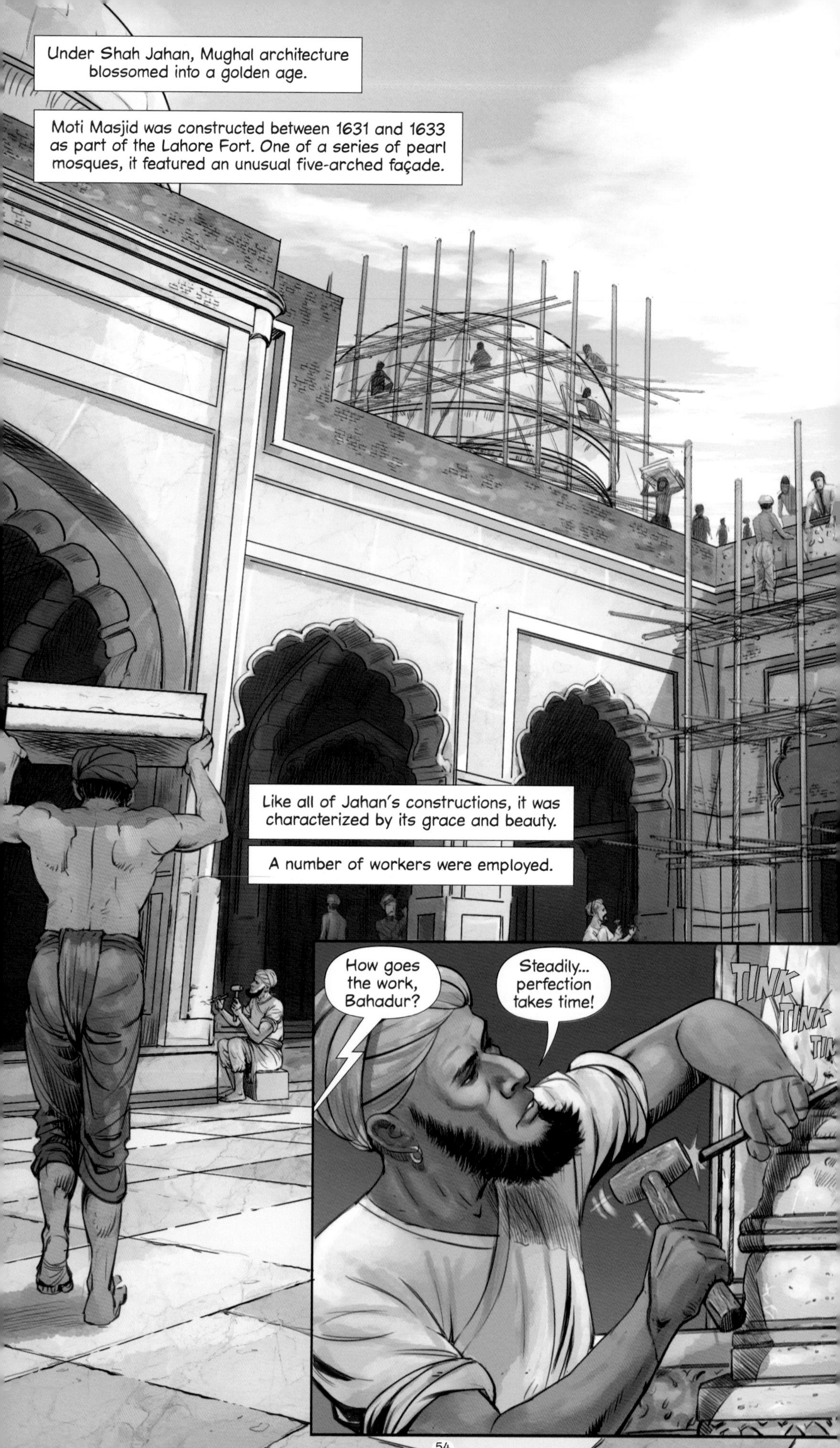
Under Shah Jahan, Mughal architecture blossomed into a golden age.
Moti Masjid was constructed between 1631 and 1633 as part of the Lahore Fort. One of a series of pearl mosques, it featured an unusual five-arched façade.
Like all of Jahan's constructions, it was characterized by its grace and beauty.
A number of workers were employed.
How goes the work, Bahadur?
Steadily... perfection takes time!
TINK
TINK

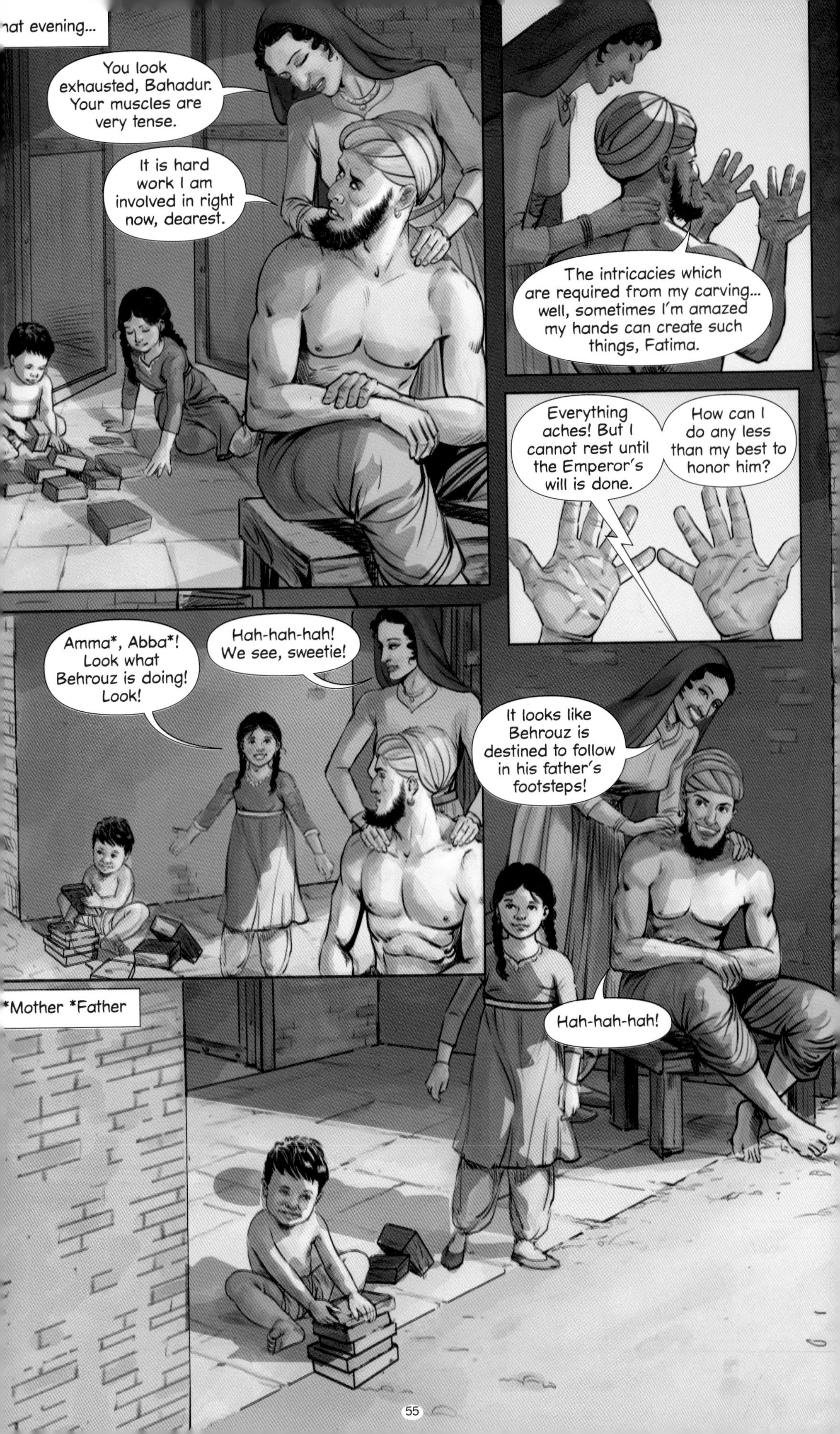

hat evening...
You look exhausted, Bahadur. Your muscles are very tense.
It is hard work I am involved in right now, dearest.
The intricacies which are required from my carving... well, sometimes I'm amazed my hands can create such things, Fatima.
Everything aches! But I cannot rest until the Emperor's will is done.
How can I do any less than my best to honor him?
Amma*, Abba*! Look what Behrouz is doing! Look!
Hah-hah-hah! We see, sweetie!
It looks like Behrouz is destined to follow in his father's footsteps!
Hah-hah-hah!
*Mother *Father

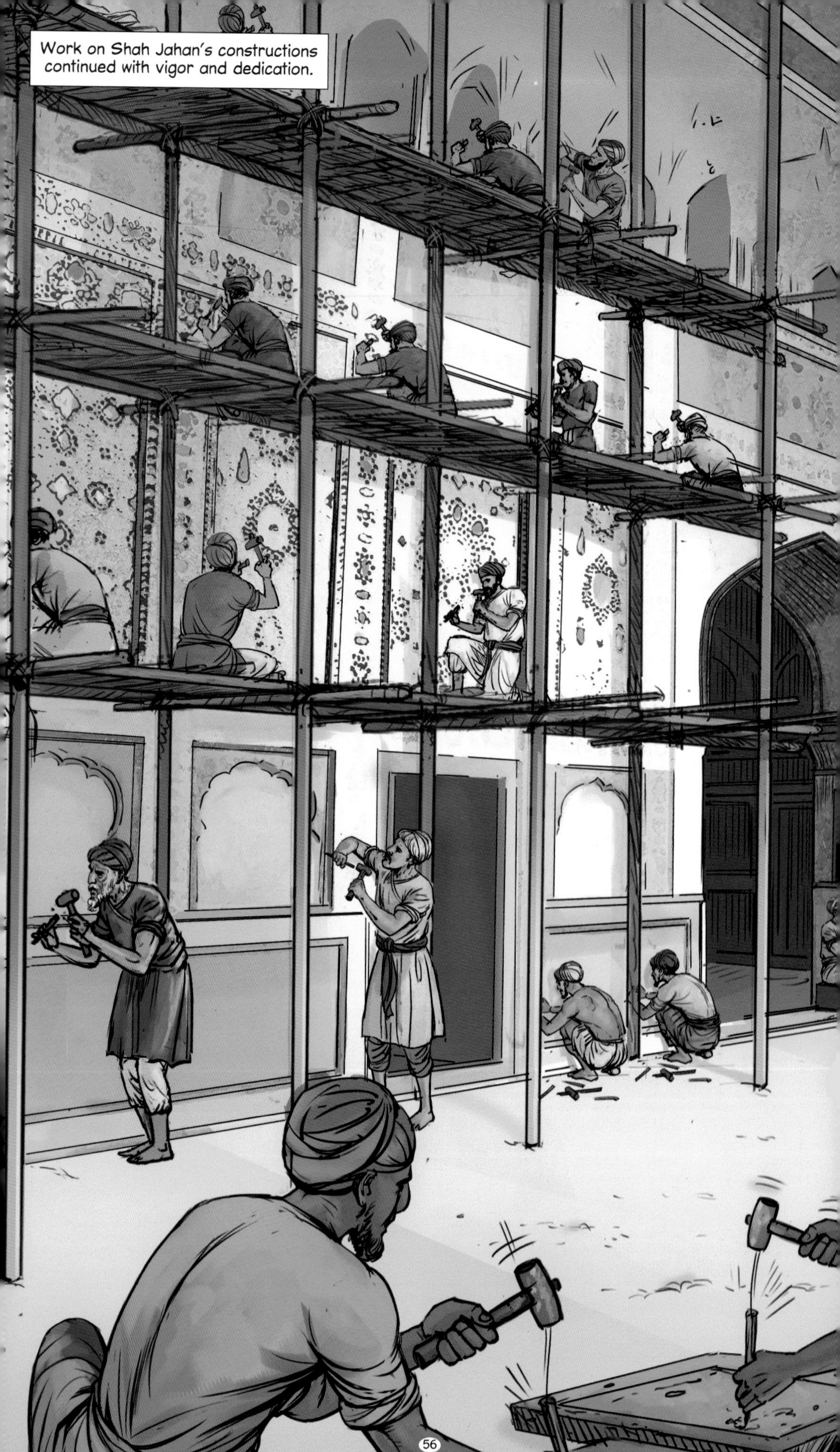
Work on Shah Jahan's constructions continued with vigor and dedication.

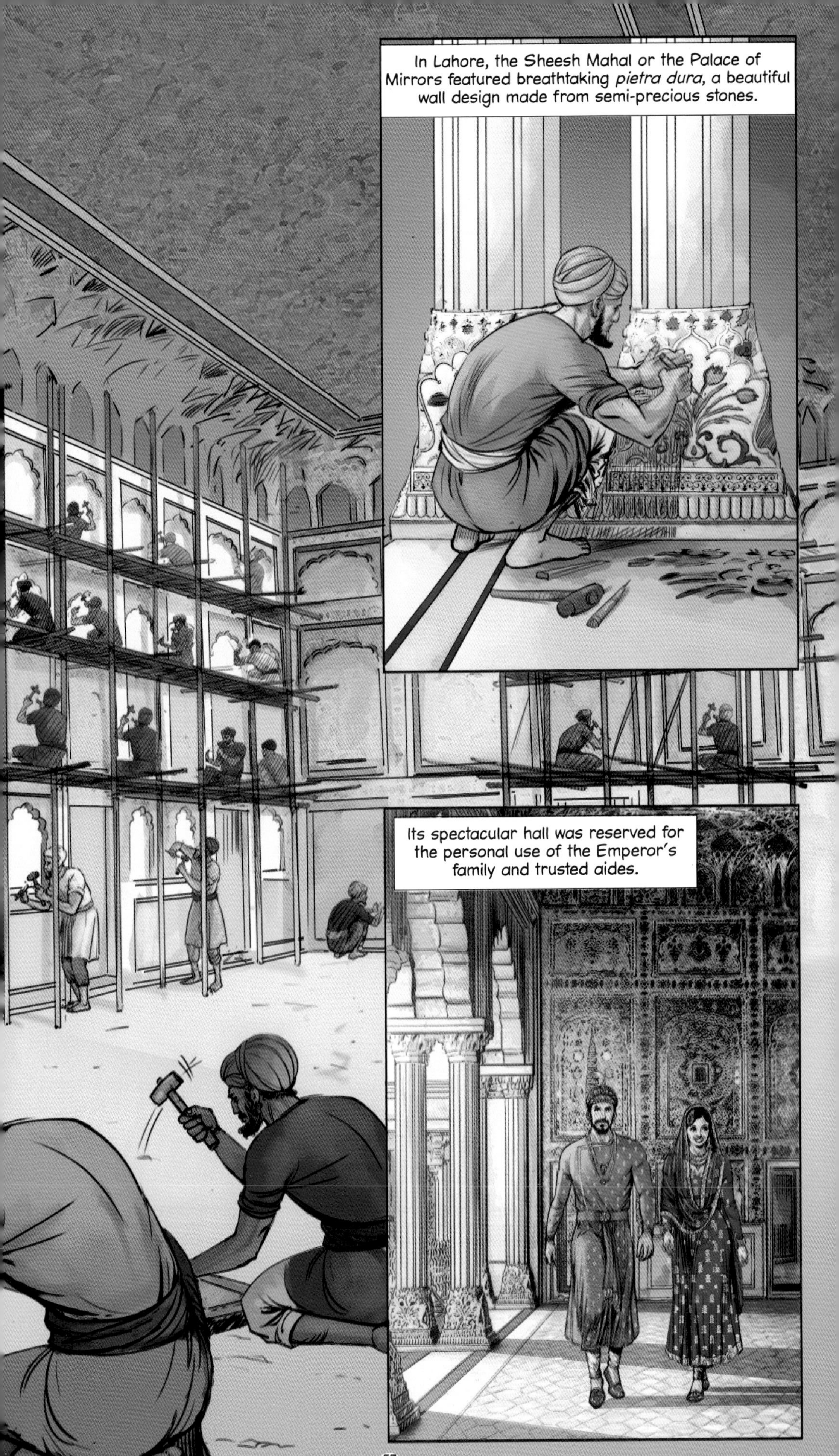
In Lahore, the Sheesh Mahal or the Palace of Mirrors featured breathtaking *pietra dura*, a beautiful wall design made from semi-precious stones.
Its spectacular hall was reserved for the personal use of the Emperor's family and trusted aides.

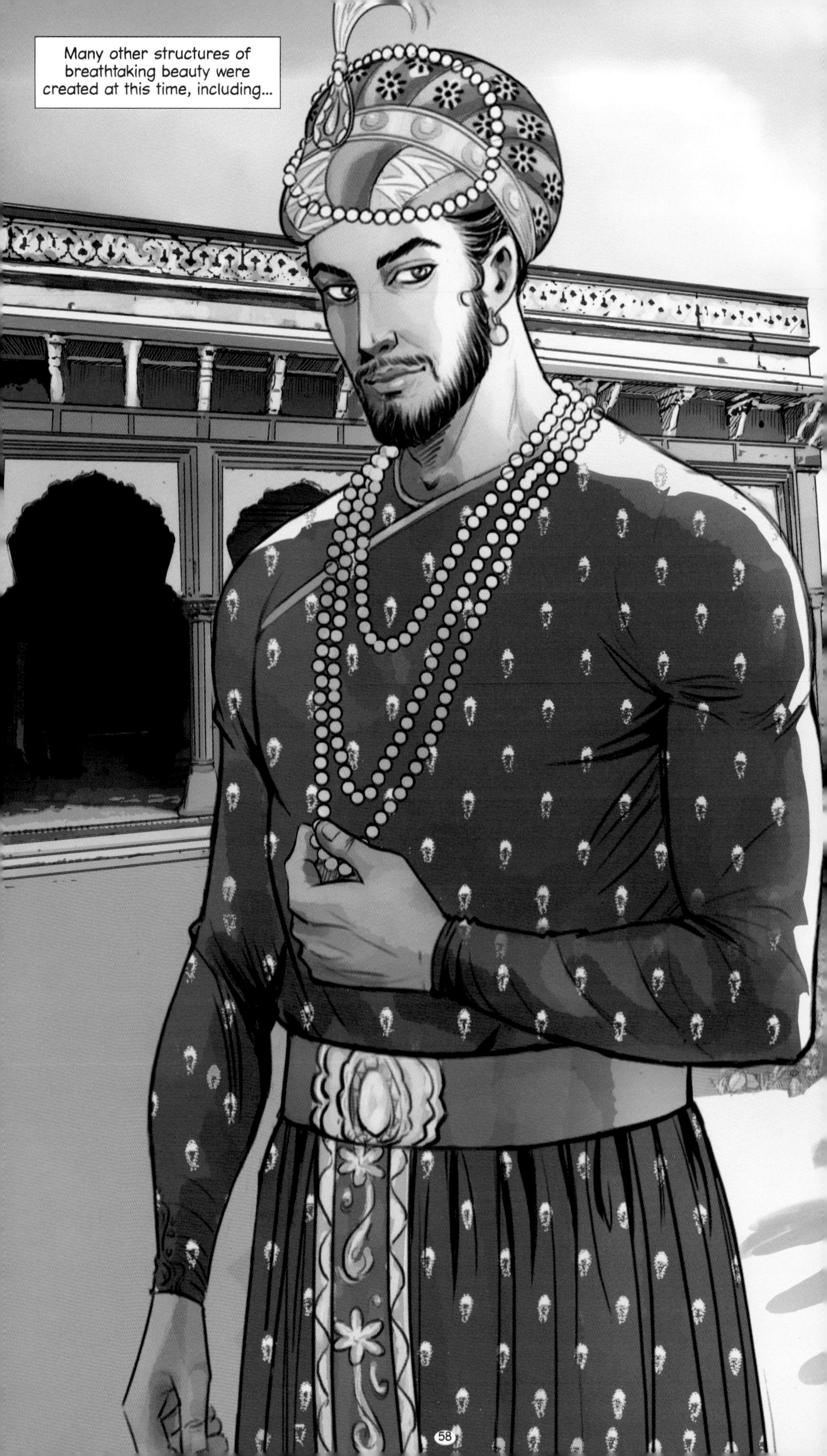
Many other structures of breathtaking beauty were created at this time, including...

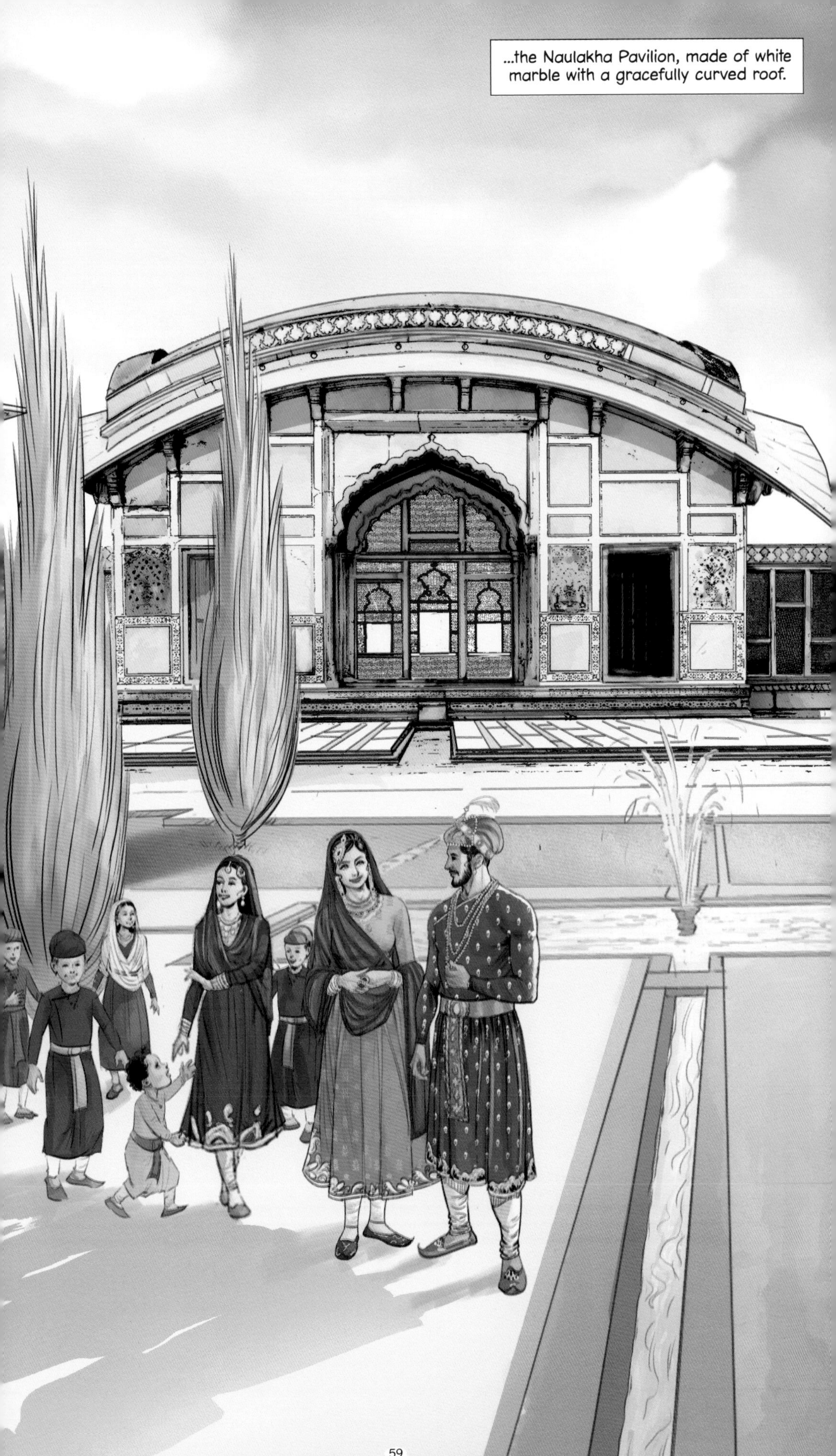
...the Naulakha Pavilion, made of white marble with a gracefully curved roof.

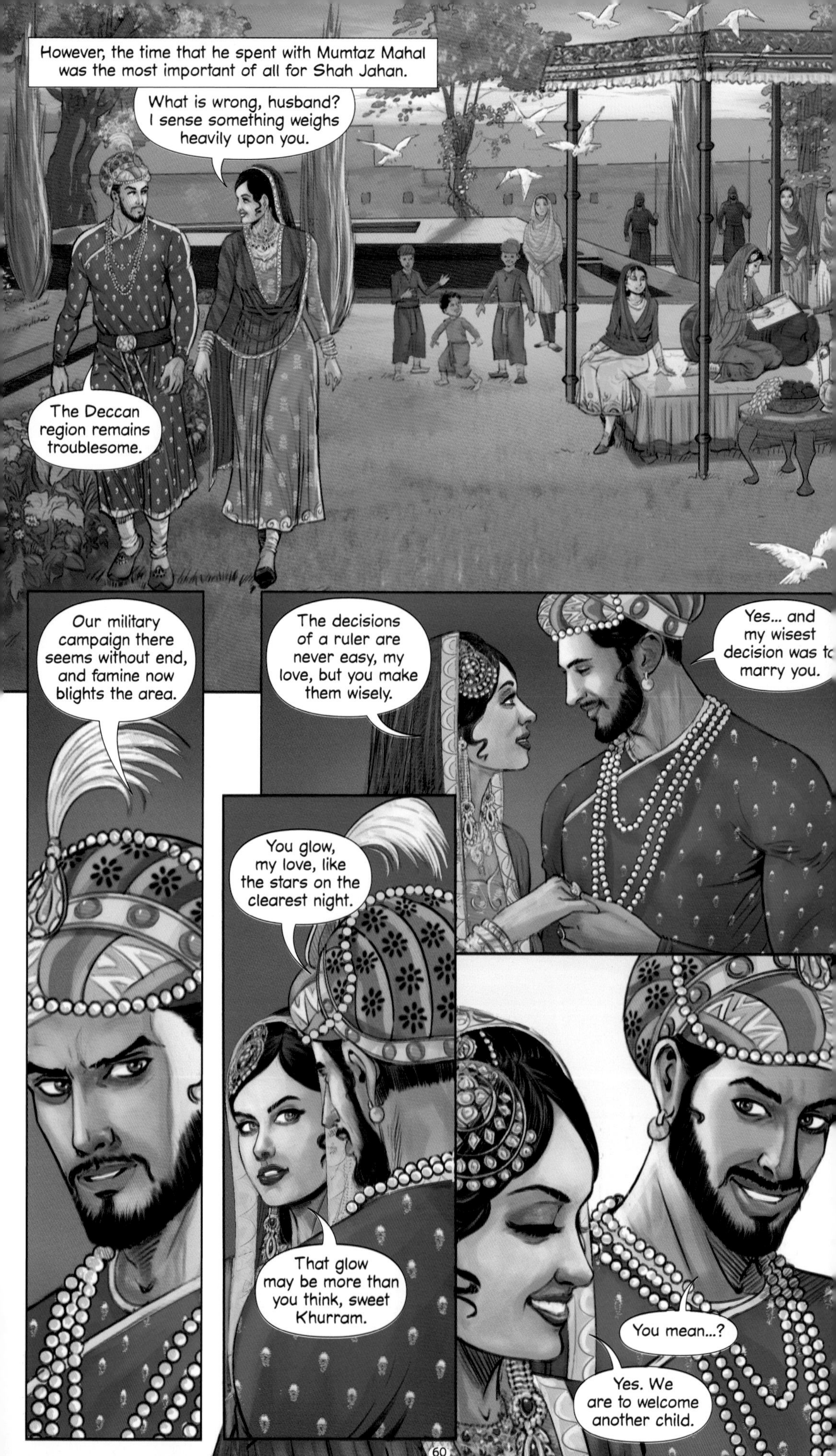
However, the time that he spent with Mumtaz Mahal was the most important of all for Shah Jahan.
What is wrong, husband? I sense something weighs heavily upon you.
The Deccan region remains troublesome.
Our military campaign there seems without end, and famine now blights the area.
The decisions of a ruler are never easy, my love, but you make them wisely.
Yes... and my wisest decision was to marry you.
You glow, my love, like the stars on the clearest night.
That glow may be more than you think, sweet Khurram.
You mean...?
Yes. We are to welcome another child.

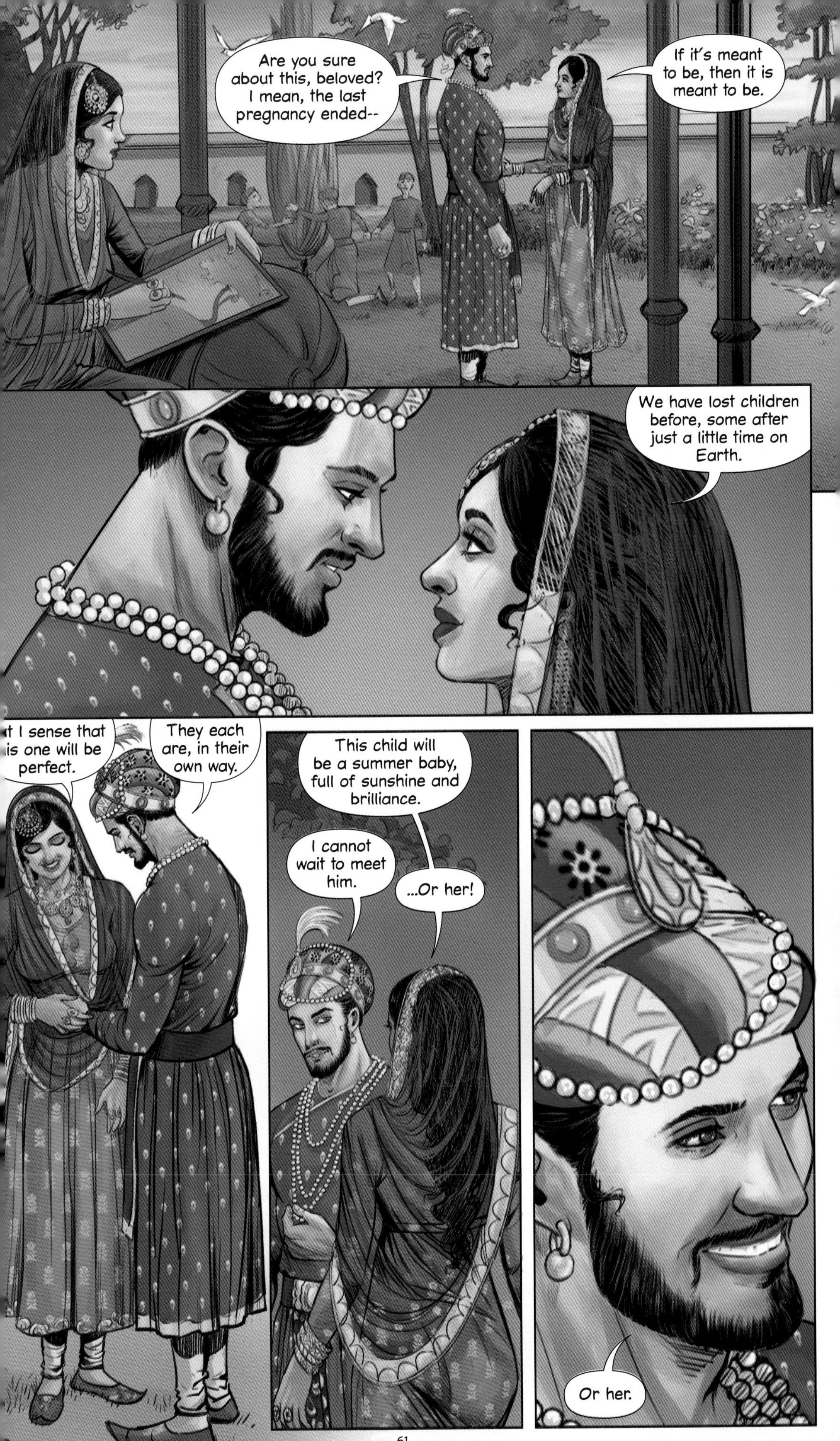
Are you sure about this, beloved? I mean, the last pregnancy ended--
If it's meant to be, then it is meant to be.
We have lost children before, some after just a little time on Earth.
t I sense that is one will be perfect.
They each are, in their own way.
This child will be a summer baby, full of sunshine and brilliance.
I cannot wait to meet him.
...Or her!
Or her.

Chapter 3 The Tragic Birth of Gauhar Ara Begum

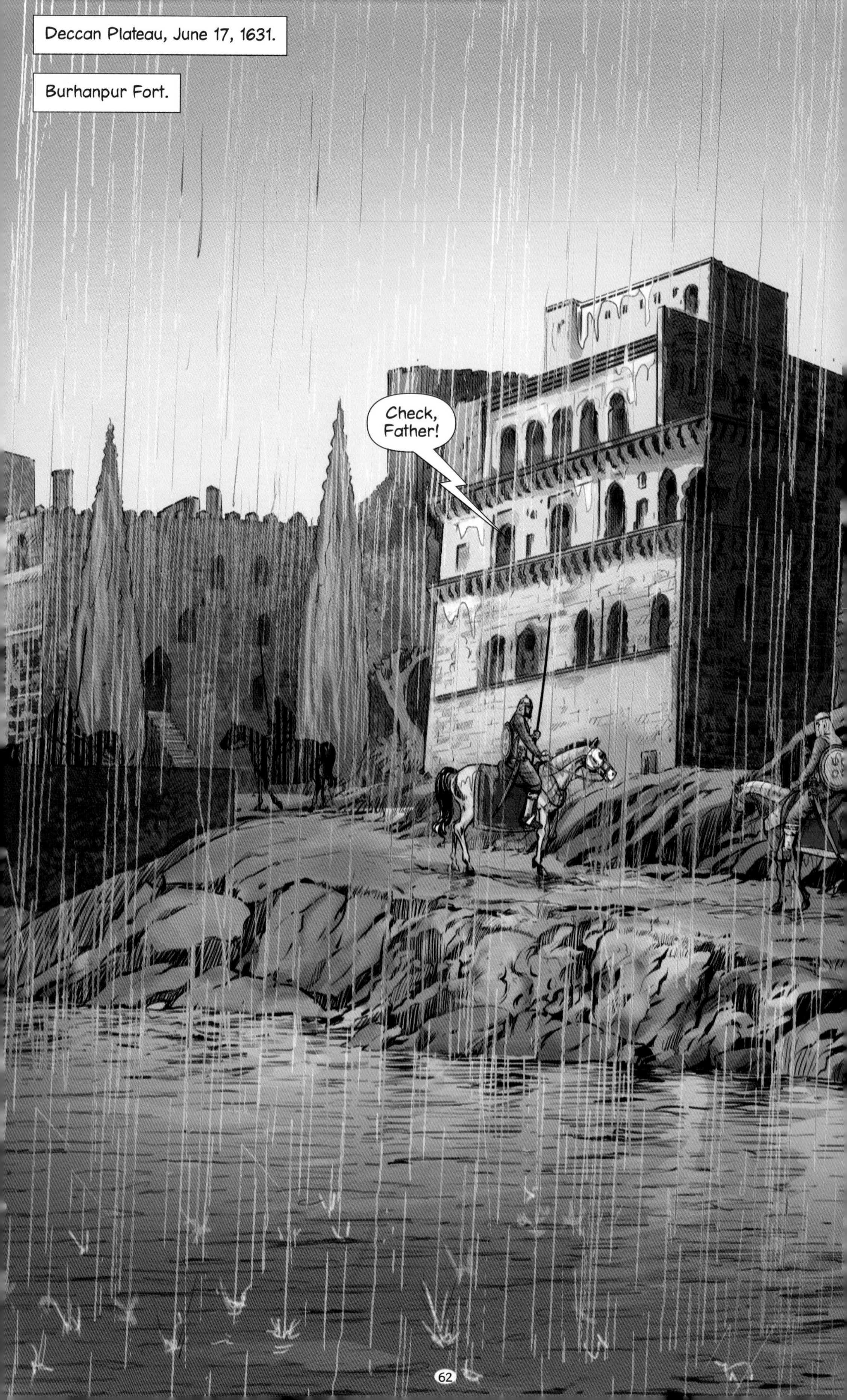
Deccan Plateau, June 17, 1631.
Burhanpur Fort.
Check, Father!

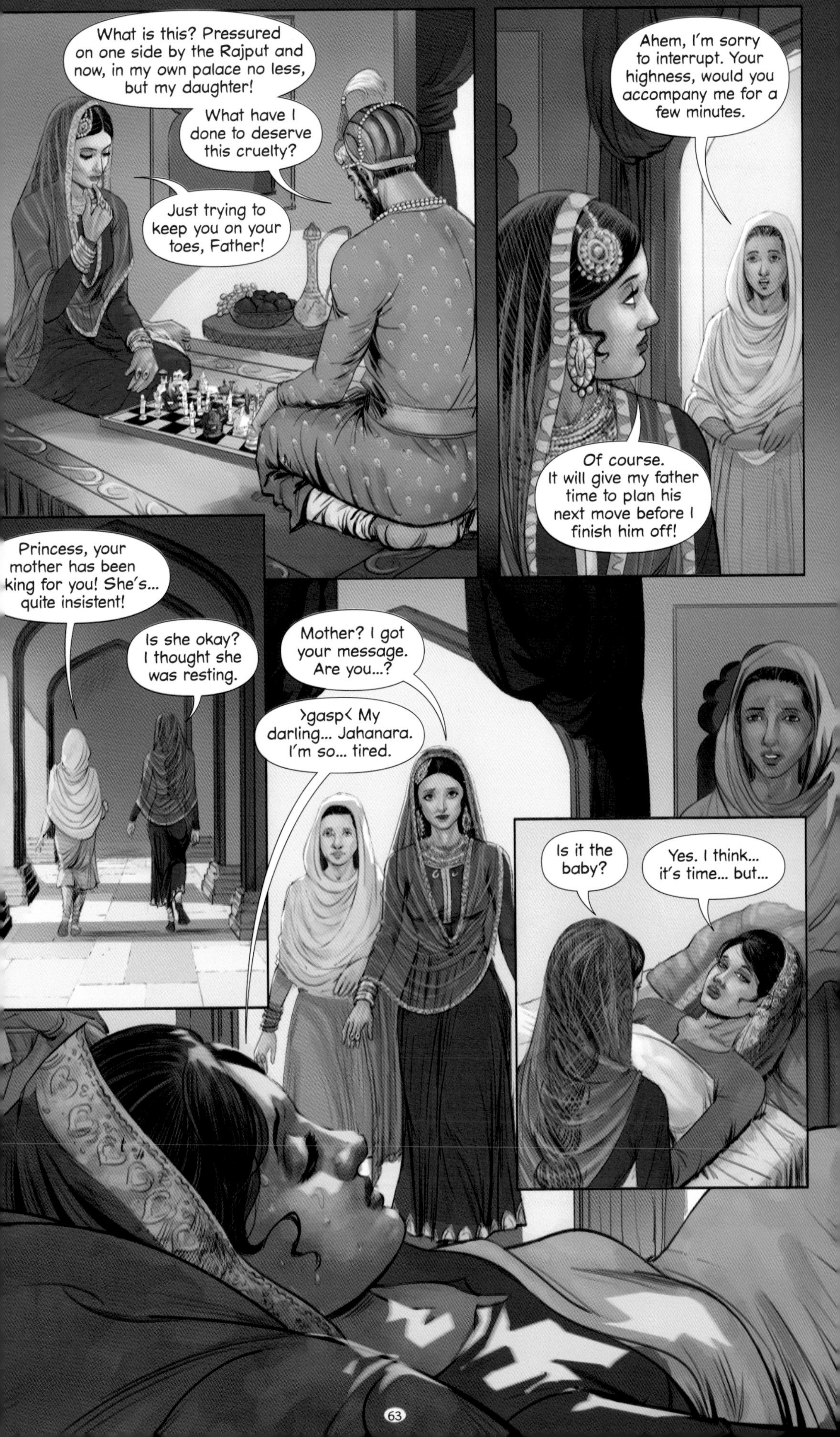

What is this? Pressured on one side by the Rajput and now, in my own palace no less, but my daughter!
What have I done to deserve this cruelty?
Just trying to keep you on your toes, Father!
Ahem, I'm sorry to interrupt. Your highness, would you accompany me for a few minutes.
Of course. It will give my father time to plan his next move before I finish him off!
Princess, your mother has been king for you! She's... quite insistent!
Is she okay? I thought she was resting.
Mother? I got your message. Are you...?
>gasp< My darling... Jahanara. I'm so... tired.
Is it the baby?
Yes. I think... it's time... but...

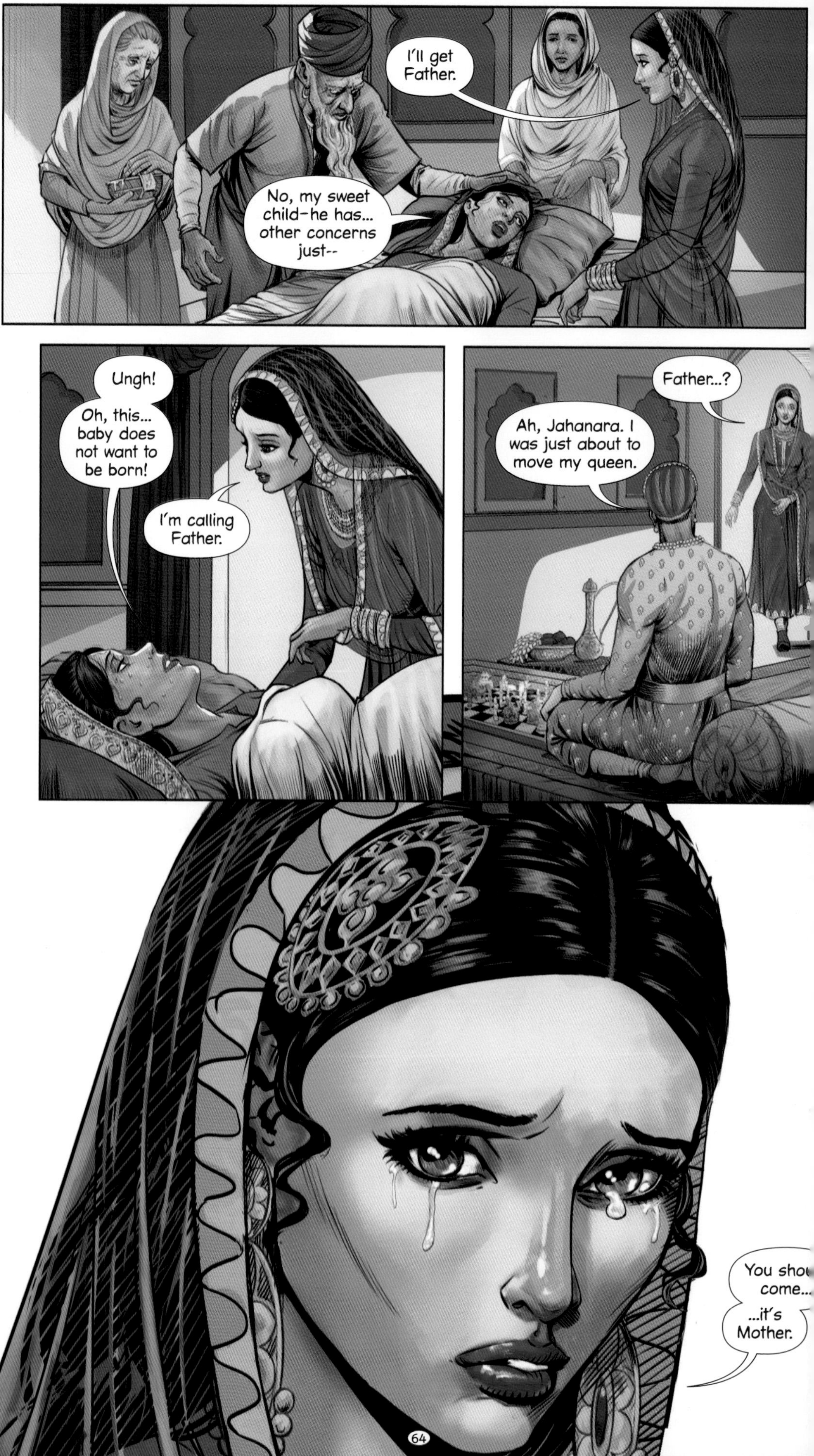
I'll get Father.
No, my sweet child–he has... other concerns just--
Ungh!
Oh, this... baby does not want to be born!
I'm calling Father.
Father...?
Ah, Jahanara. I was just about to move my queen.
You sho
come...
...it's Mother.

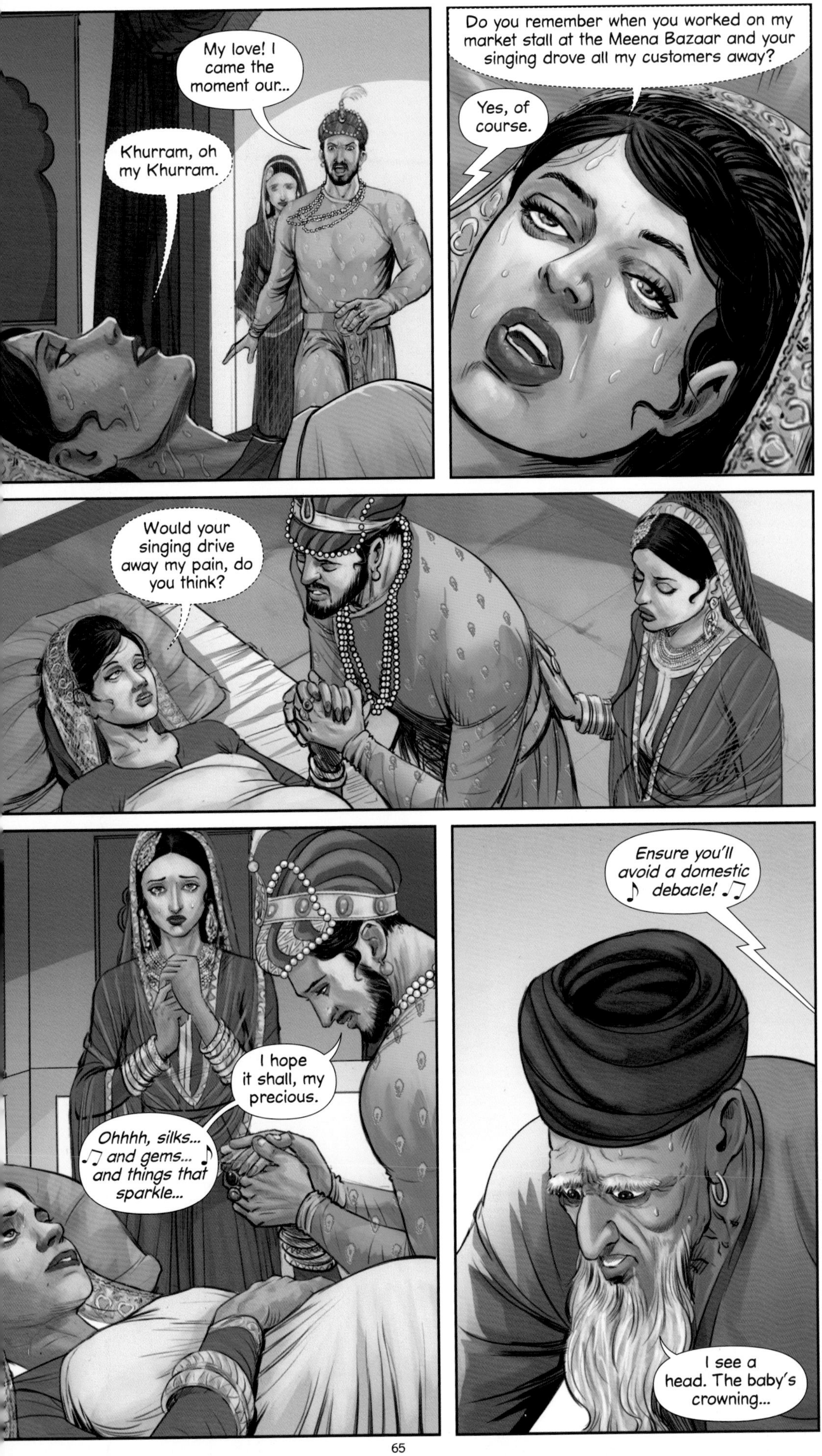

Khurram, oh my Khurram.
My love! I came the moment our...
Do you remember when you worked on my market stall at the Meena Bazaar and your singing drove all my customers away?
Yes, of course.
Would your singing drive away my pain, do you think?
Ohhhh, silks... ♫ and gems... ♪ and things that sparkle...
I hope it shall, my precious.
Ensure you'll avoid a domestic ♪ debacle! ♫
I see a head. The baby's crowning...

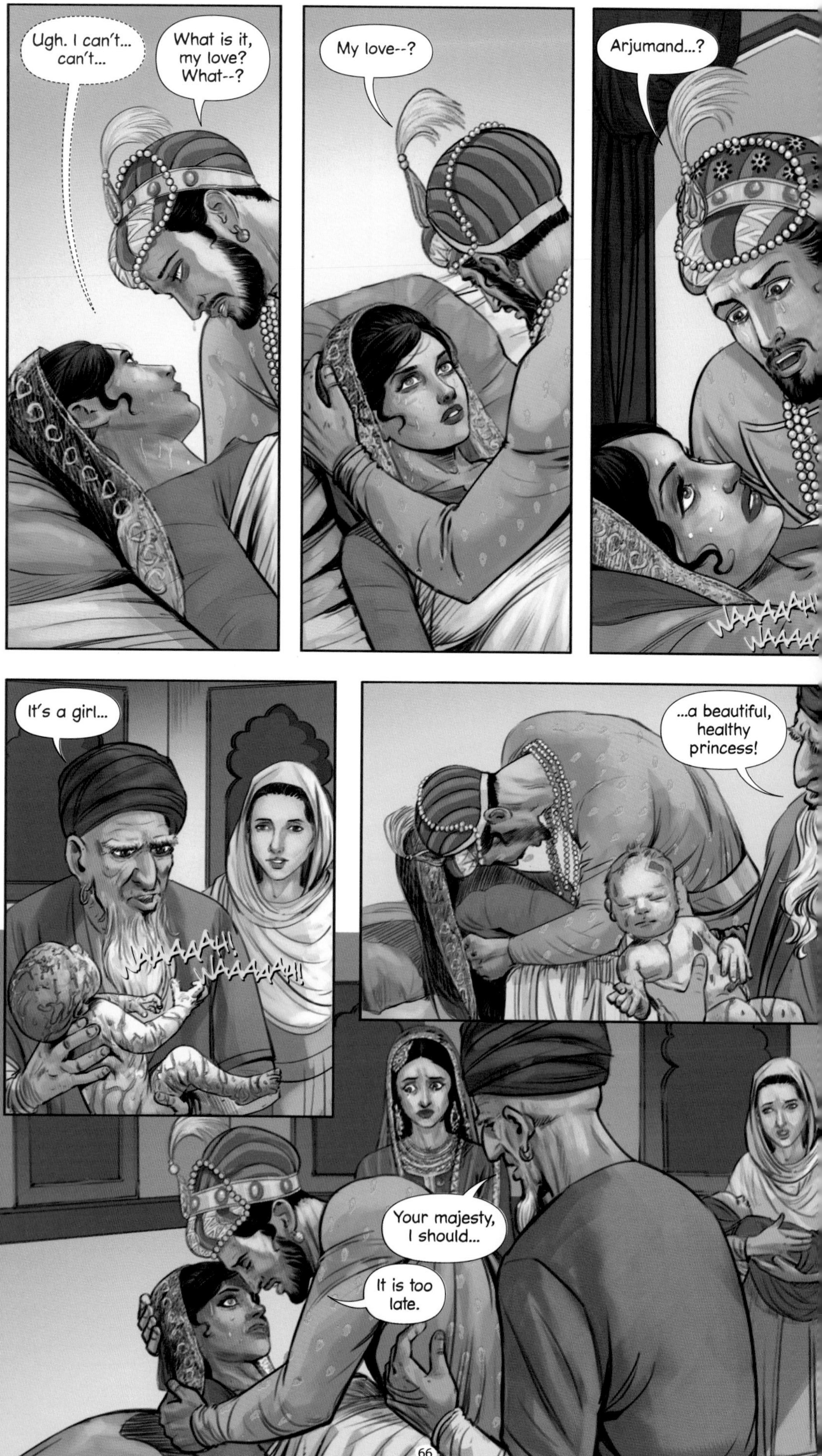
Ugh. I can't... can't...
What is it, my love? What--?
My love--?
Arjumand...?
WAAAAAH! WAAAA
It's a girl...
WAAAAAH! WAAAAAH!!
...a beautiful, healthy princess!
Your majesty, I should...
It is too late.

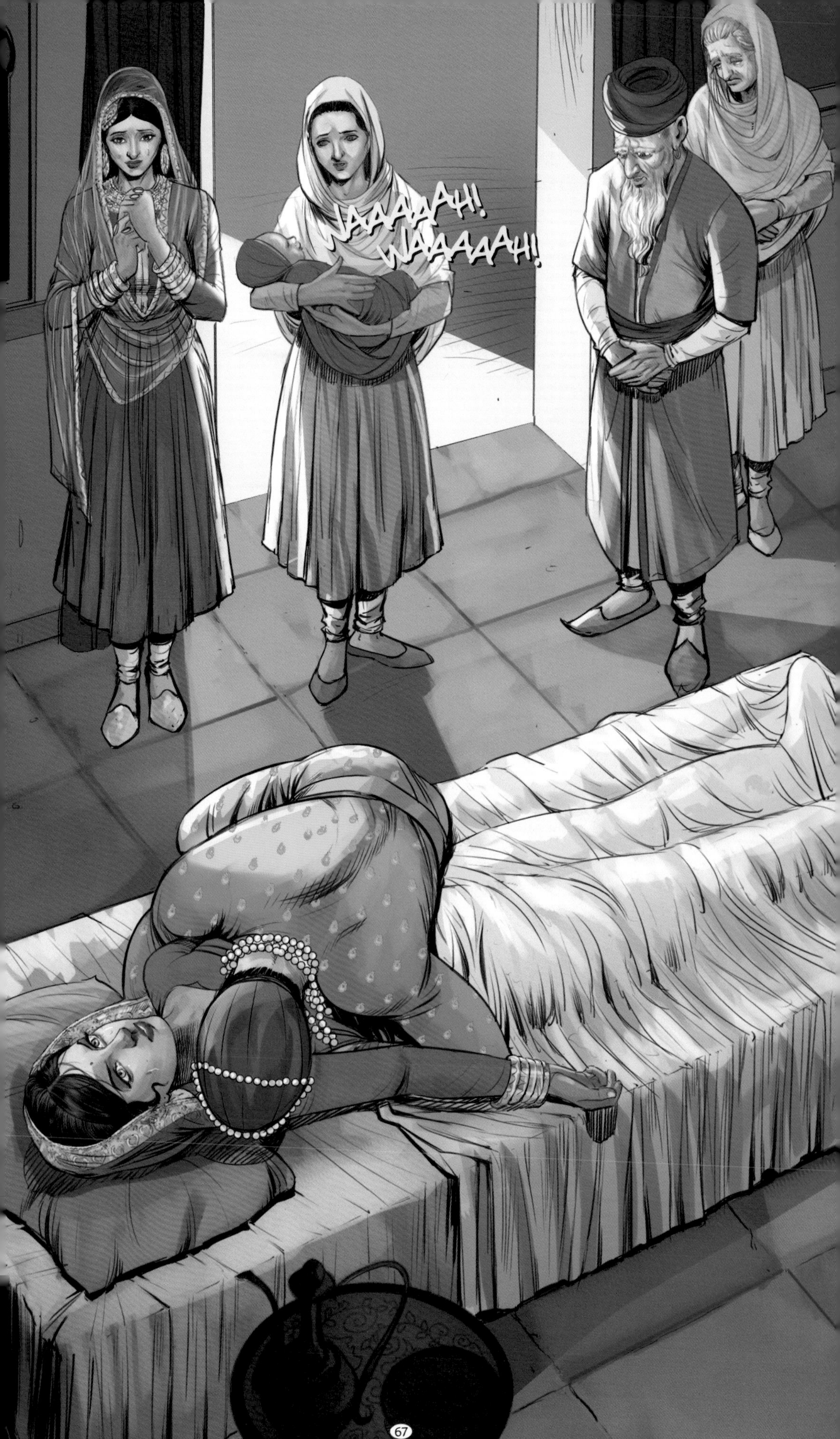
WAAAAAH!
WAAAAAH!

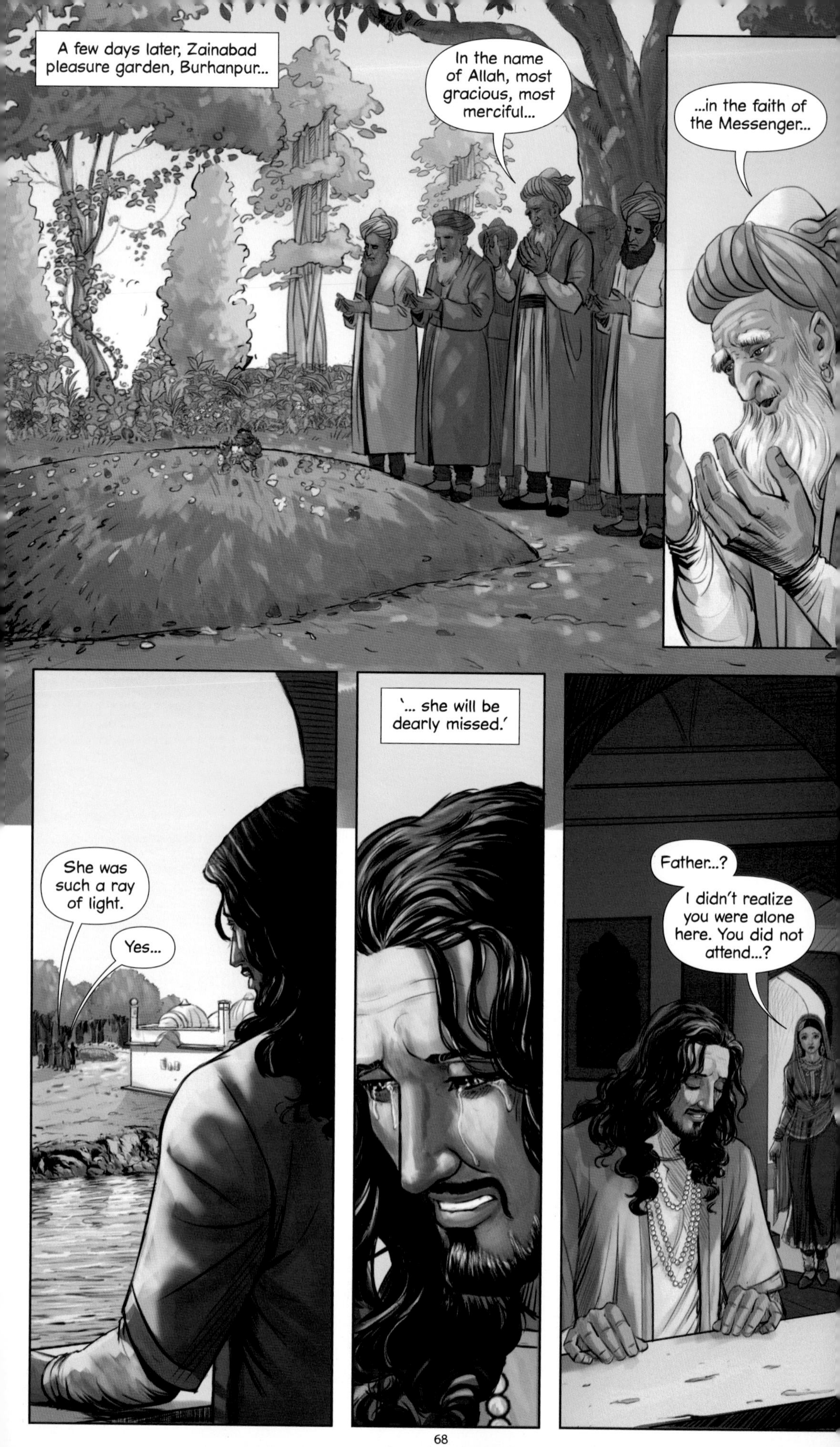
A few days later, Zainabad pleasure garden, Burhanpur...
In the name of Allah, most gracious, most merciful...
...in the faith of the Messenger...
She was such a ray of light.
Yes...
'... she will be dearly missed.'
Father...?
I didn't realize you were alone here. You did not attend...?

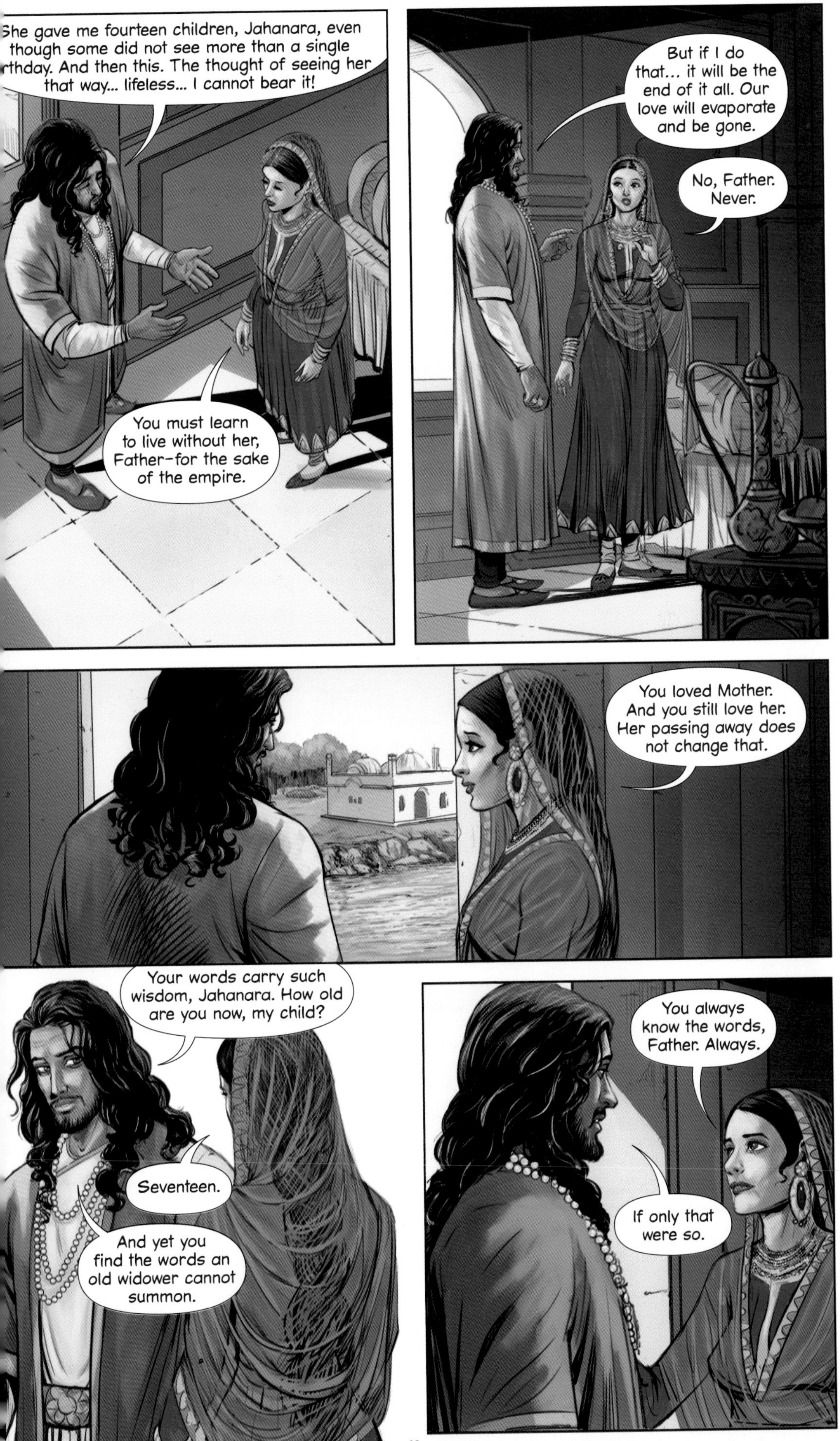

She gave me fourteen children, Jahanara, even though some did not see more than a single birthday. And then this. The thought of seeing her that way... lifeless... I cannot bear it!
You must learn to live without her, Father—for the sake of the empire.
But if I do that... it will be the end of it all. Our love will evaporate and be gone.
No, Father. Never.
You loved Mother. And you still love her. Her passing away does not change that.
Your words carry such wisdom, Jahanara. How old are you now, my child?
Seventeen.
And yet you find the words an old widower cannot summon.
You always know the words, Father. Always.
If only that were so.

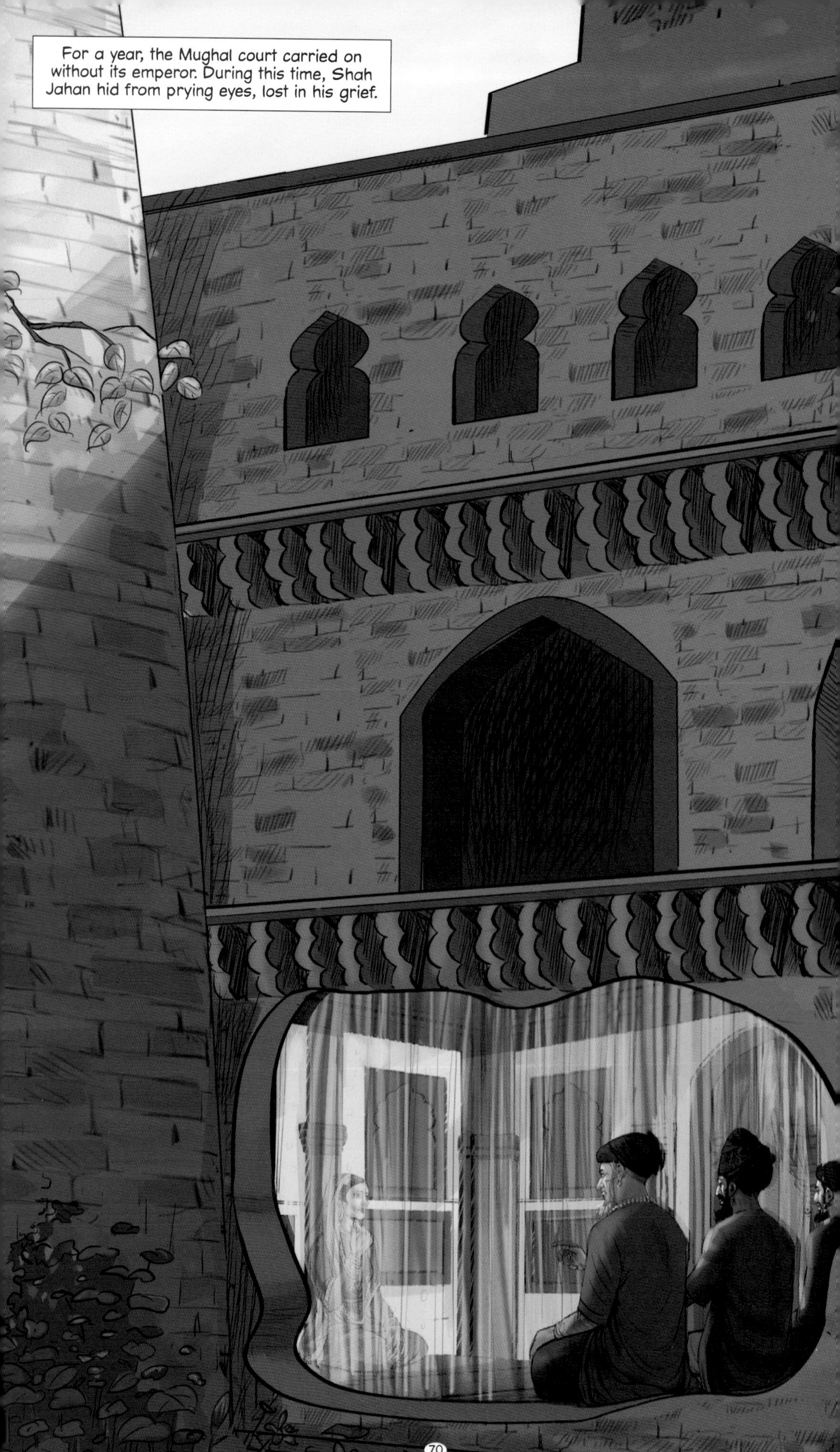
For a year, the Mughal court carried on without its emperor. During this time, Shah Jahan hid from prying eyes, lost in his grief.

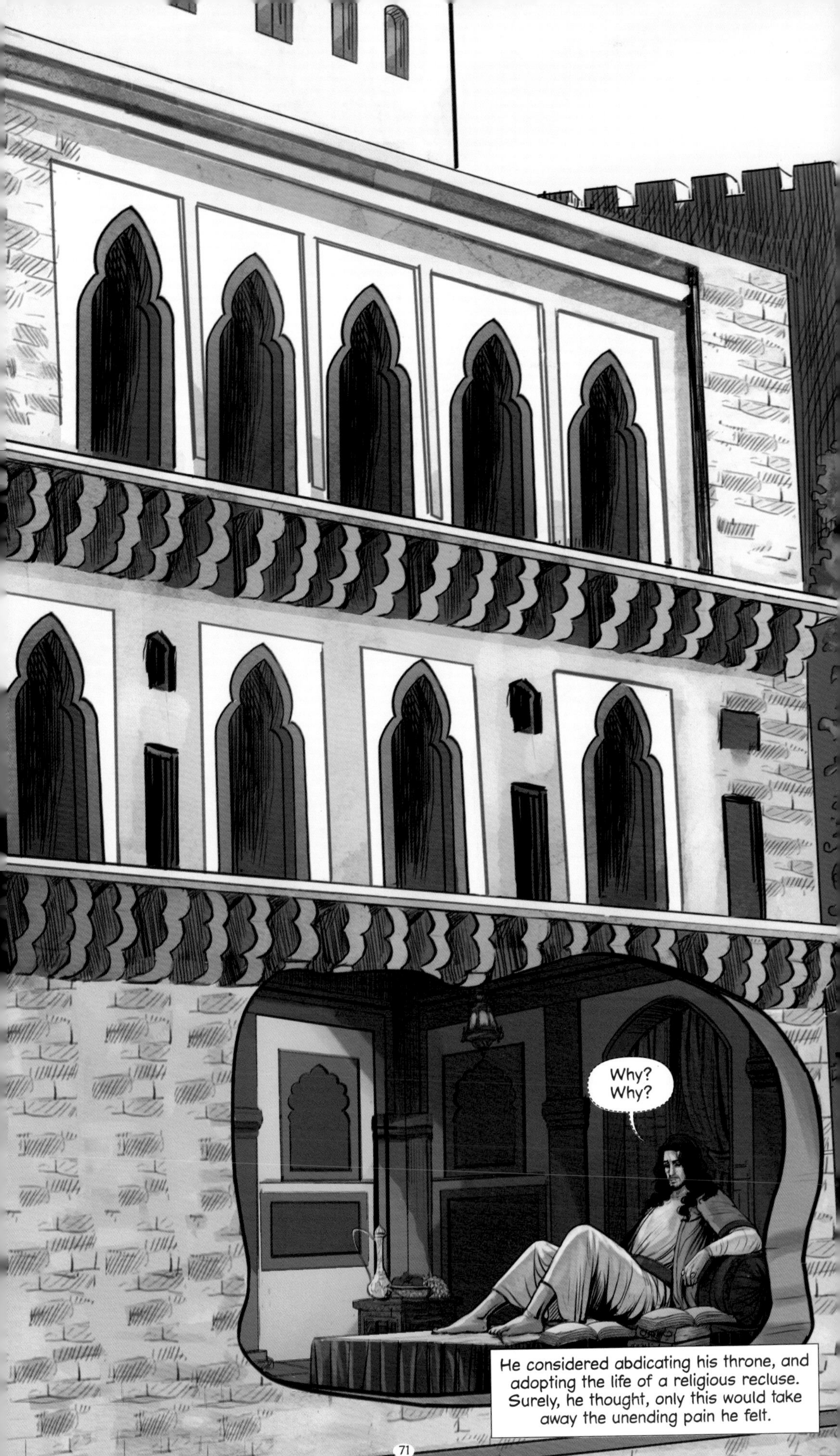
Why? Why?
He considered abdicating his throne, and adopting the life of a religious recluse. Surely, he thought, only this would take away the unending pain he felt.

Chapter 4 A Vision of Paradise

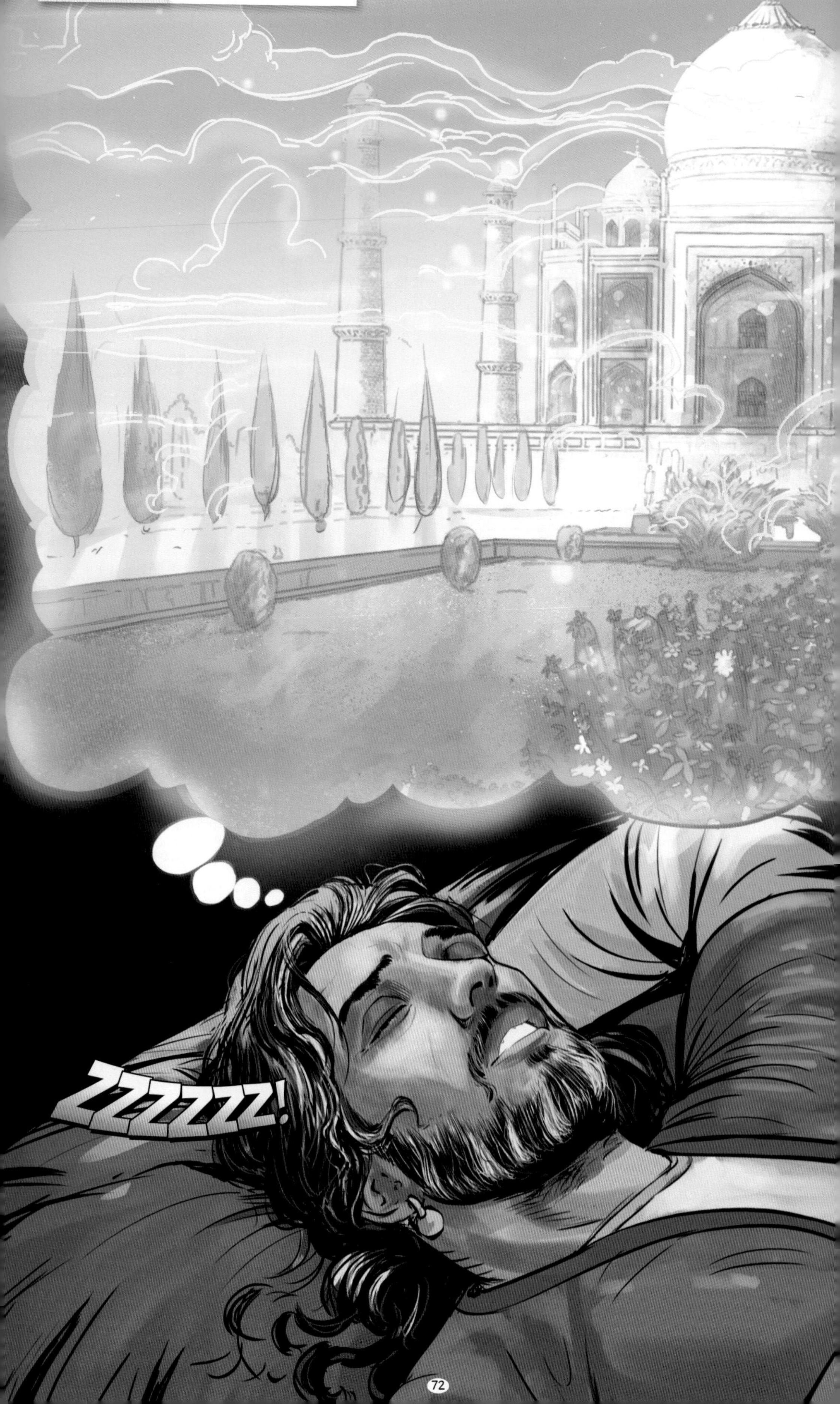
ZZZZZZ!

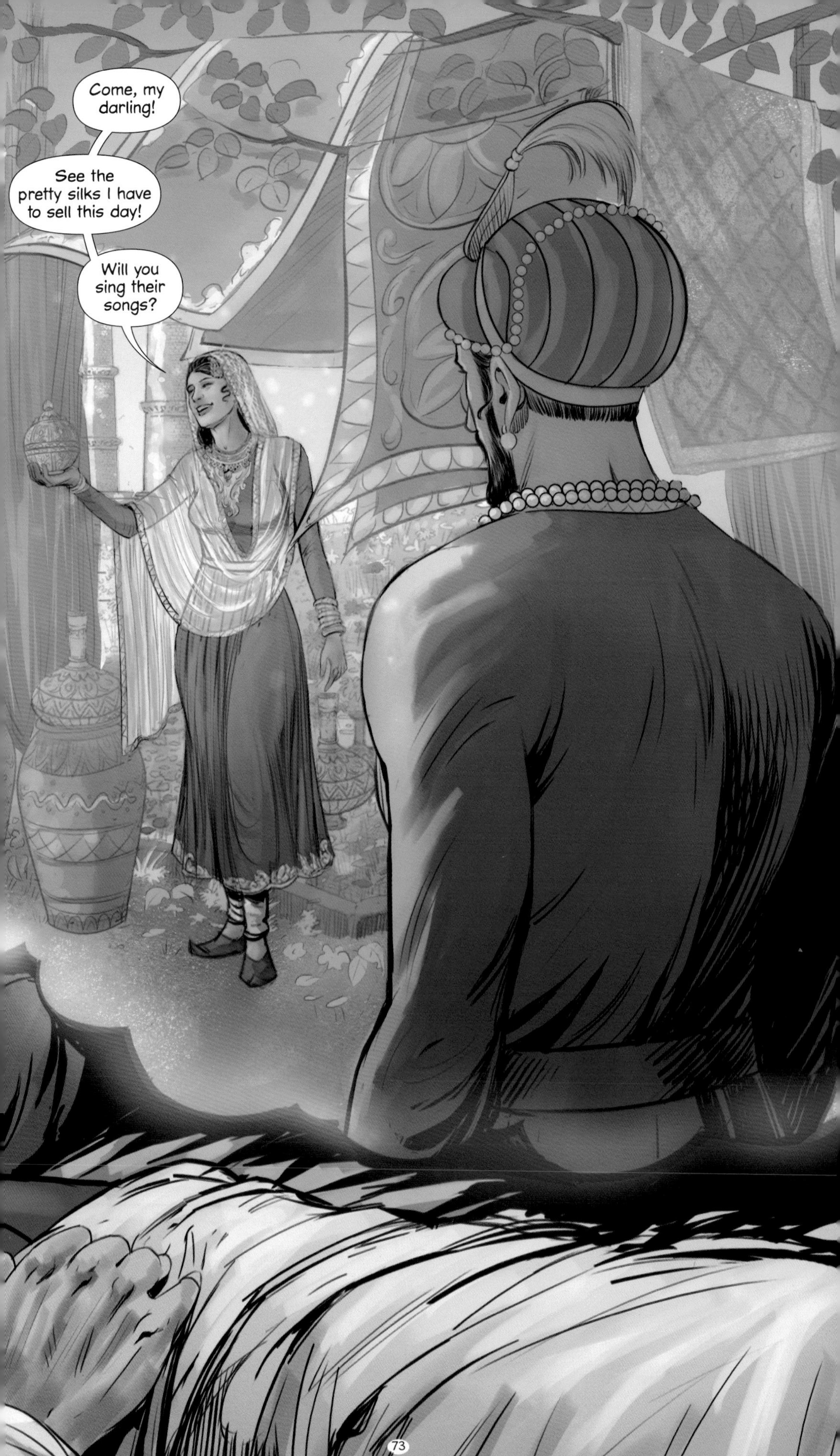
Come, my darling!
See the pretty silks I have to sell this day!
Will you sing their songs?

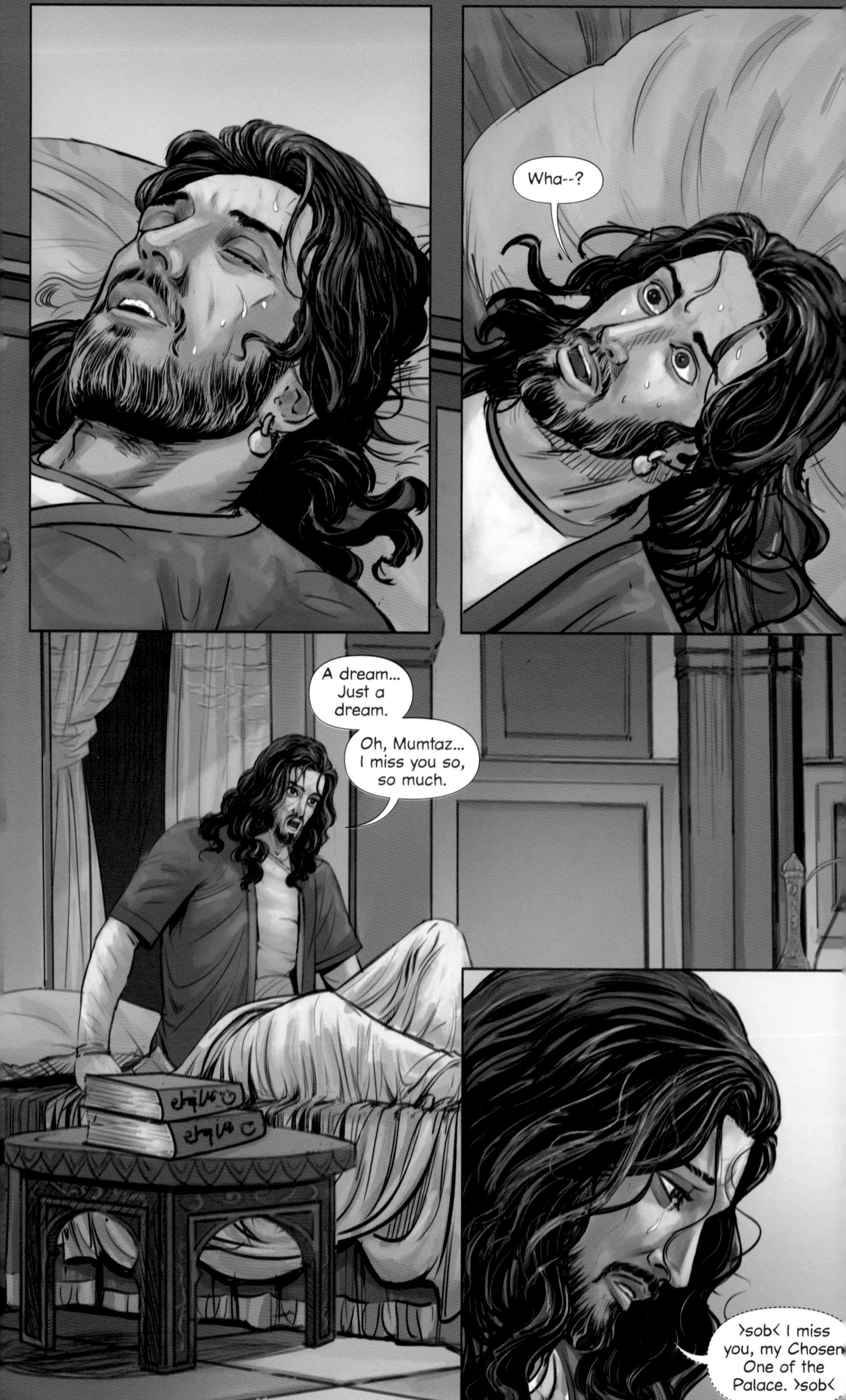
Wha--?
A dream... Just a dream.
Oh, Mumtaz... I miss you so, so much.
>sob< I miss you, my Chosen One of the Palace. >sob<

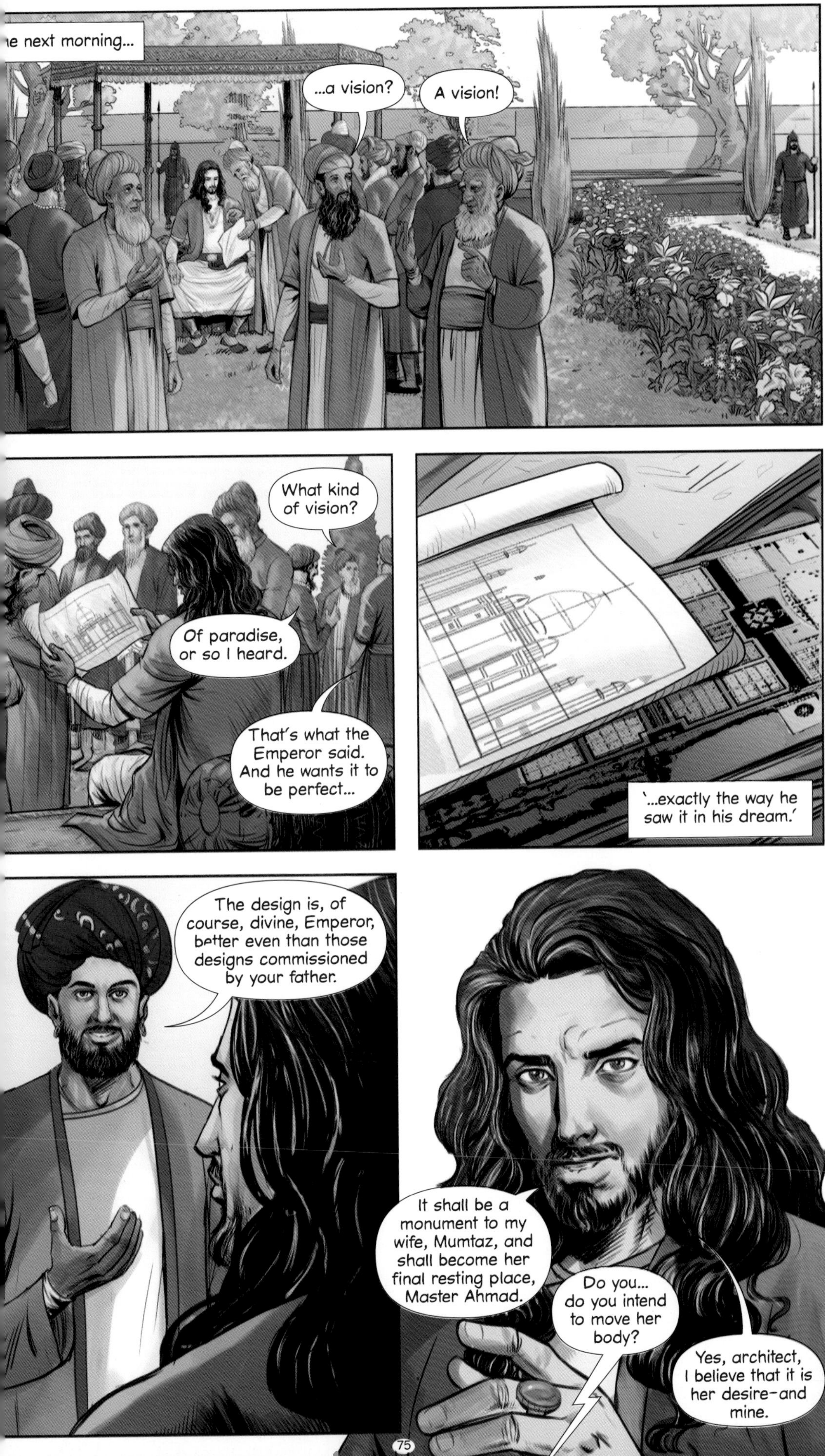
ie next morning...
...a vision?
A vision!
What kind of vision?
Of paradise, or so I heard.
That's what the Emperor said. And he wants it to be perfect...
'...exactly the way he saw it in his dream.'
The design is, of course, divine, Emperor, better even than those designs commissioned by your father.
It shall be a monument to my wife, Mumtaz, and shall become her final resting place, Master Ahmad.
Do you... do you intend to move her body?
Yes, architect, I believe that it is her desire–and mine.

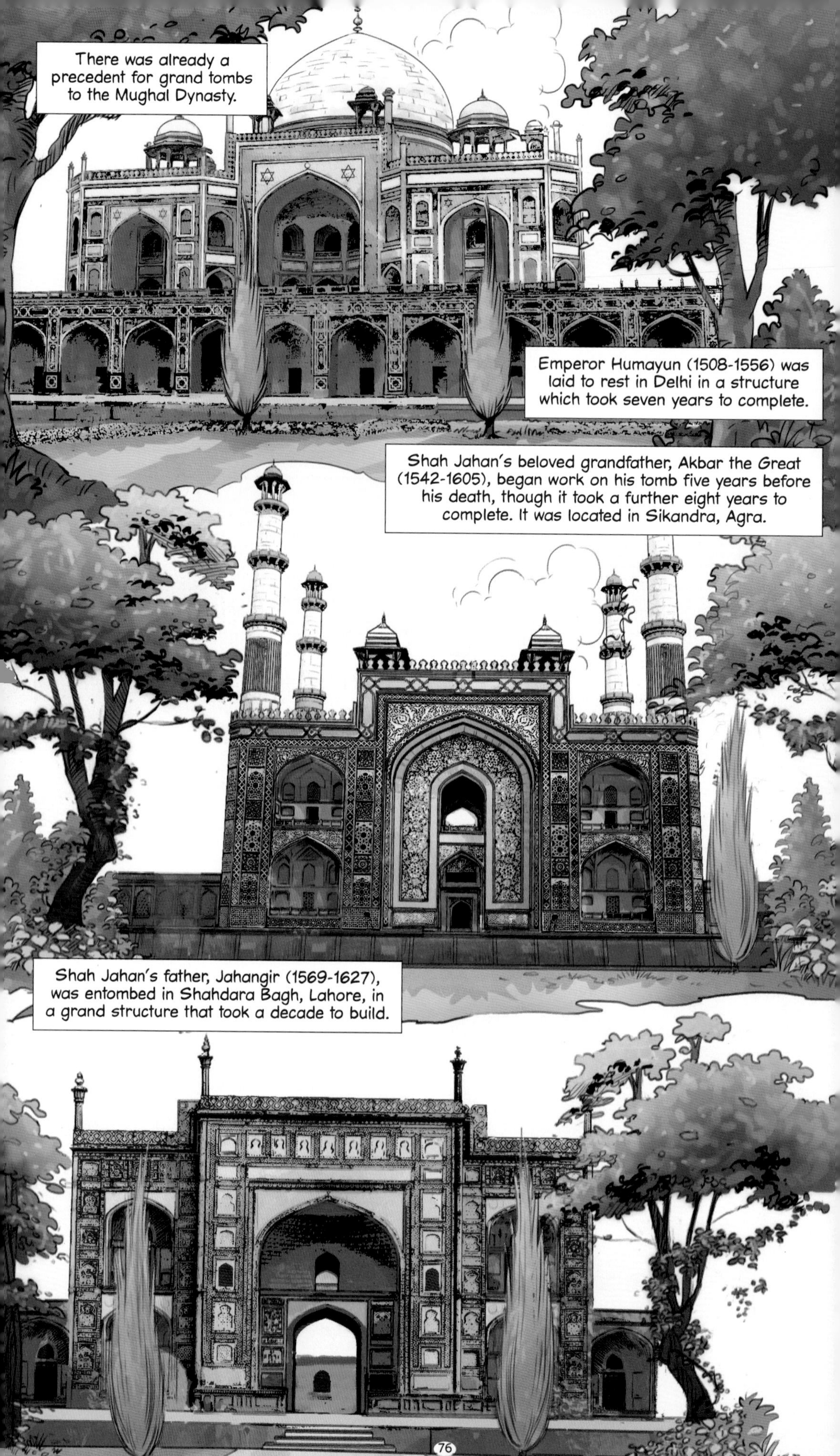

There was already a precedent for grand tombs to the Mughal Dynasty.
Emperor Humayun (1508-1556) was laid to rest in Delhi in a structure which took seven years to complete.
Shah Jahan's beloved grandfather, Akbar the Great (1542-1605), began work on his tomb five years before his death, though it took a further eight years to complete. It was located in Sikandra, Agra.
Shah Jahan's father, Jahangir (1569-1627), was entombed in Shahdara Bagh, Lahore, in a grand structure that took a decade to build.

Shah Jahan searched for the perfect [loc]ation for his monument to Mumtaz Mahal, [det]ermined to bring his vision of paradise to [e]arth in her name. He finally settled on...

...Agra, Yes, this is it, overlooking the Yamuna River. The sense of tranquility is exactly as I felt it in my vision.

This place is owned by Maharaja Jai Singh. He can drive a hard bargain.

Let him bargain, Ahmad Lahauri. You are my chief architect—it is your task to design this dream for me.

A deal was struck with the Maharaja, who exchanged the land overlooking the Yamuna River for a large palace in the center of Agra.

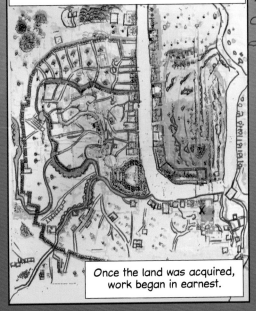

Once the land was acquired, work began in earnest.

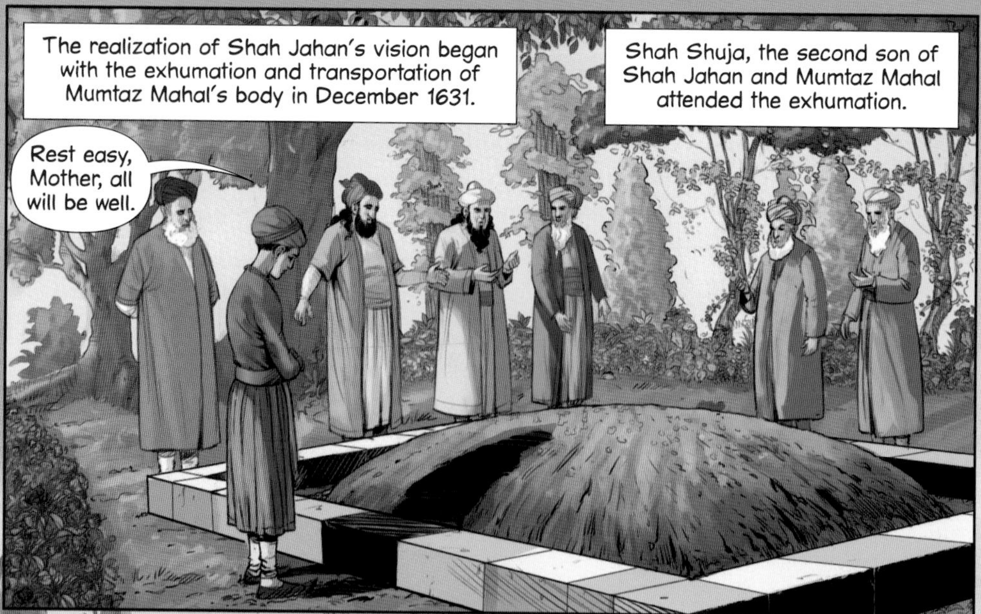
The realization of Shah Jahan's vision began with the exhumation and transportation of Mumtaz Mahal's body in December 1631.
Shah Shuja, the second son of Shah Jahan and Mumtaz Mahal attended the exhumation.
Rest easy, Mother, all will be well.

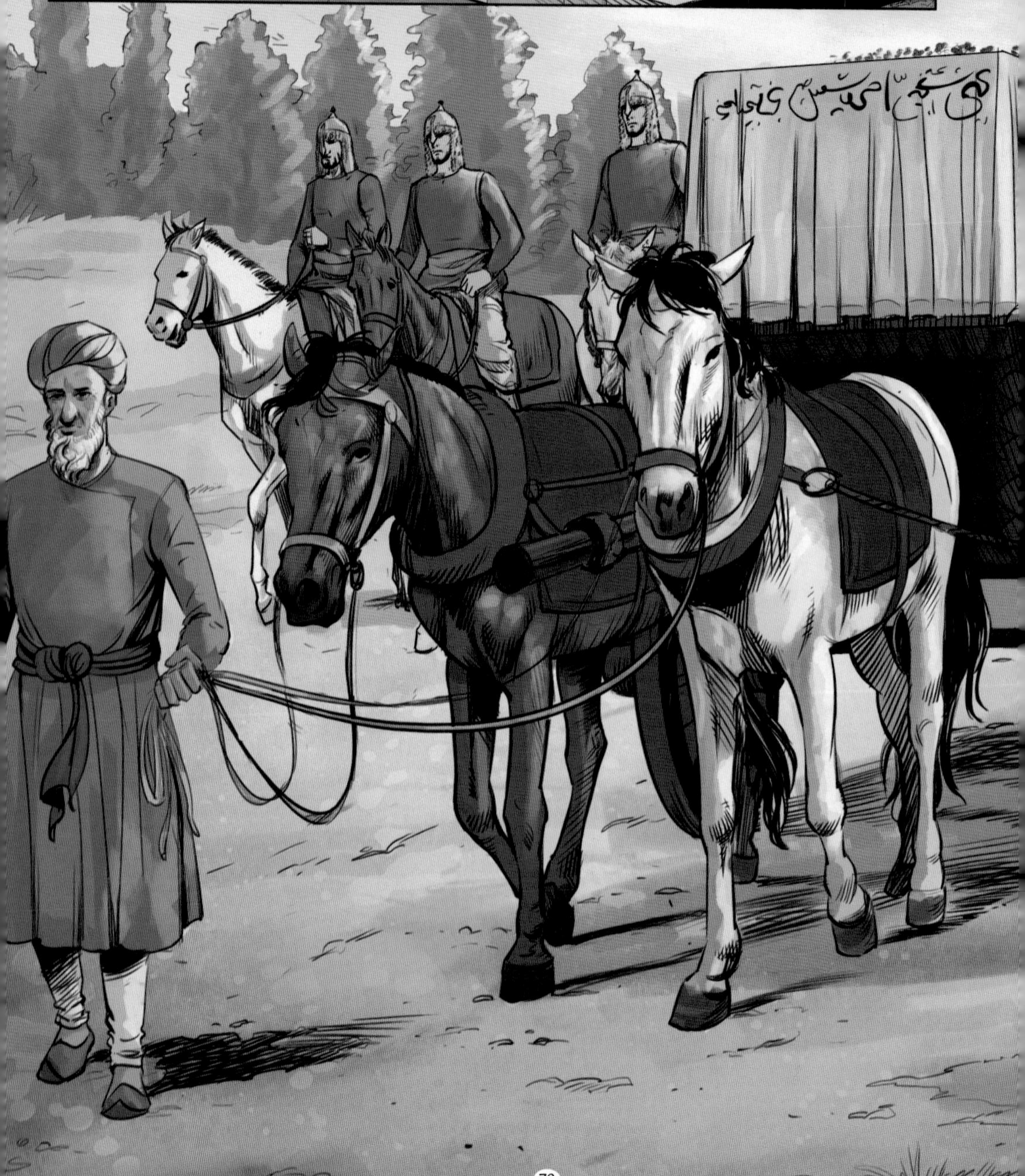

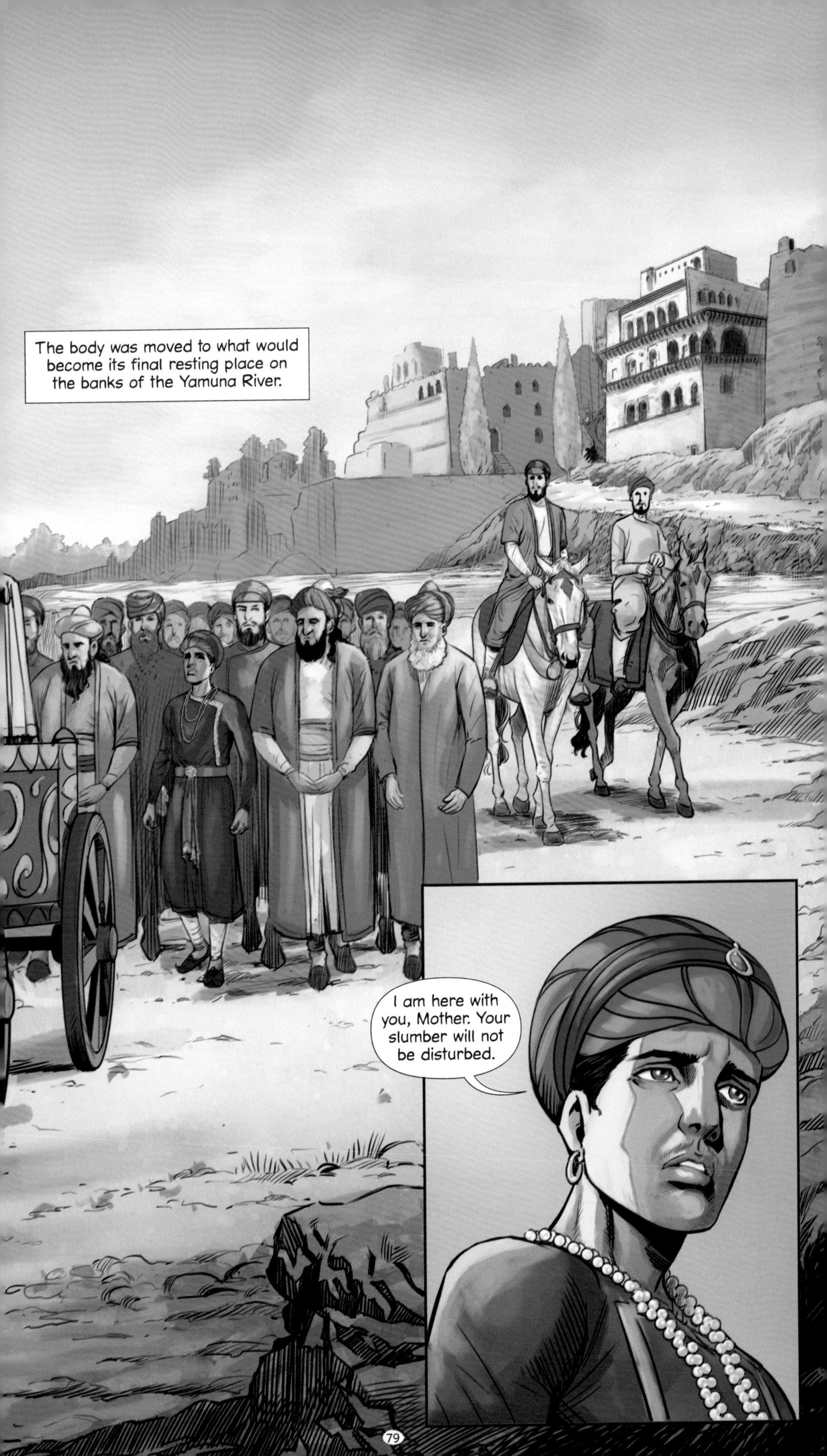
The body was moved to what would become its final resting place on the banks of the Yamuna River.
I am here with you, Mother. Your slumber will not be disturbed.

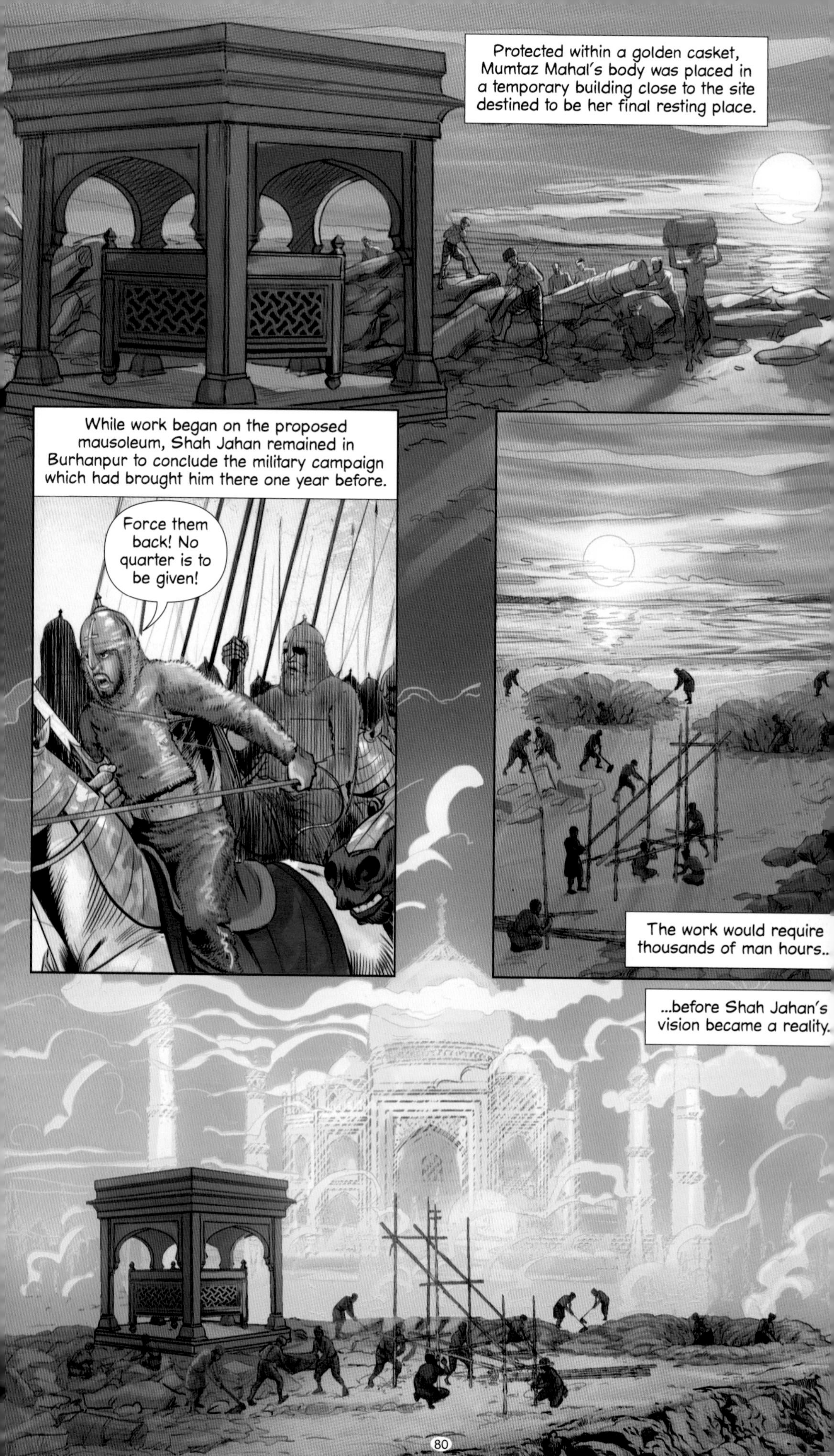

Protected within a golden casket, Mumtaz Mahal's body was placed in a temporary building close to the site destined to be her final resting place.
While work began on the proposed mausoleum, Shah Jahan remained in Burhanpur to conclude the military campaign which had brought him there one year before.
Force them back! No quarter is to be given!
The work would require thousands of man hours..
...before Shah Jahan's vision became a reality.

Shah Jahan returned to Agra in June, 1632.

He continued devoting all of his time to realizing his vision, and all the while the affairs of the court trundled on.

Father...?

Jahanara, come in.

Father, I think it's time.

You have hidden yourself away, since the day... that day in Zainabad. It has been two years...

Two years? It feels so much longer.

I think you should come back to the court. It is time. For your absence to last longer would be too much.

Jahanara, my precious daughter, you have shown me such patience and kindness, reminding me so much of your mother...

...but I am not ready.

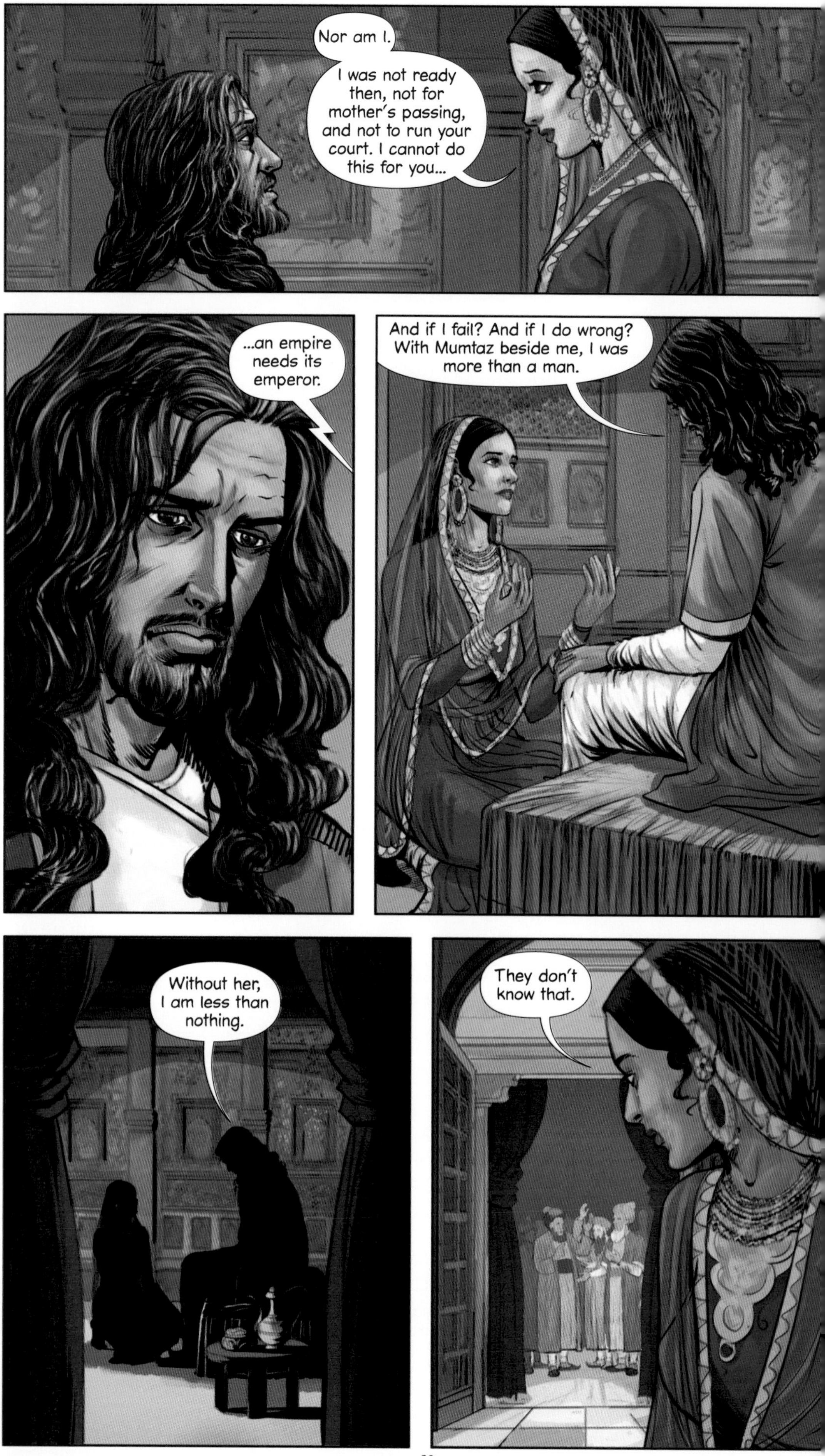
Nor am I.
I was not ready then, not for mother's passing, and not to run your court. I cannot do this for you...
...an empire needs its emperor.
And if I fail? And if I do wrong? With Mumtaz beside me, I was more than a man.
Without her, I am less than nothing.
They don't know that.

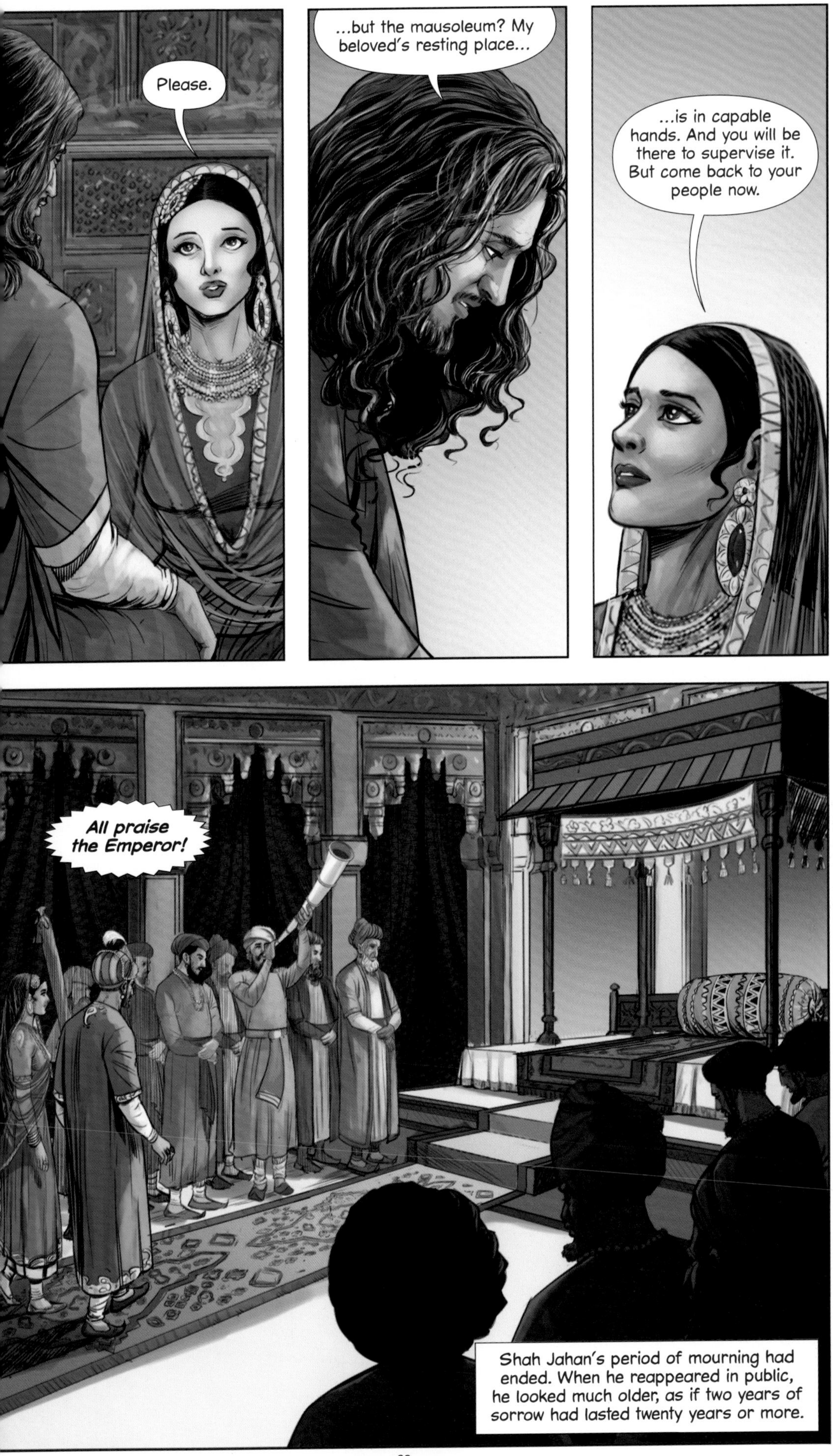
Please.
...but the mausoleum? My beloved's resting place...
...is in capable hands. And you will be there to supervise it. But come back to your people now.
All praise the Emperor!
Shah Jahan's period of mourning had ended. When he reappeared in public, he looked much older, as if two years of sorrow had lasted twenty years or more.

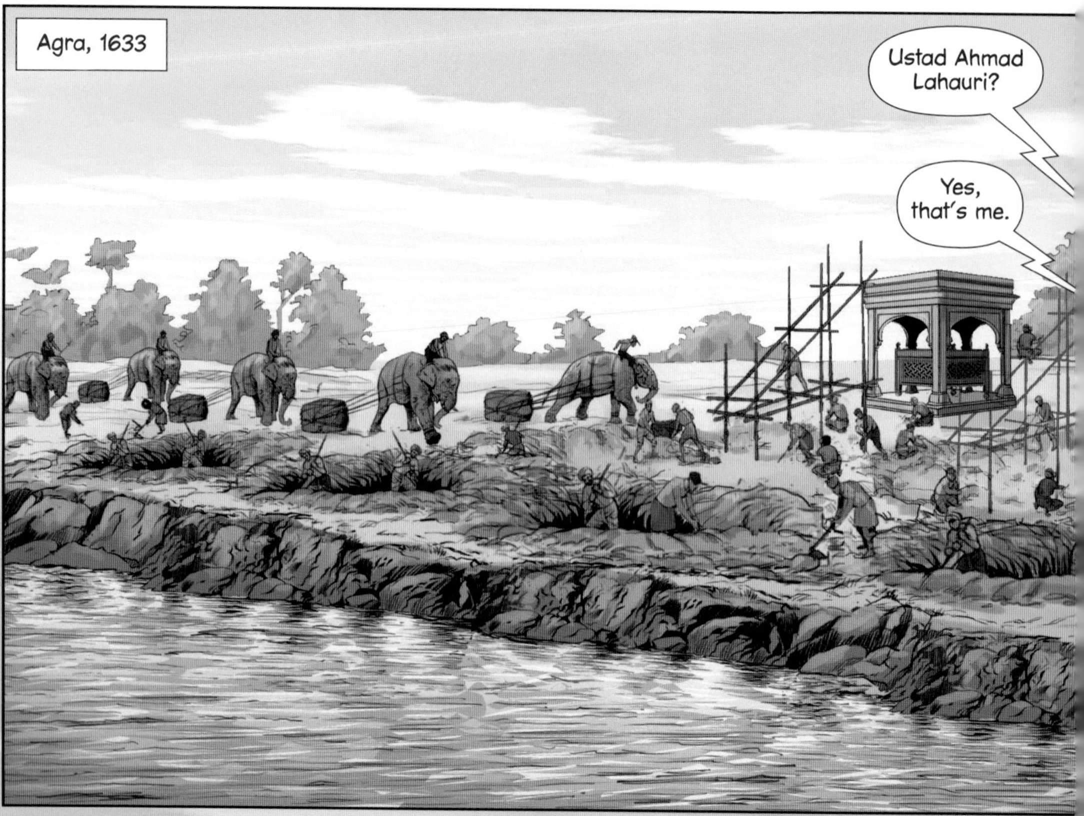
Agra, 1633
Ustad Ahmad Lahauri?
Yes, that's me.

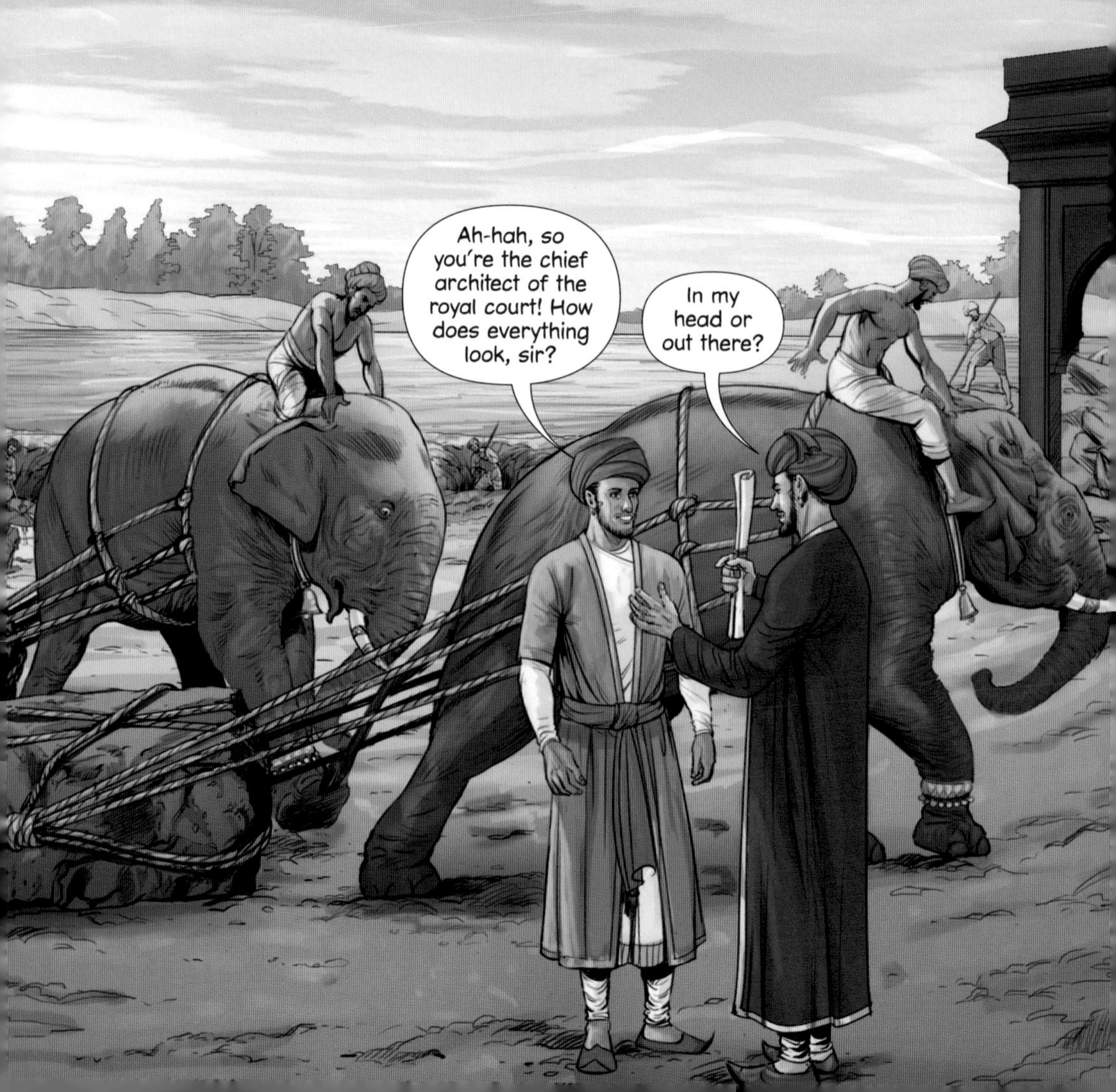
Ah-hah, so you're the chief architect of the royal court! How does everything look, sir?
In my head or out there?

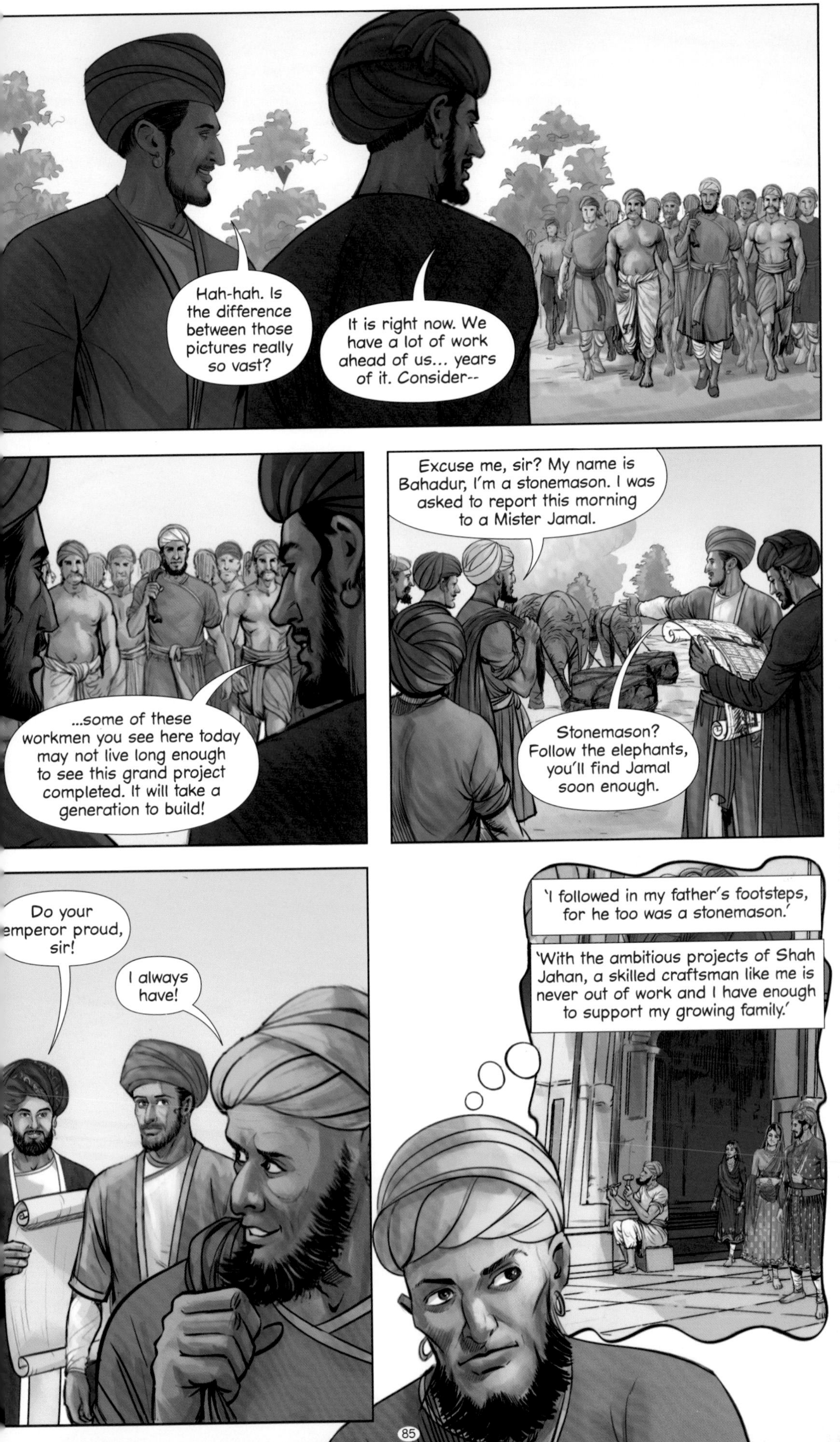

Hah-hah. Is the difference between those pictures really so vast?
It is right now. We have a lot of work ahead of us... years of it. Consider--
...some of these workmen you see here today may not live long enough to see this grand project completed. It will take a generation to build!
Excuse me, sir? My name is Bahadur, I'm a stonemason. I was asked to report this morning to a Mister Jamal.
Stonemason? Follow the elephants, you'll find Jamal soon enough.
Do your emperor proud, sir!
I always have!
'I followed in my father's footsteps, for he too was a stonemason.'
'With the ambitious projects of Shah Jahan, a skilled craftsman like me is never out of work and I have enough to support my growing family.'

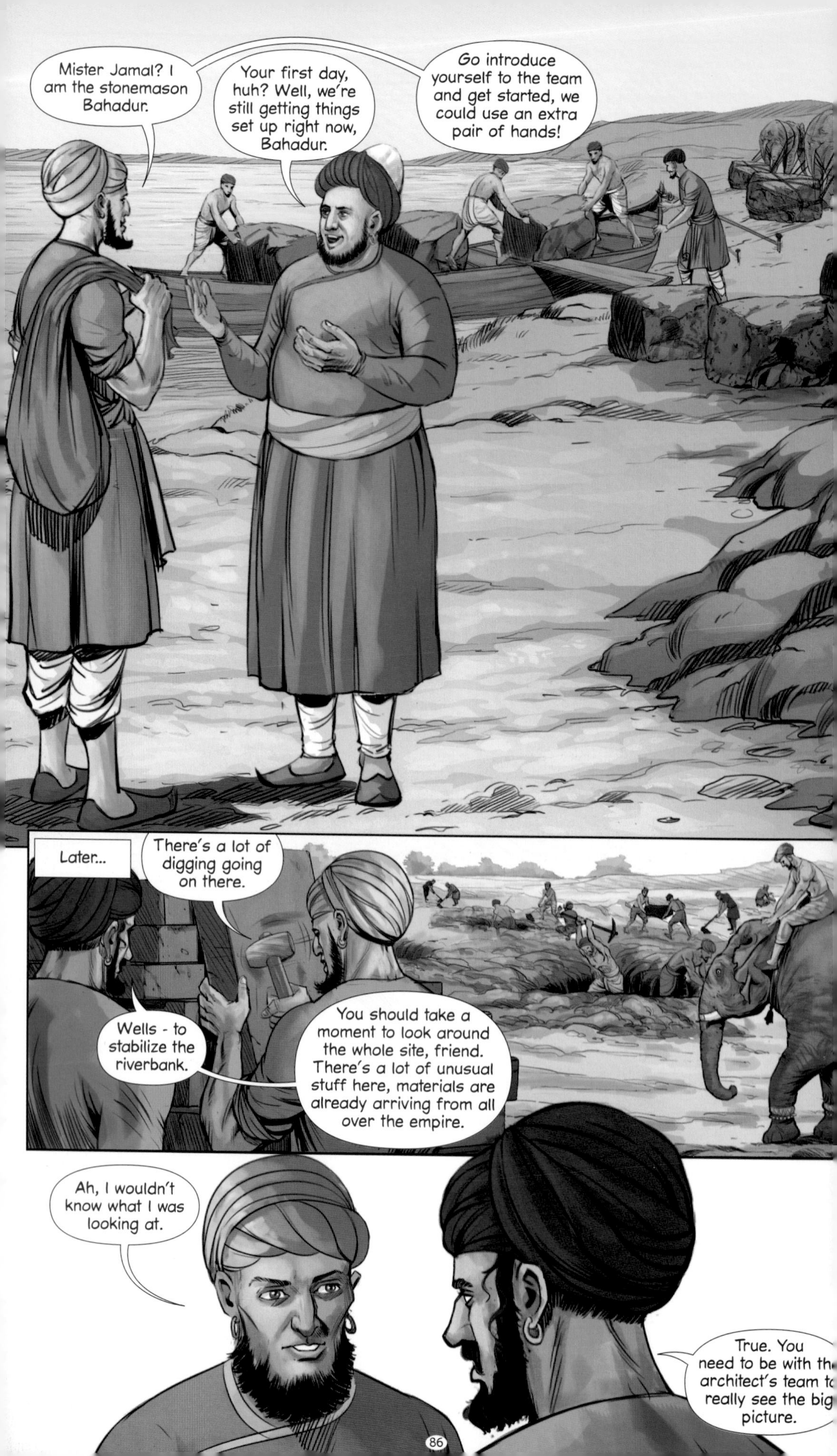

Mister Jamal? I am the stonemason Bahadur.
Your first day, huh? Well, we're still getting things set up right now, Bahadur.
Go introduce yourself to the team and get started, we could use an extra pair of hands!
Later...
There's a lot of digging going on there.
Wells - to stabilize the riverbank.
You should take a moment to look around the whole site, friend. There's a lot of unusual stuff here, materials are already arriving from all over the empire.
Ah, I wouldn't know what I was looking at.
True. You need to be with th architect's team t really see the big picture.

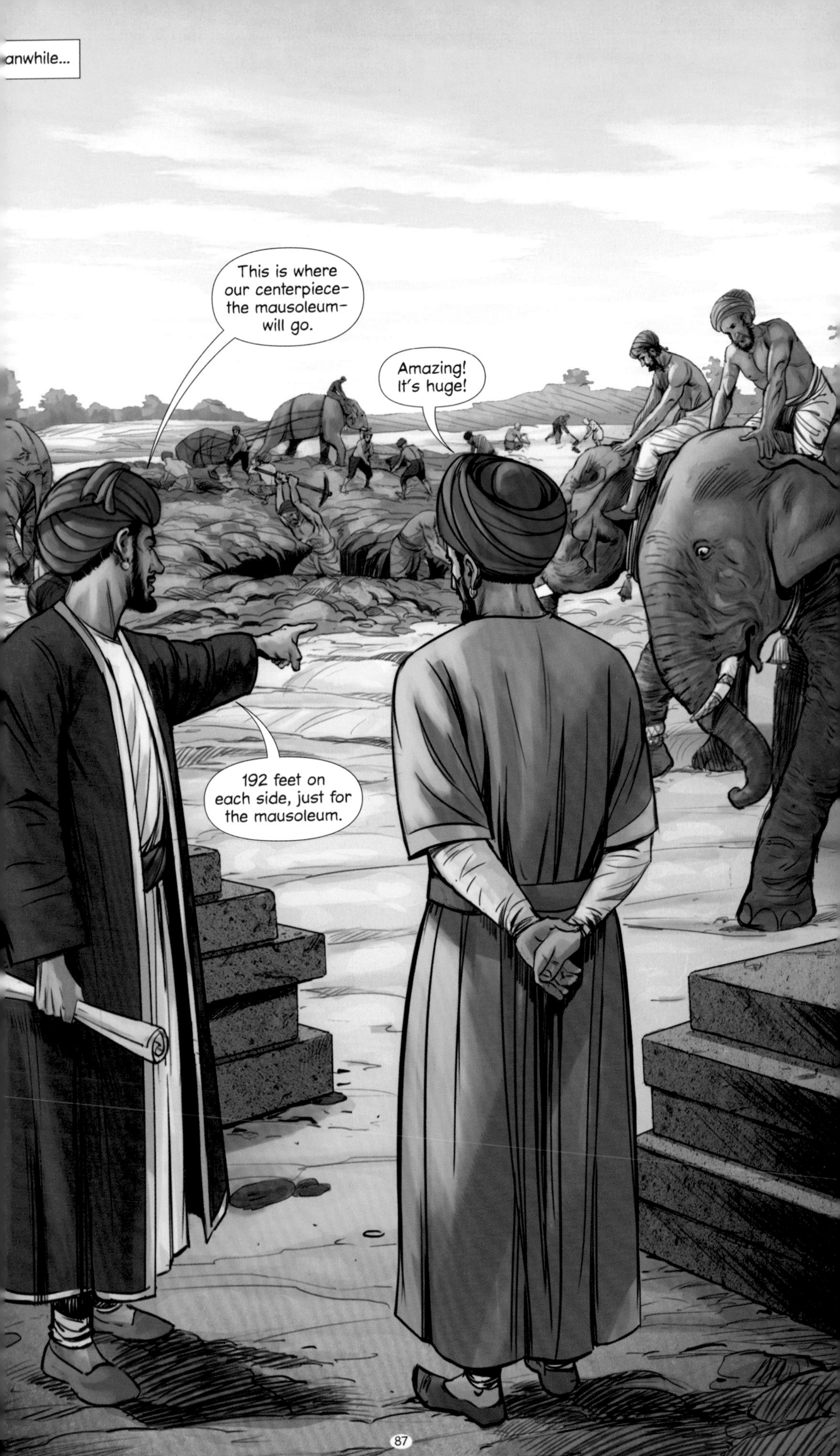
anwhile...
This is where our centerpiece- the mausoleum- will go.
Amazing! It's huge!
192 feet on each side, just for the mausoleum.

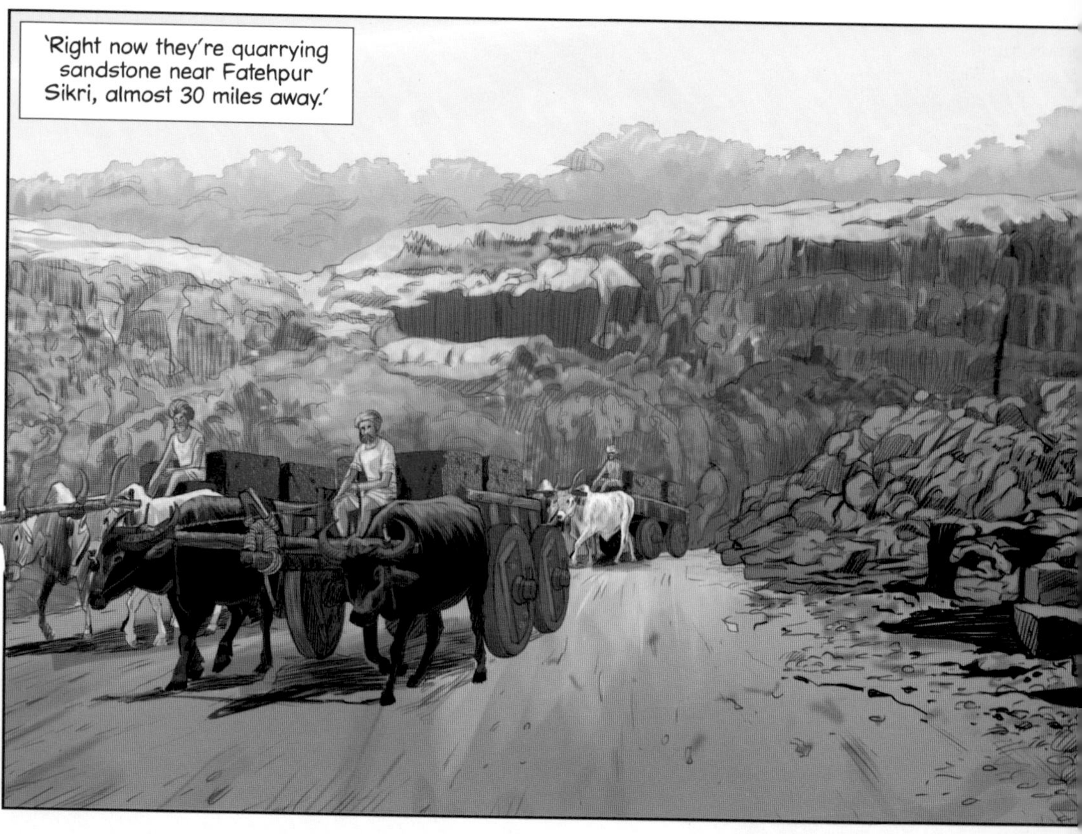
'Right now they're quarrying sandstone near Fatehpur Sikri, almost 30 miles away.'

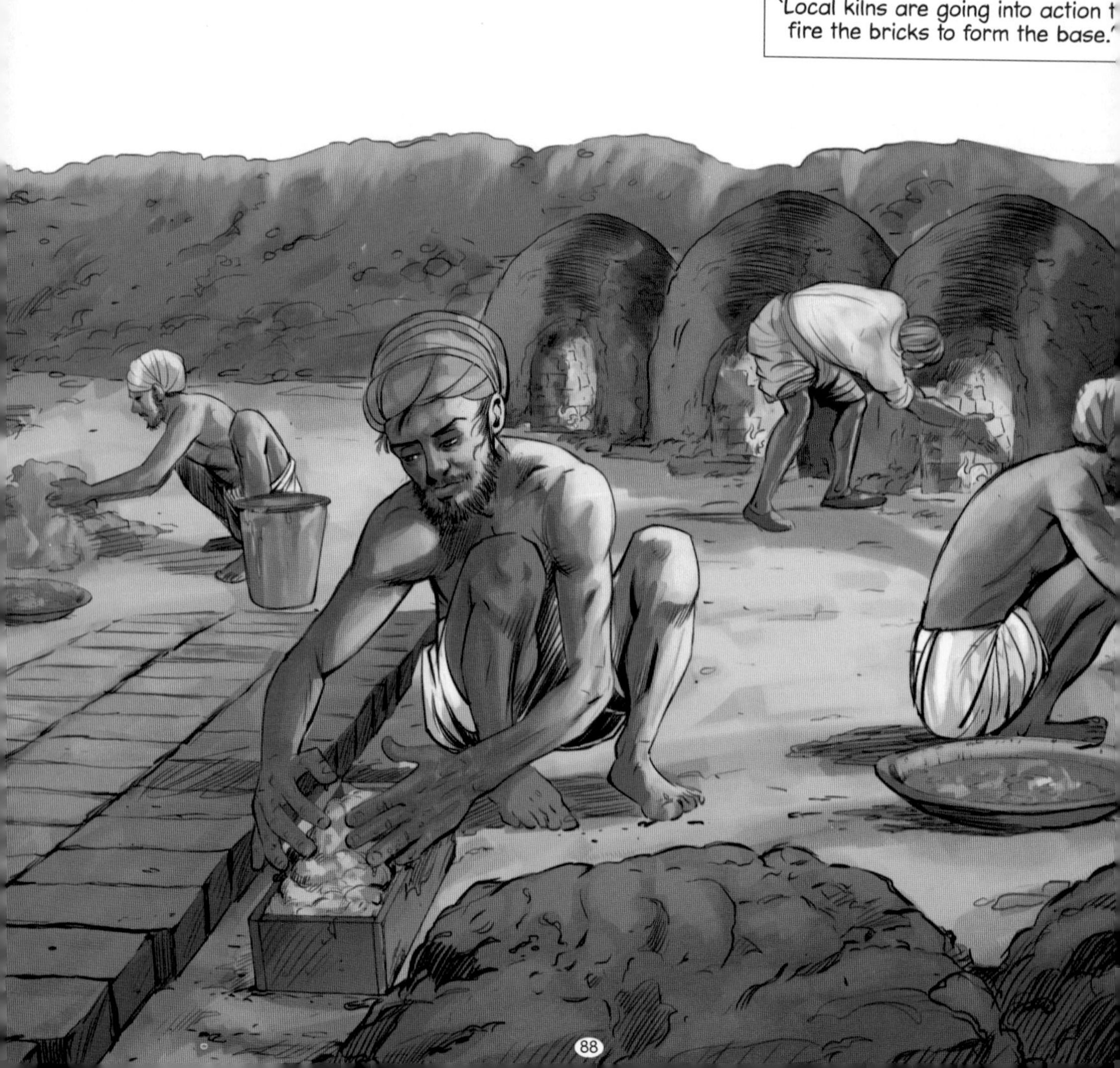
'Local kilns are going into action t
fire the bricks to form the base.'

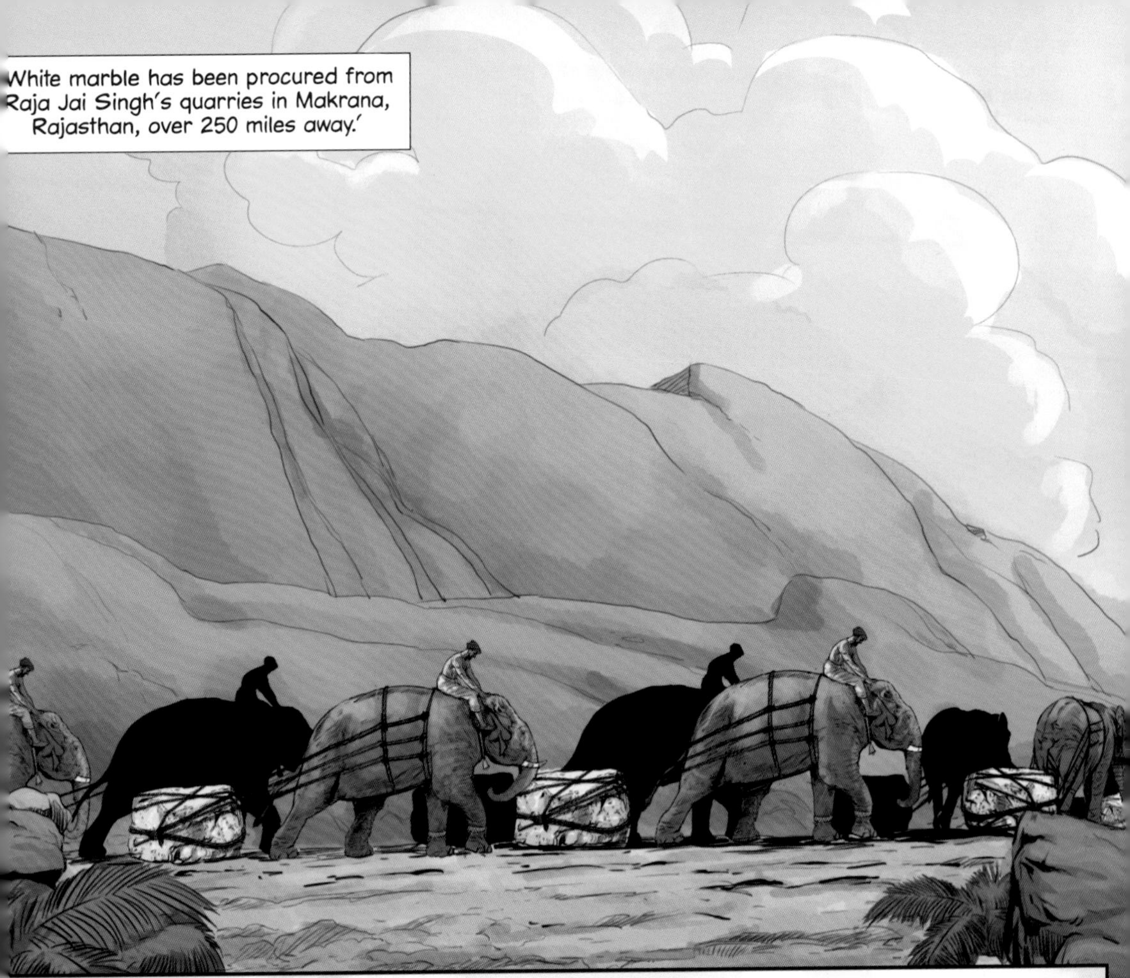
White marble has been procured from Raja Jai Singh's quarries in Makrana, Rajasthan, over 250 miles away.'

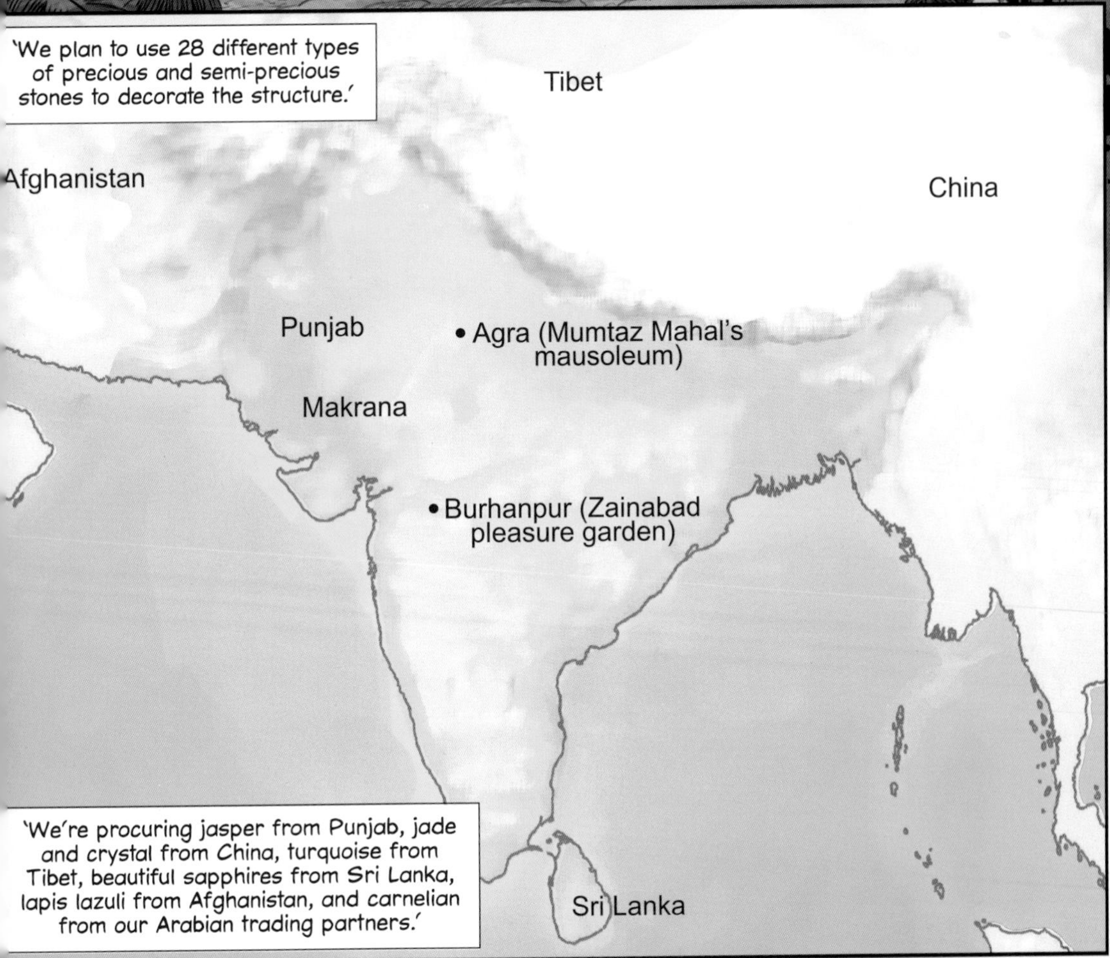
'We plan to use 28 different types of precious and semi-precious stones to decorate the structure.'
Tibet
Afghanistan
China
Punjab
• Agra (Mumtaz Mahal's mausoleum)
Makrana
• Burhanpur (Zainabad pleasure garden)
Sri Lanka
'We're procuring jasper from Punjab, jade and crystal from China, turquoise from Tibet, beautiful sapphires from Sri Lanka, lapis lazuli from Afghanistan, and carnelian from our Arabian trading partners.'

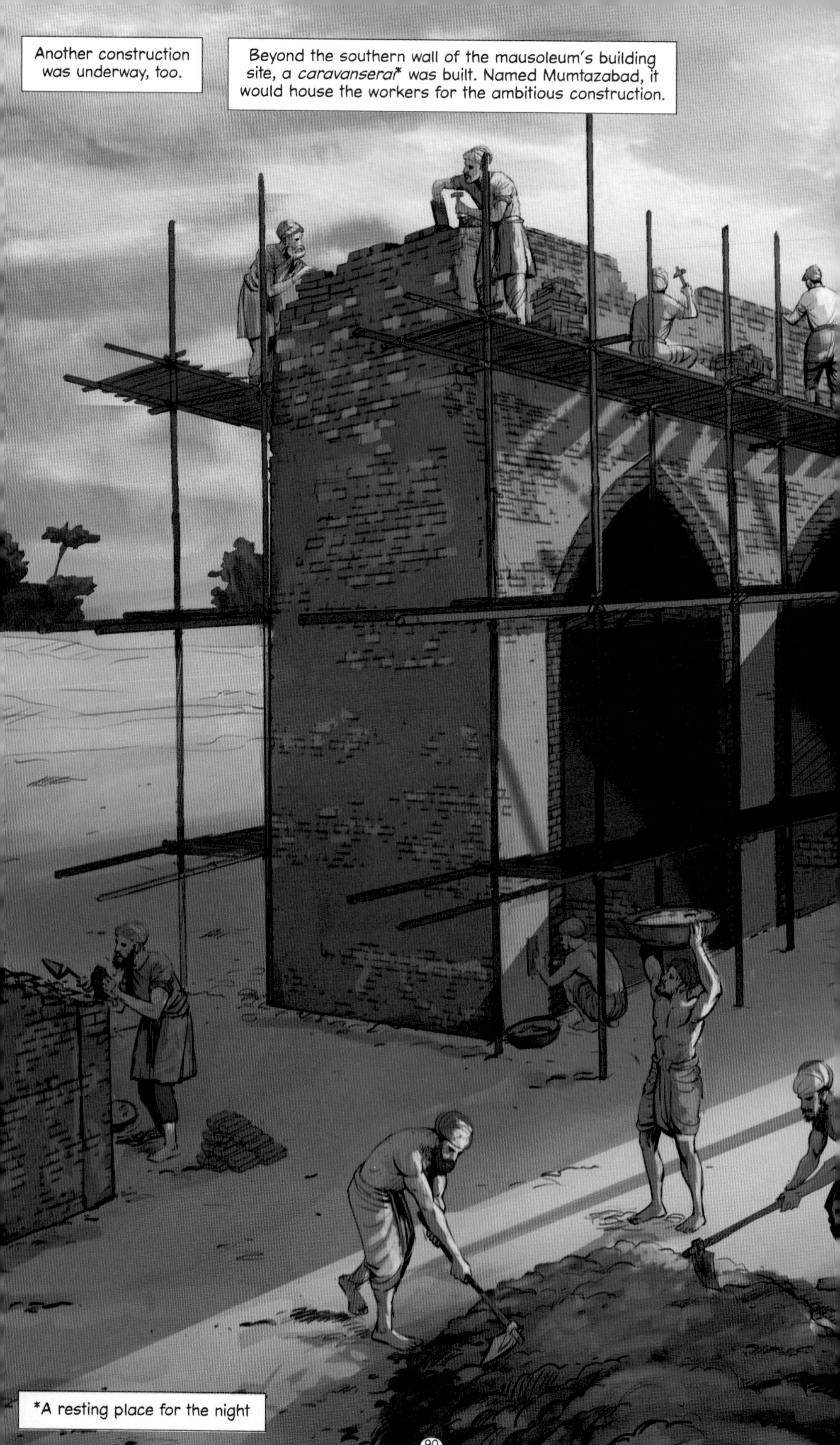
Another construction was underway, too.
Beyond the southern wall of the mausoleum's building site, a *caravanserai** was built. Named Mumtazabad, it would house the workers for the ambitious construction.
*A resting place for the night

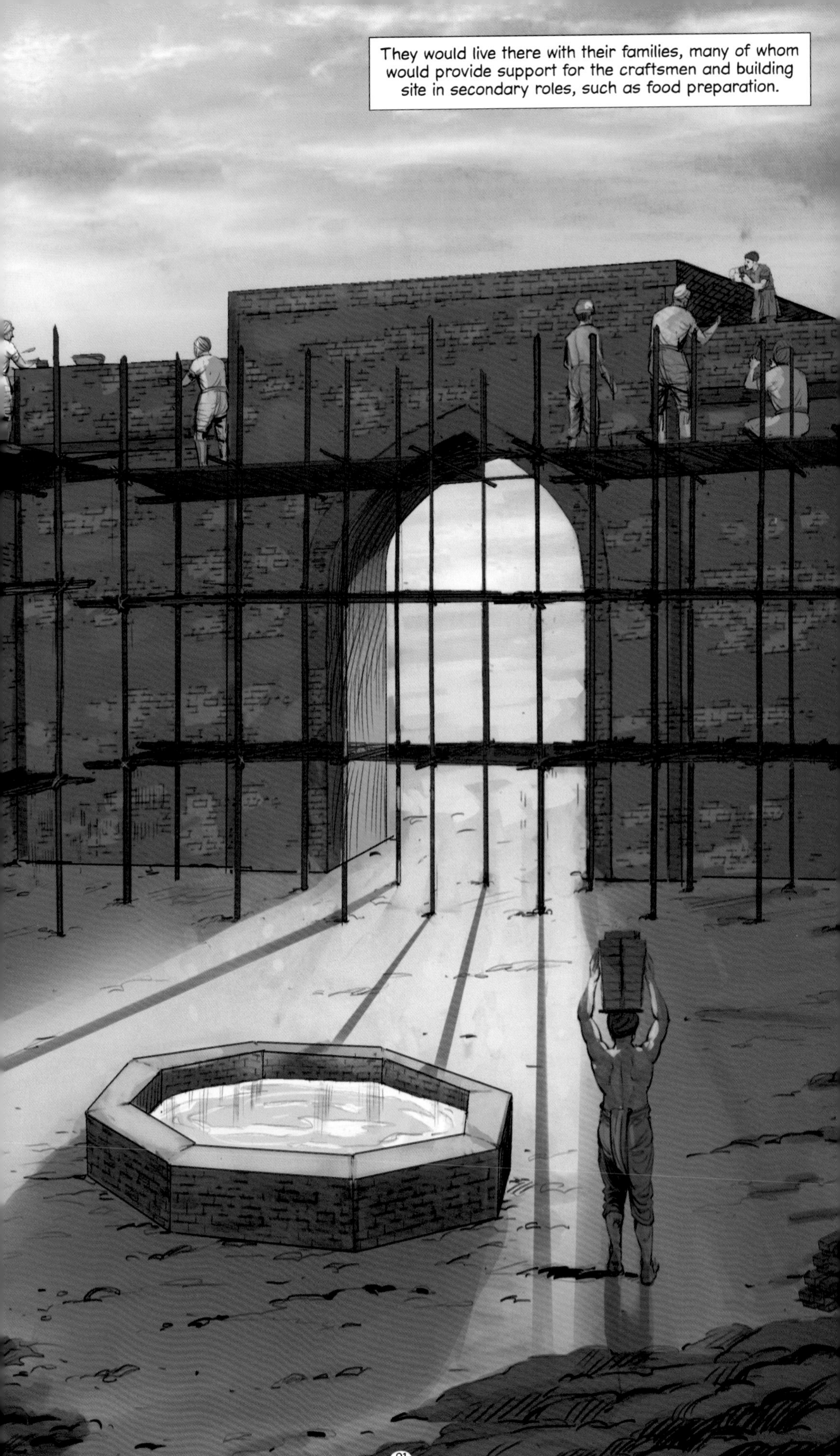
They would live there with their families, many of whom would provide support for the craftsmen and building site in secondary roles, such as food preparation.

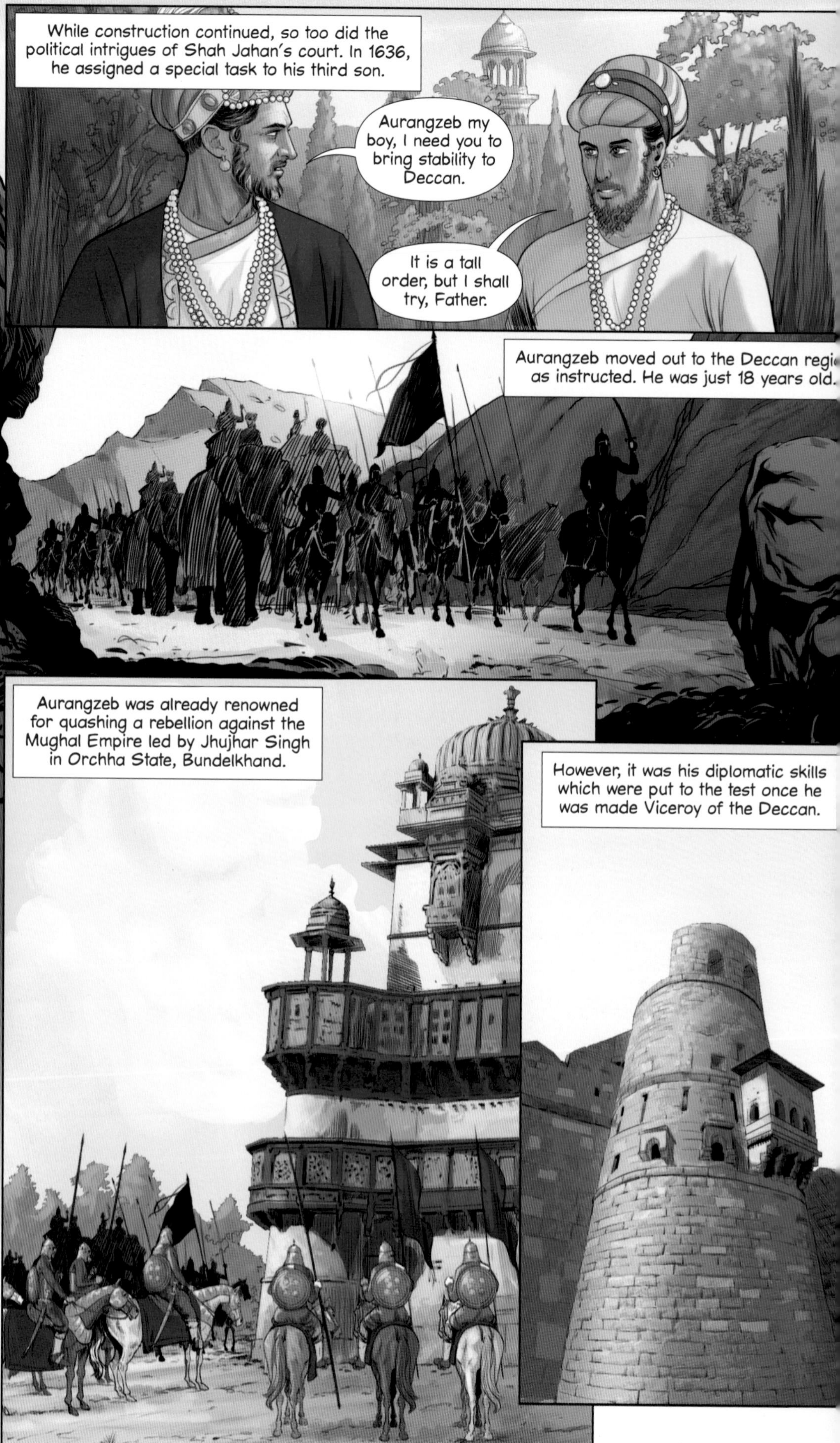
While construction continued, so too did the political intrigues of Shah Jahan's court. In 1636, he assigned a special task to his third son.
Aurangzeb my boy, I need you to bring stability to Deccan.
It is a tall order, but I shall try, Father.
Aurangzeb moved out to the Deccan regi as instructed. He was just 18 years old.
Aurangzeb was already renowned for quashing a rebellion against the Mughal Empire led by Jhujhar Singh in Orchha State, Bundelkhand.
However, it was his diplomatic skills which were put to the test once he was made Viceroy of the Deccan.

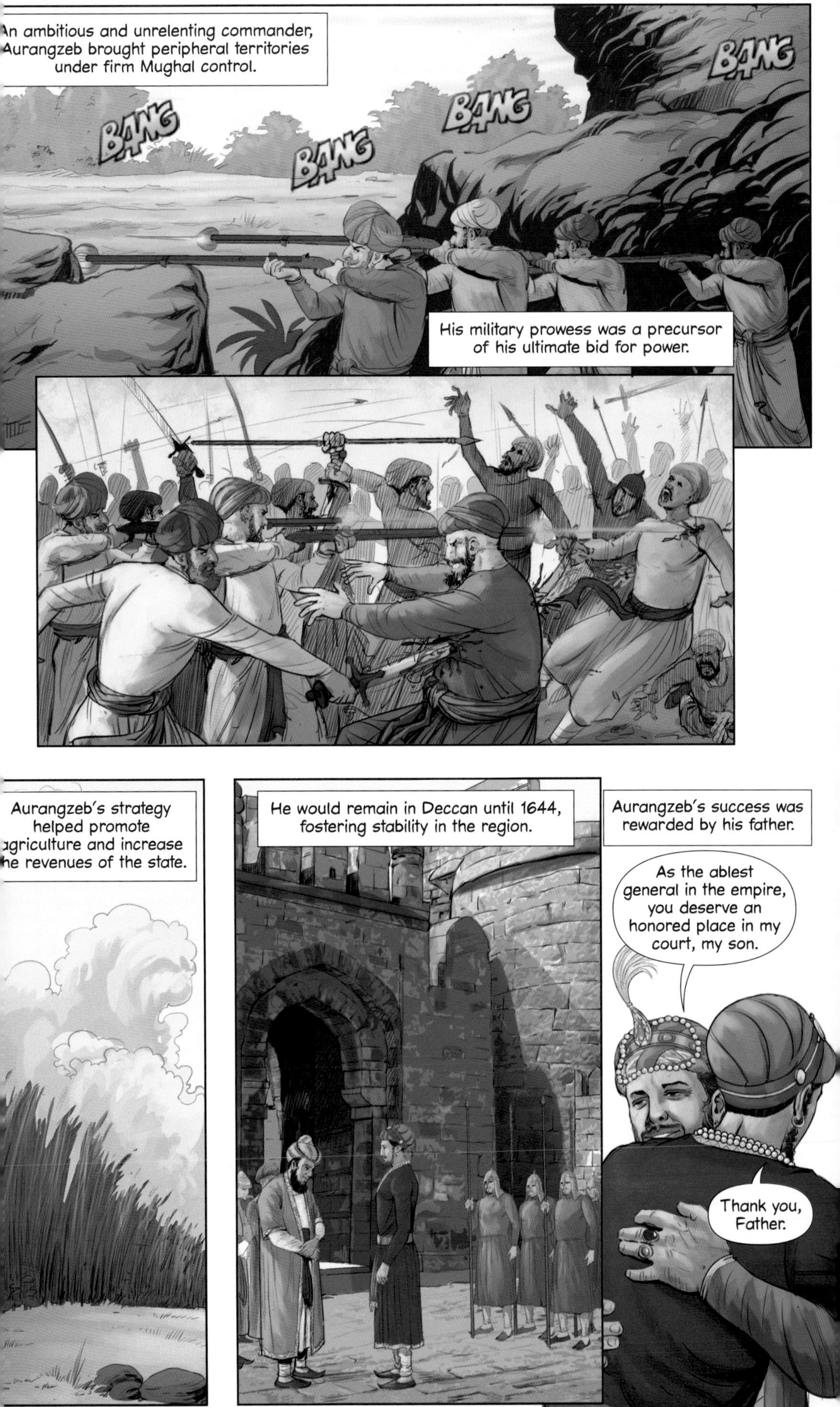

An ambitious and unrelenting commander, Aurangzeb brought peripheral territories under firm Mughal control.
BANG
BANG
BANG
BANG
His military prowess was a precursor of his ultimate bid for power.
Aurangzeb's strategy helped promote agriculture and increase the revenues of the state.
He would remain in Deccan until 1644, fostering stability in the region.
Aurangzeb's success was rewarded by his father.
As the ablest general in the empire, you deserve an honored place in my court, my son.
Thank you, Father.

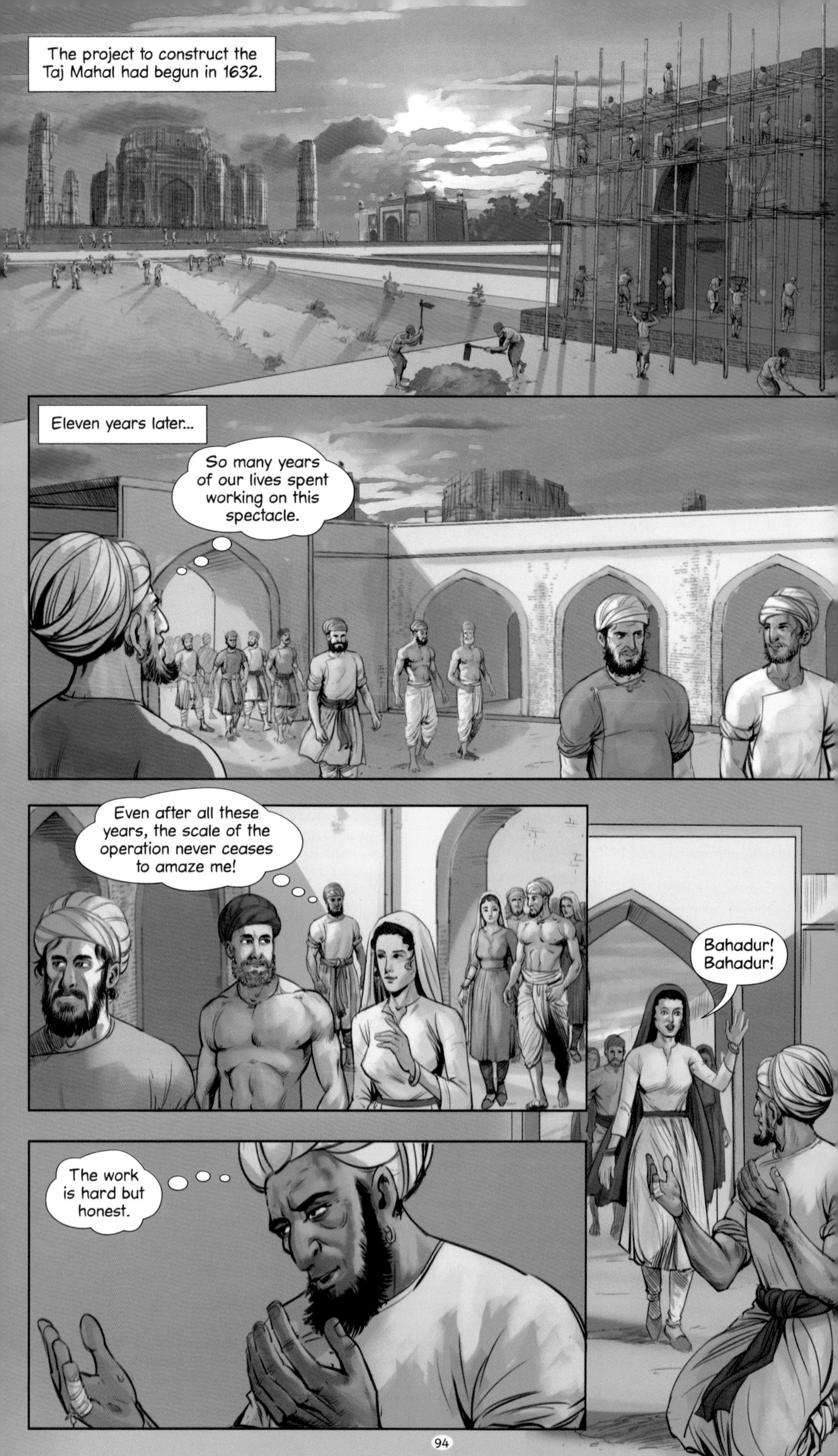

The project to construct the Taj Mahal had begun in 1632.
Eleven years later...
So many years of our lives spent working on this spectacle.
Even after all these years, the scale of the operation never ceases to amaze me!
Bahadur! Bahadur!
The work is hard but honest.

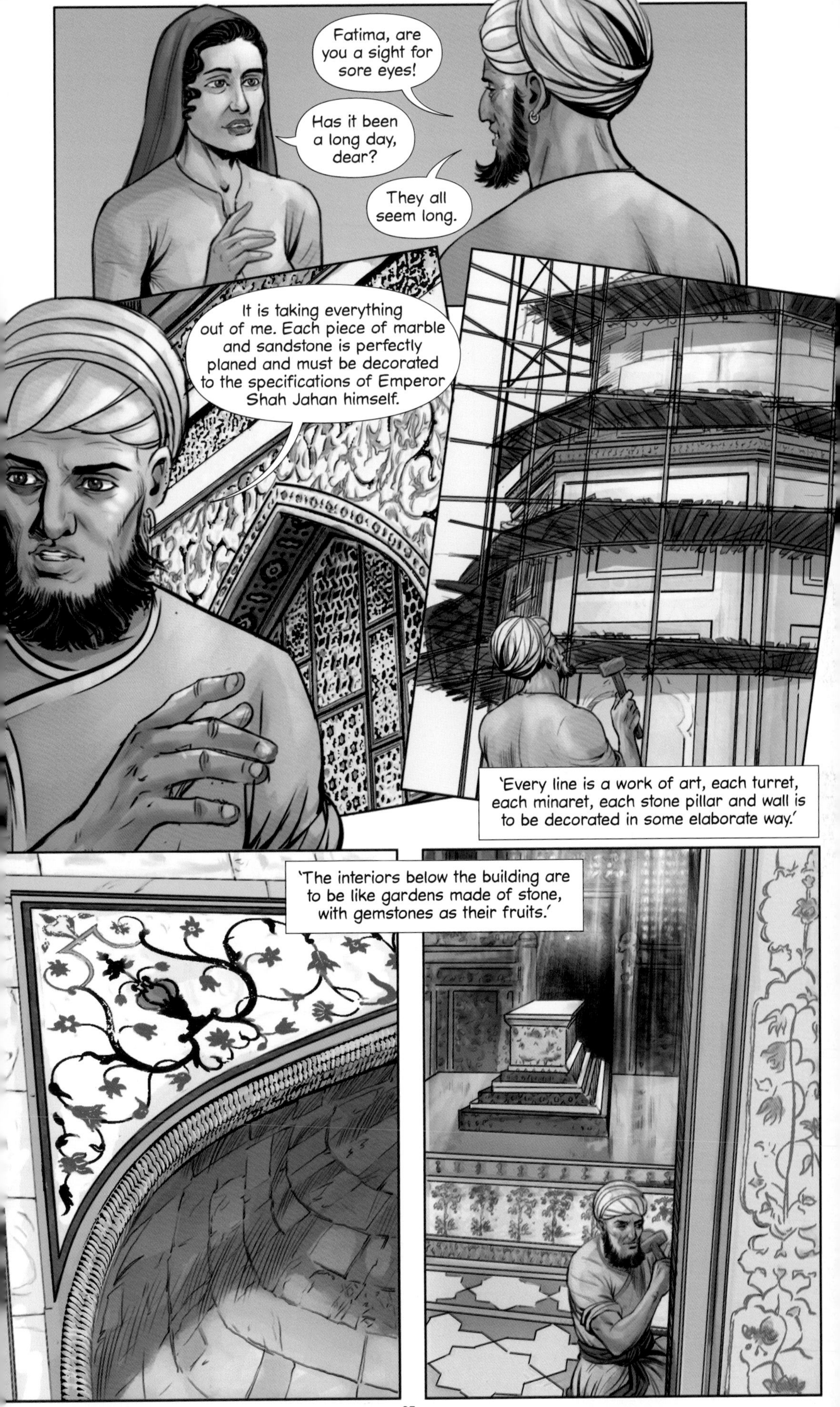

Fatima, are you a sight for sore eyes!
Has it been a long day, dear?
They all seem long.
It is taking everything out of me. Each piece of marble and sandstone is perfectly planed and must be decorated to the specifications of Emperor Shah Jahan himself.
'Every line is a work of art, each turret, each minaret, each stone pillar and wall is to be decorated in some elaborate way.'
'The interiors below the building are to be like gardens made of stone, with gemstones as their fruits.'

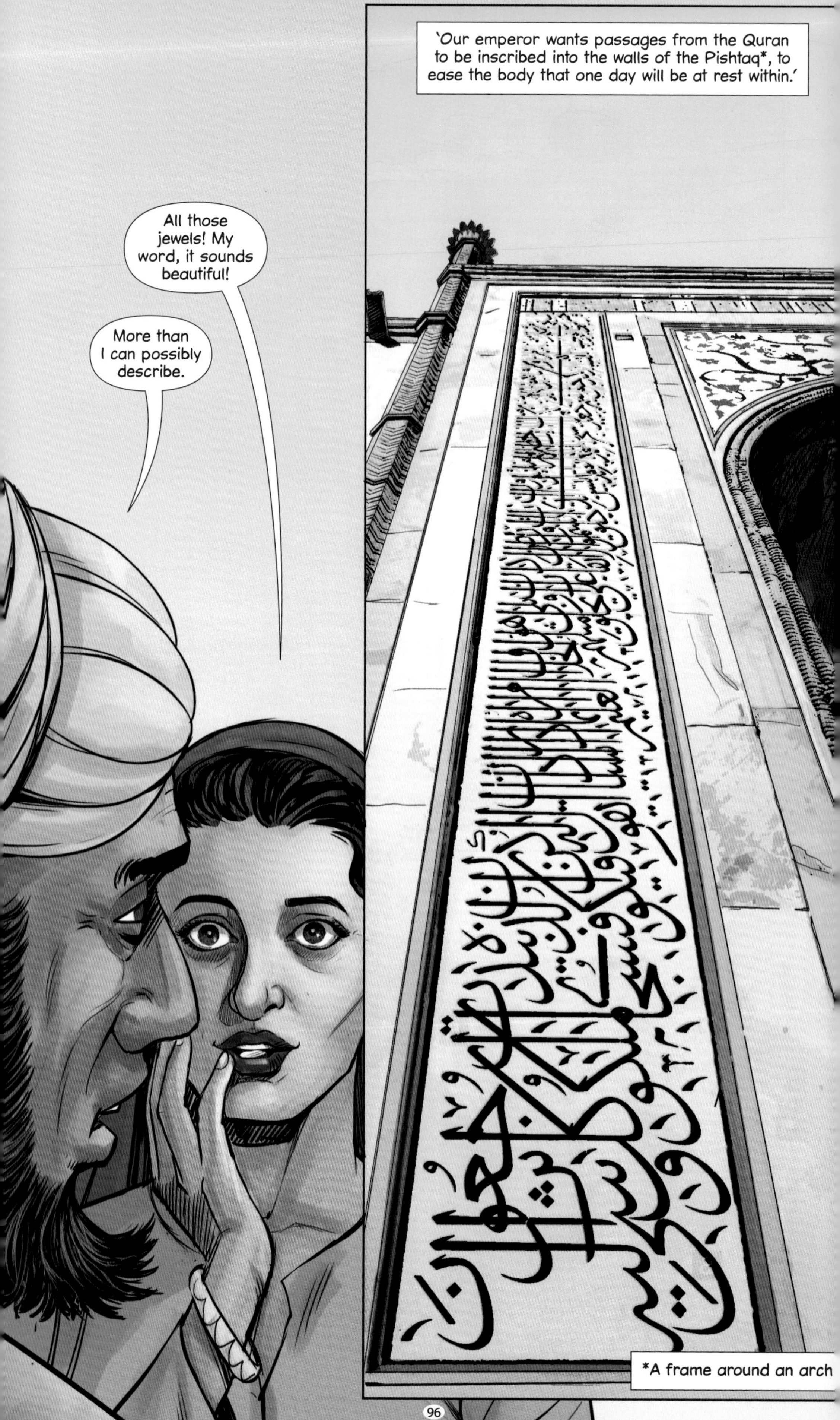
'Our emperor wants passages from the Quran to be inscribed into the walls of the Pishtaq*, to ease the body that one day will be at rest within.'
All those jewels! My word, it sounds beautiful!
More than I can possibly describe.
*A frame around an arch

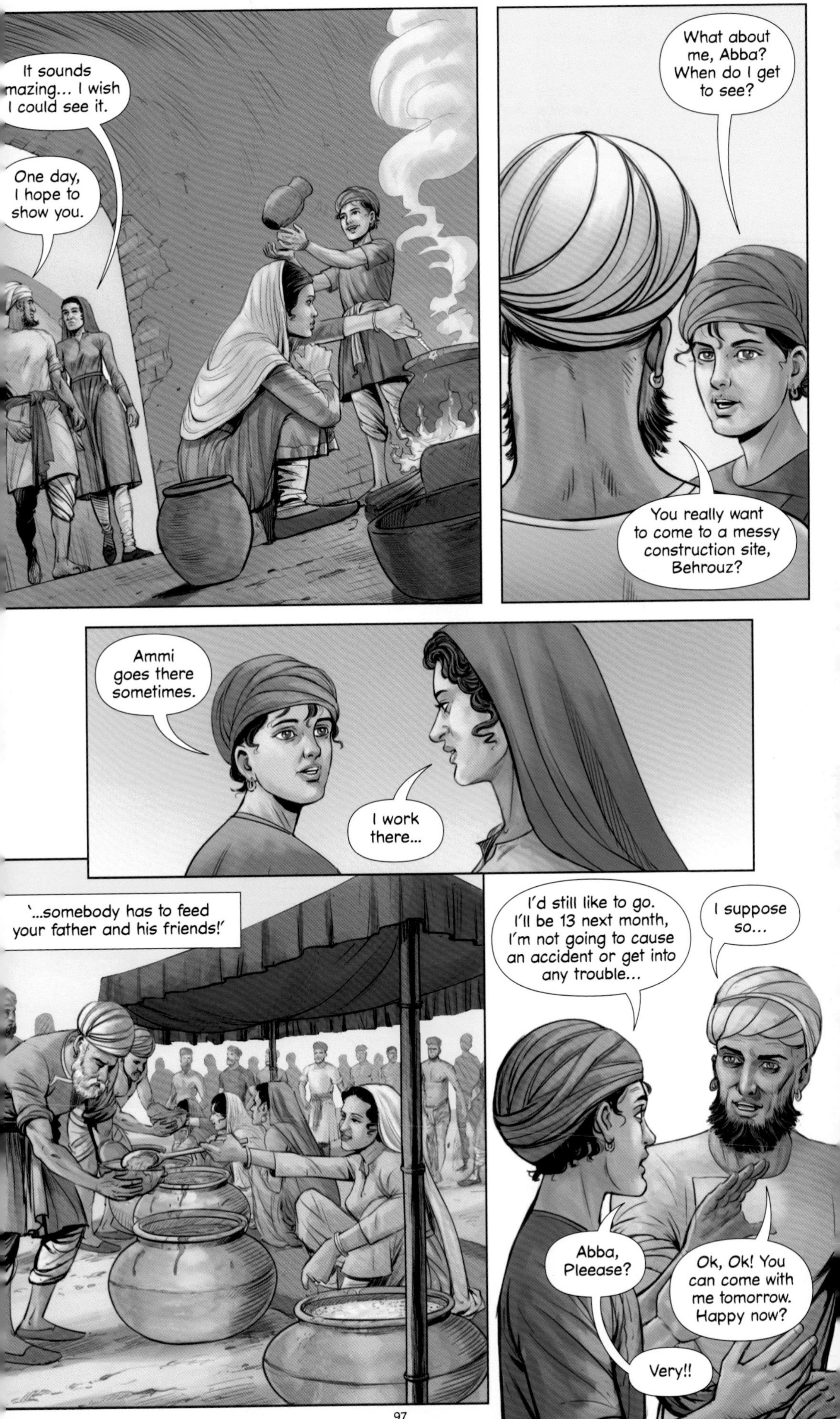
It sounds mazing... I wish I could see it.
One day, I hope to show you.
What about me, Abba? When do I get to see?
You really want to come to a messy construction site, Behrouz?
Ammi goes there sometimes.
I work there...
'...somebody has to feed your father and his friends!'
I'd still like to go. I'll be 13 next month, I'm not going to cause an accident or get into any trouble...
I suppose so...
Abba, Pleease?
Ok, Ok! You can come with me tomorrow. Happy now?
Very!!

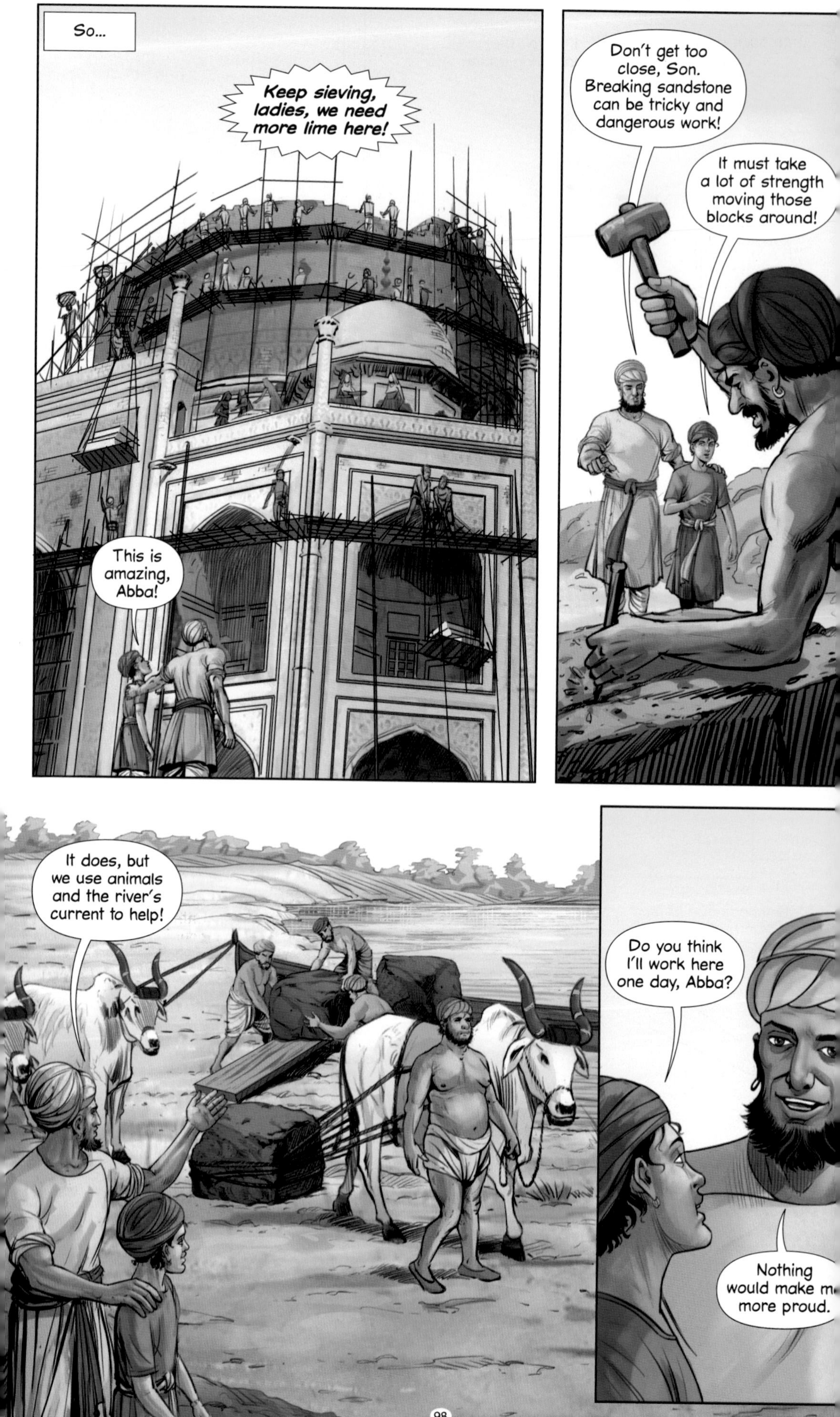
So...
Keep sieving, ladies, we need more lime here!
This is amazing, Abba!
Don't get too close, Son. Breaking sandstone can be tricky and dangerous work!
It must take a lot of strength moving those blocks around!
It does, but we use animals and the river's current to help!
Do you think I'll work here one day, Abba?
Nothing would make m
more proud.

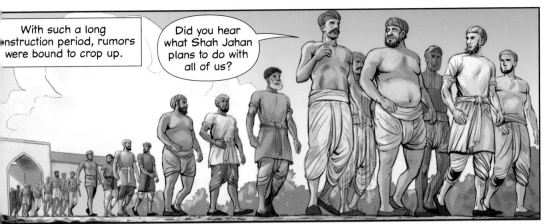

With such a long construction period, rumors were bound to crop up.

Did you hear what Shah Jahan plans to do with all of us?

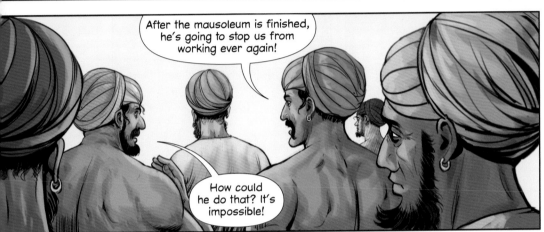

After the mausoleum is finished, he's going to stop us from working ever again!

How could he do that? It's impossible!

He could put us all to death so we could never build another monument like this one!

Or he could just cut our hands off. That would stop us from ever working again.

I think I'm going to be sick!

I should go check on him.

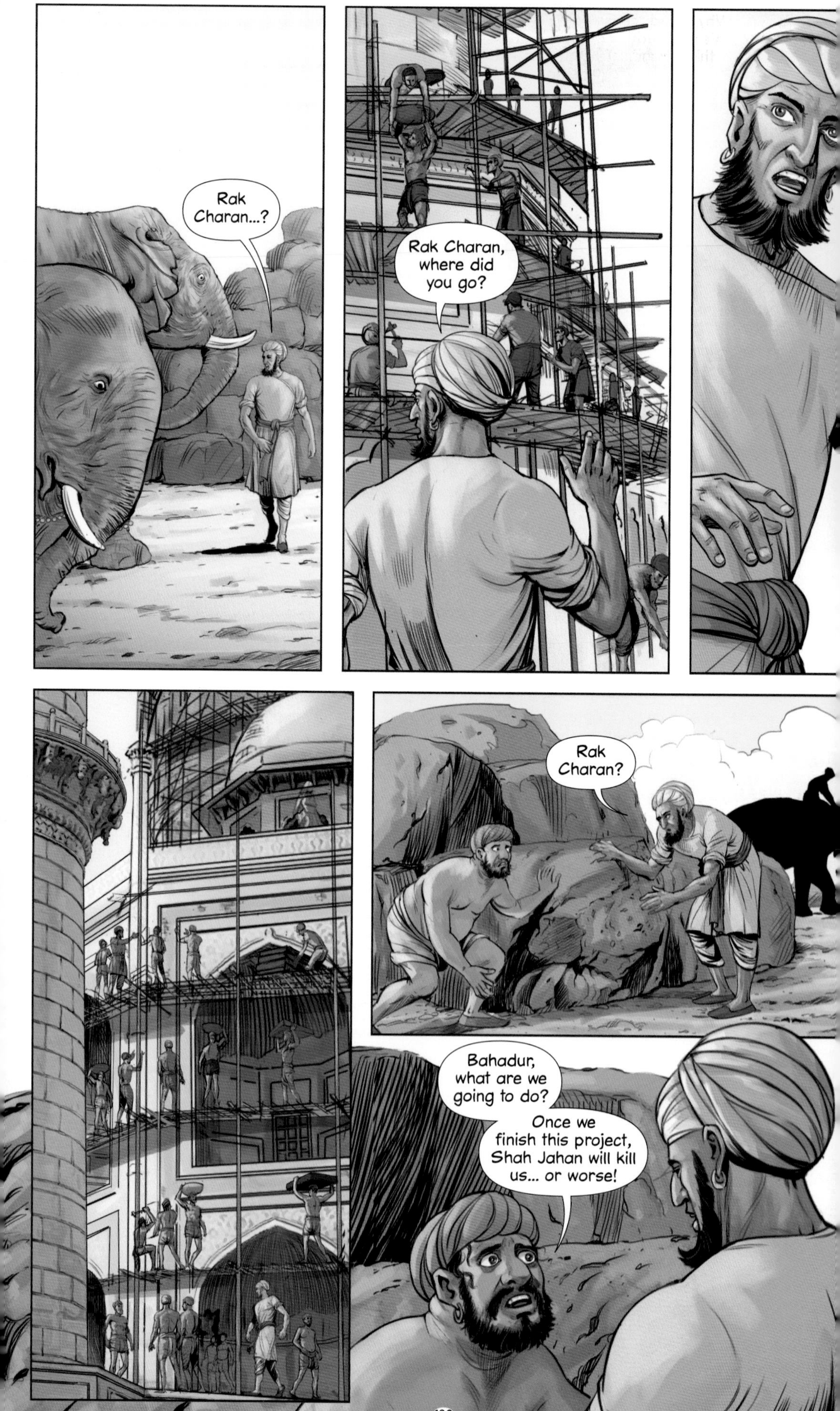

Rak Charan...?
Rak Charan, where did you go?
Rak Charan?
Bahadur, what are we going to do?
Once we finish this project, Shah Jahan will kill us... or worse!

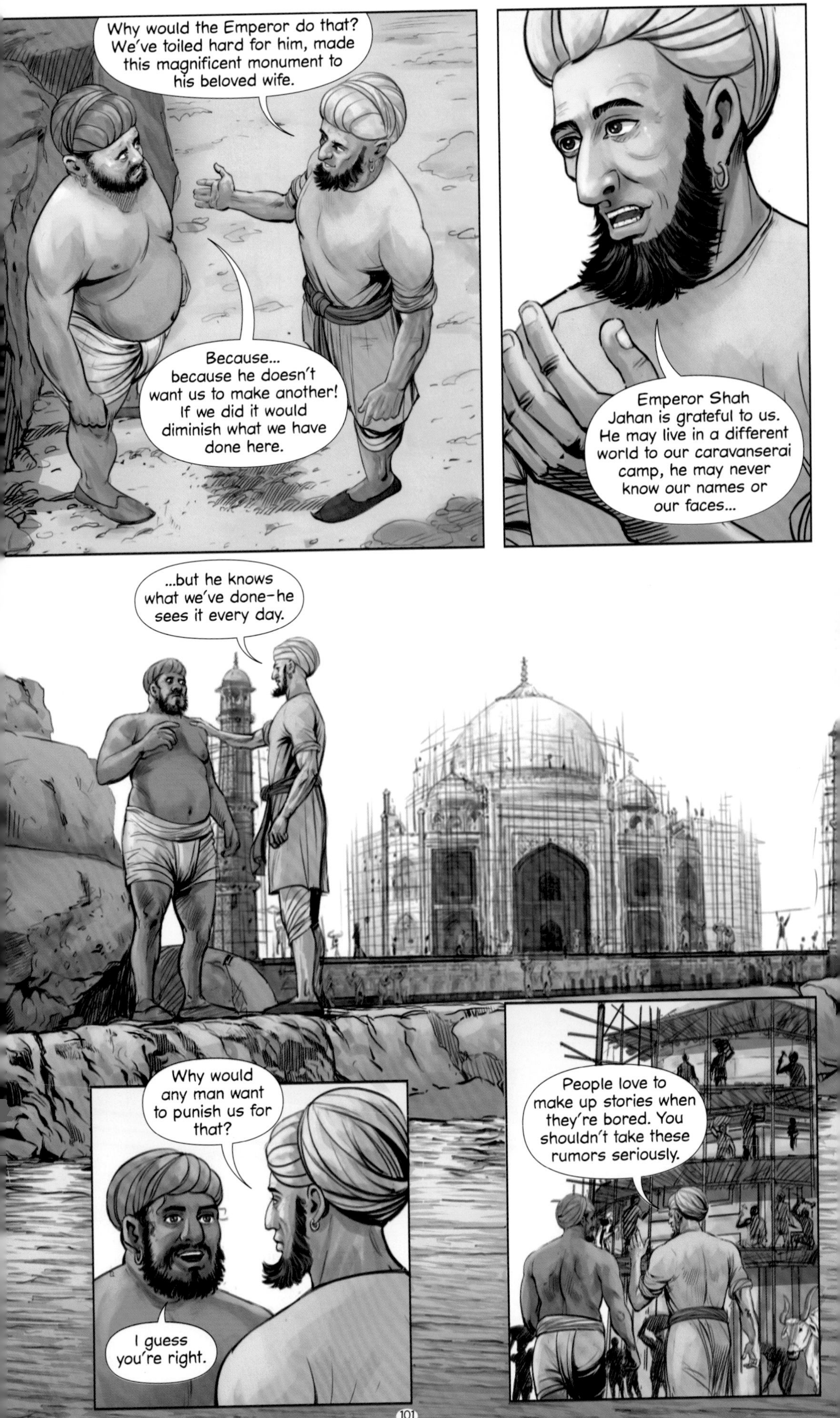
Why would the Emperor do that? We've toiled hard for him, made this magnificent monument to his beloved wife.
Because... because he doesn't want us to make another! If we did it would diminish what we have done here.
Emperor Shah Jahan is grateful to us. He may live in a different world to our caravanserai camp, he may never know our names or our faces...
...but he knows what we've done—he sees it every day.
Why would any man want to punish us for that?
I guess you're right.
People love to make up stories when they're bored. You shouldn't take these rumors seriously.

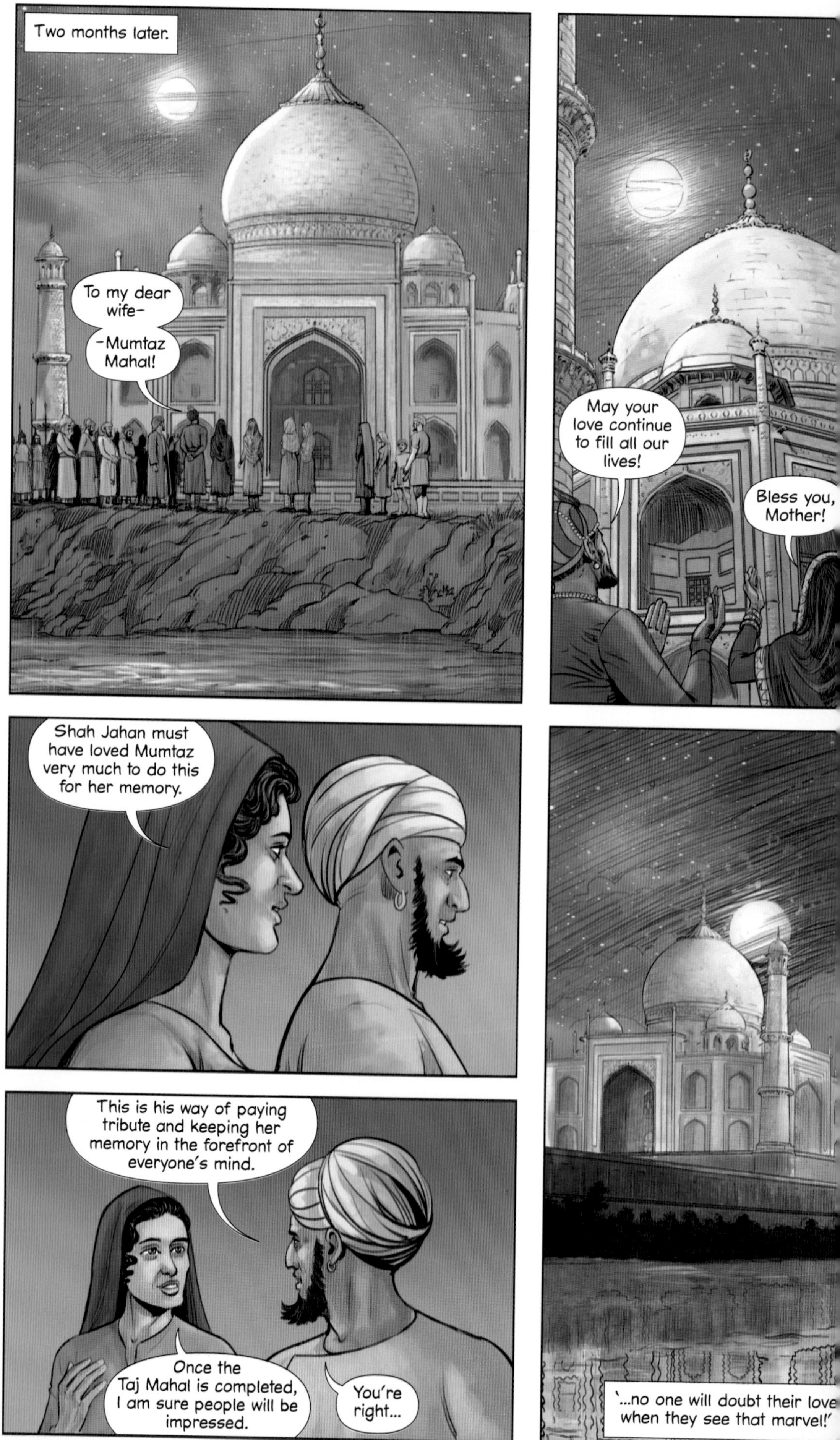
Two months later.
To my dear wife-
-Mumtaz Mahal!
May your love continue to fill all our lives!
Bless you, Mother!
Shah Jahan must have loved Mumtaz very much to do this for her memory.
This is his way of paying tribute and keeping her memory in the forefront of everyone's mind.
Once the Taj Mahal is completed, I am sure people will be impressed.
You're right...
'...no one will doubt their love when they see that marvel!'

hapter 5 Finishing Touches

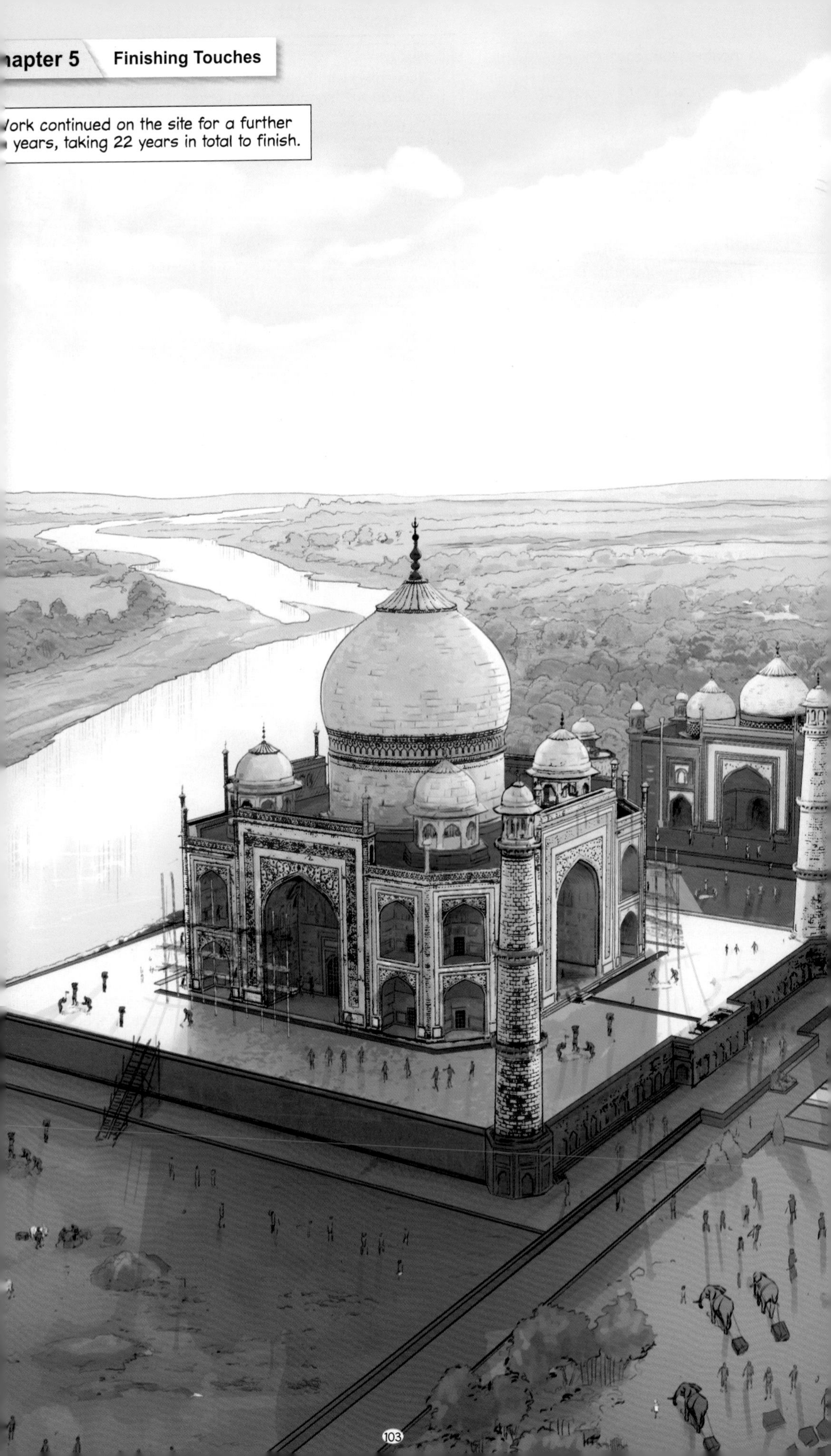
ork continued on the site for a further
years, taking 22 years in total to finish.

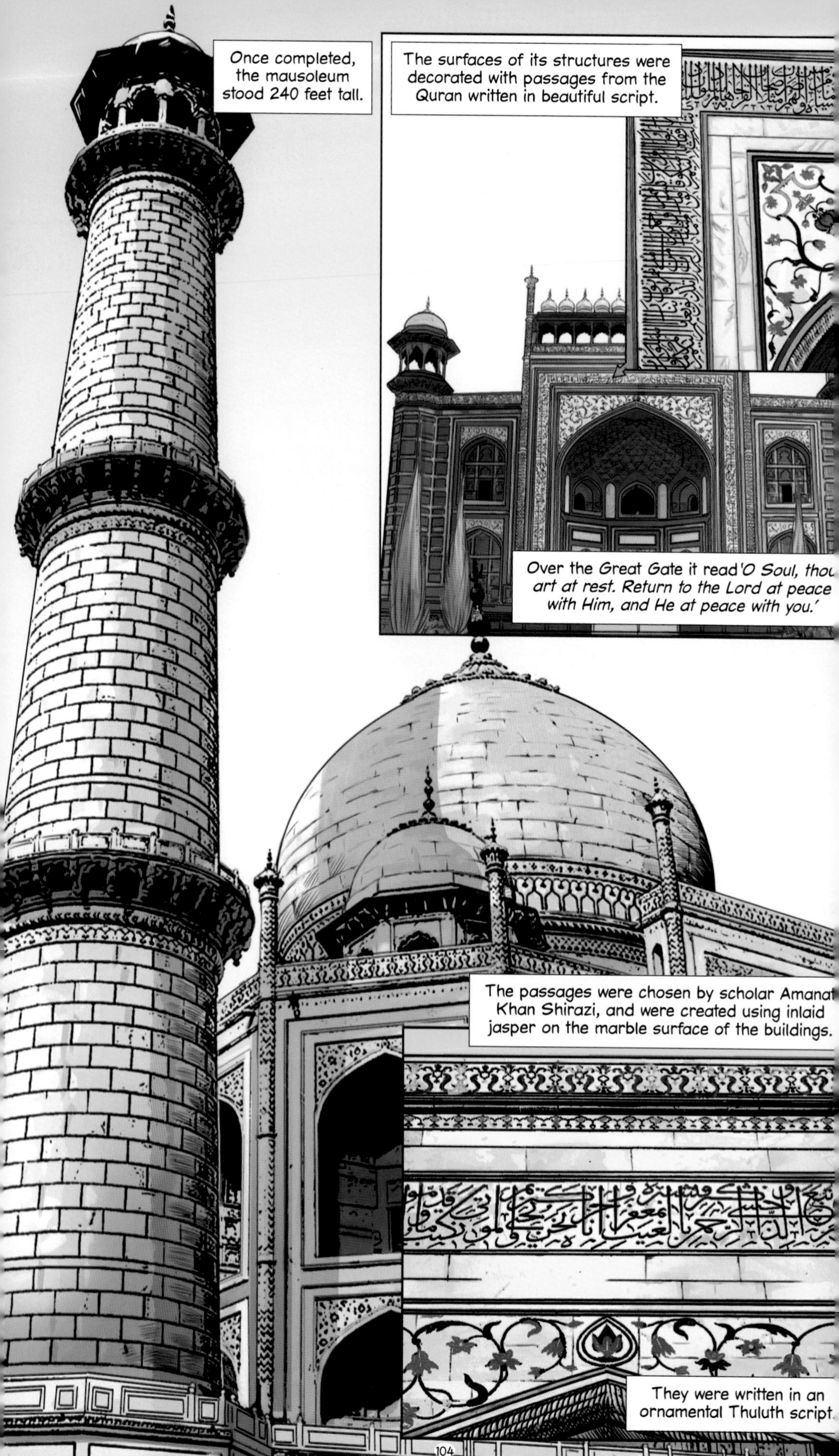
Once completed, the mausoleum stood 240 feet tall.
The surfaces of its structures were decorated with passages from the Quran written in beautiful script.
Over the Great Gate it read 'O Soul, thou art at rest. Return to the Lord at peace with Him, and He at peace with you.'
The passages were chosen by scholar Amanat Khan Shirazi, and were created using inlaid jasper on the marble surface of the buildings.
They were written in an ornamental Thuluth script.

The interior was elaborately decorated with inlay work of precious and semiprecious stones.

The ambition and workmanship was without peer.

Respectful of Muslim tradition, Mumtaz's crypt was kept plain and located beneath the inner chamber, her face turned right towards Mecca.

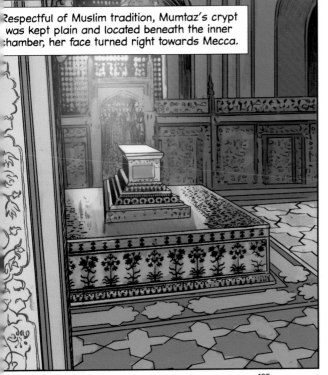

Its sides were decorated with the ninety names of God. These include 'O Noble', 'O Magnificent', 'O Unique', 'O Eternal', 'O Glorious.'

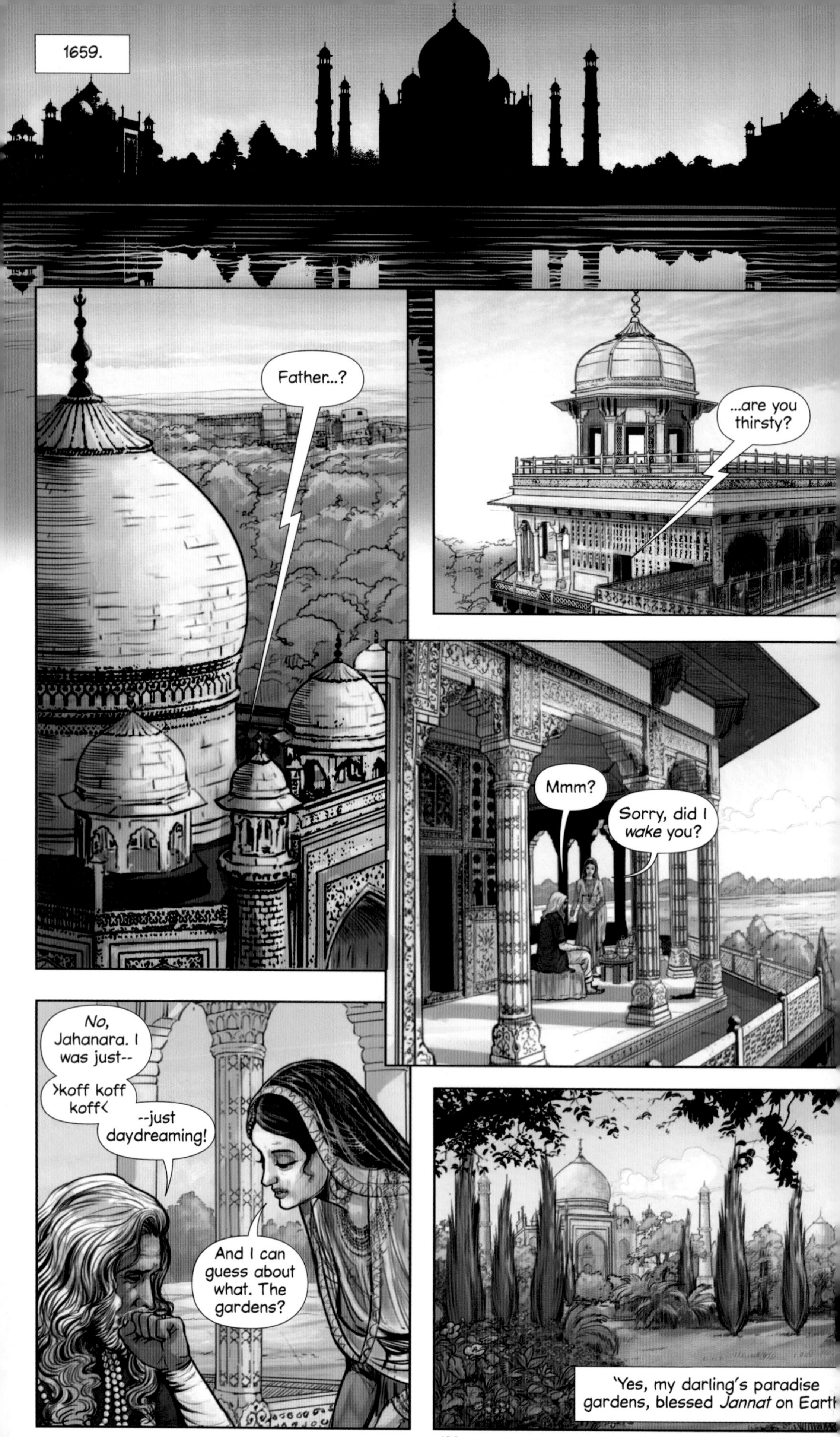
1659.
Father...?
...are you thirsty?
Mmm?
Sorry, did I *wake* you?
No, Jahanara. I was just--
>koff koff koff<
--just daydreaming!
And I can guess about what. The gardens?
'Yes, my darling's paradise gardens, blessed *Jannat* on Eart

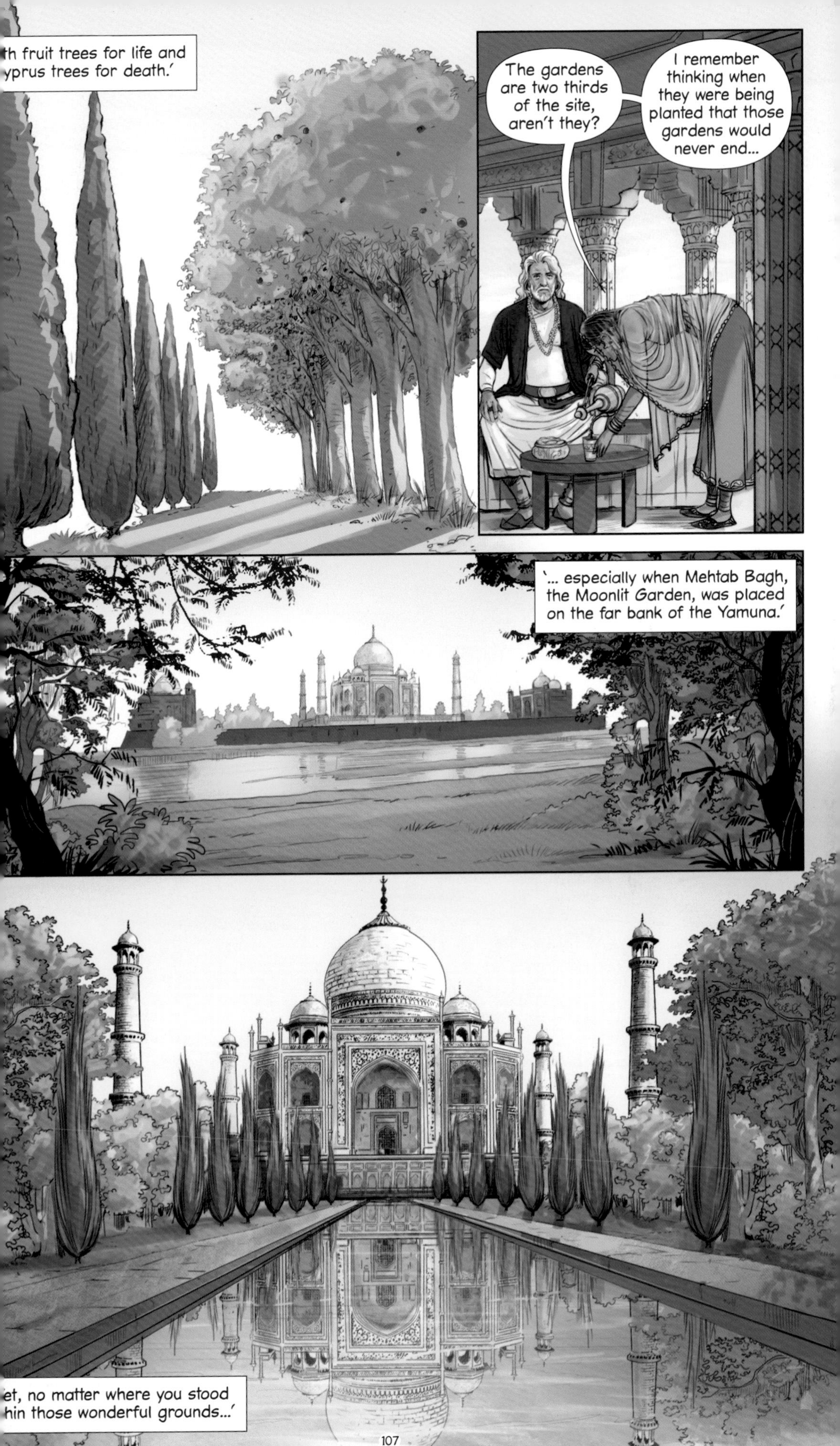

th fruit trees for life and
yprus trees for death.'
The gardens are two thirds of the site, aren't they?
I remember thinking when they were being planted that those gardens would never end...
'... especially when Mehtab Bagh, the Moonlit Garden, was placed on the far bank of the Yamuna.'
et, no matter where you stood
hin those wonderful grounds...'

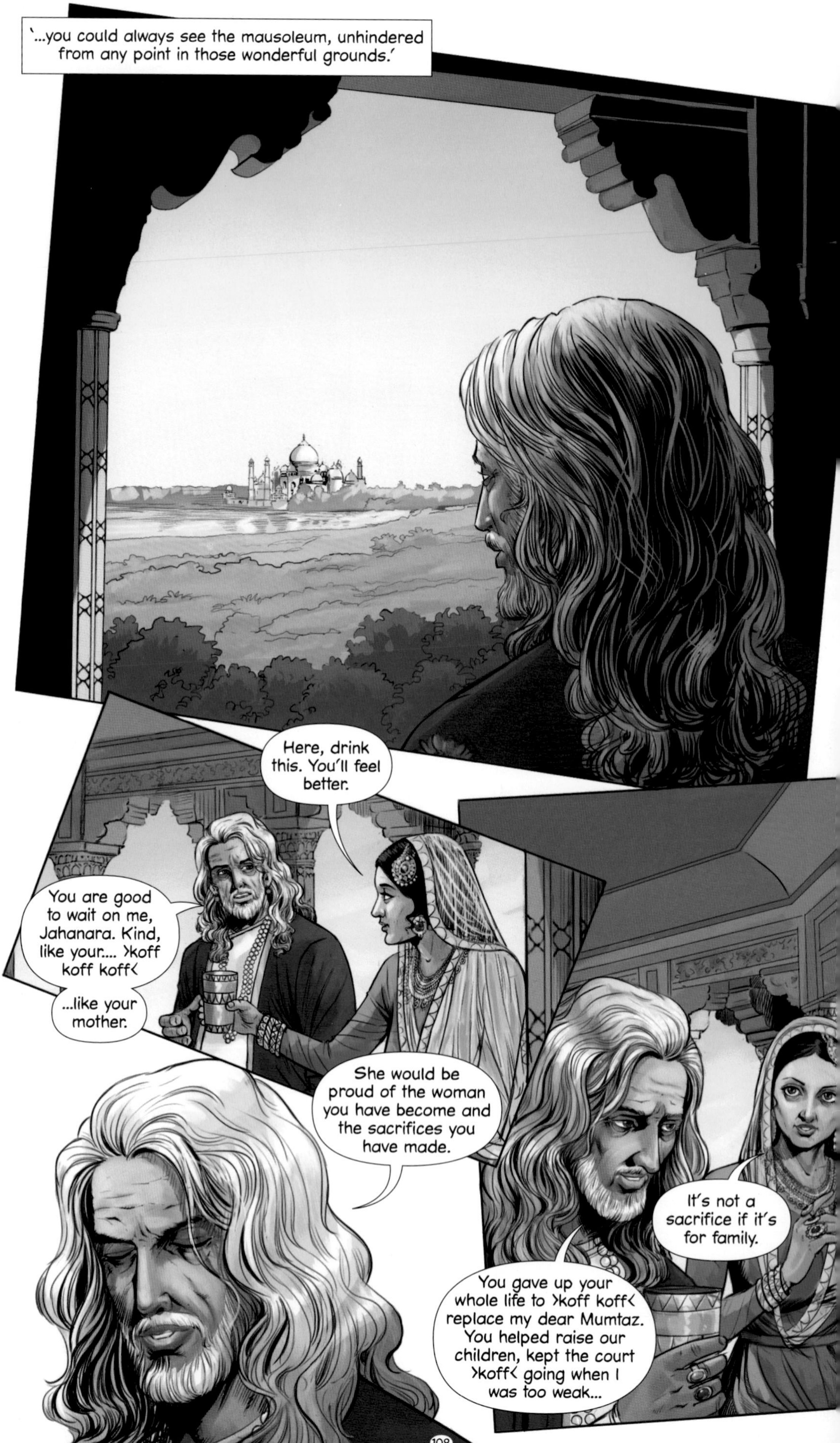
'...you could always see the mausoleum, unhindered from any point in those wonderful grounds.'
Here, drink this. You'll feel better.
You are good to wait on me, Jahanara. Kind, like your.... >koff koff koff<
...like your mother.
She would be proud of the woman you have become and the sacrifices you have made.
It's not a sacrifice if it's for family.
You gave up your whole life to >koff koff< replace my dear Mumtaz. You helped raise our children, kept the court >koff< going when I was too weak...

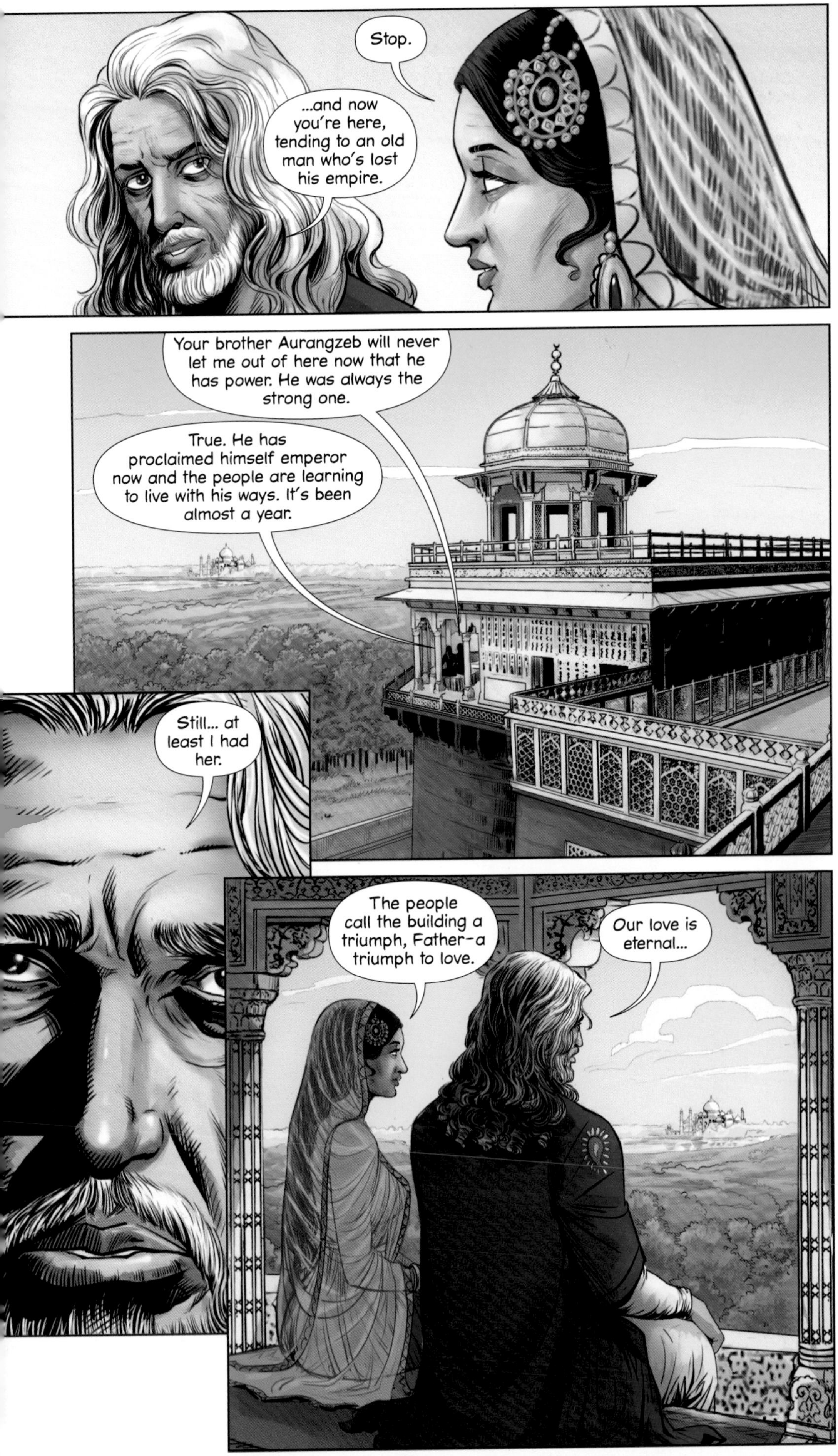
Stop.
...and now you're here, tending to an old man who's lost his empire.
Your brother Aurangzeb will never let me out of here now that he has power. He was always the strong one.
True. He has proclaimed himself emperor now and the people are learning to live with his ways. It's been almost a year.
Still... at least I had her.
The people call the building a triumph, Father–a triumph to love.
Our love is eternal...

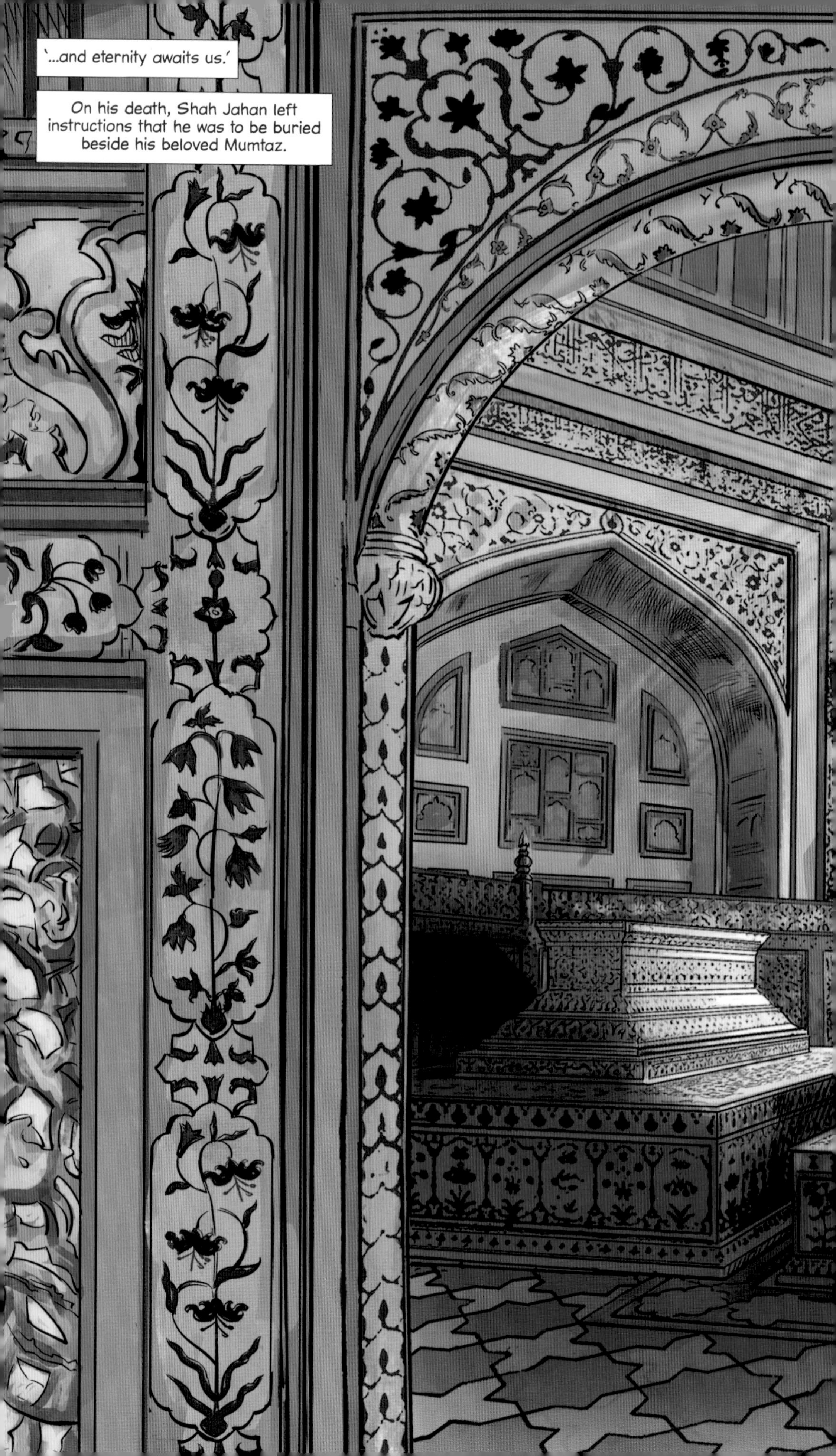
'...and eternity awaits us.'
On his death, Shah Jahan left instructions that he was to be buried beside his beloved Mumtaz.

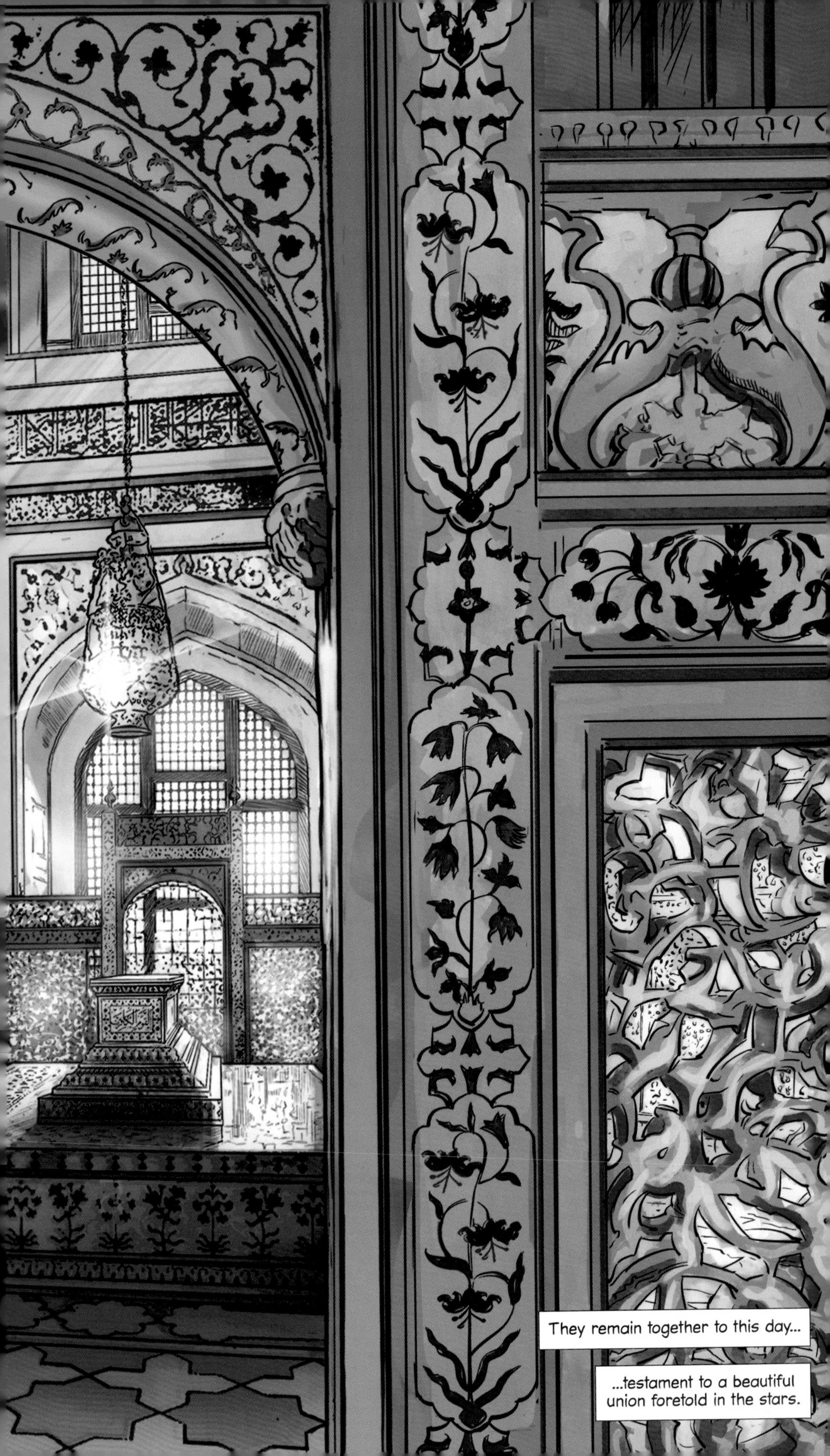
They remain together to this day...
...testament to a beautiful union foretold in the stars.

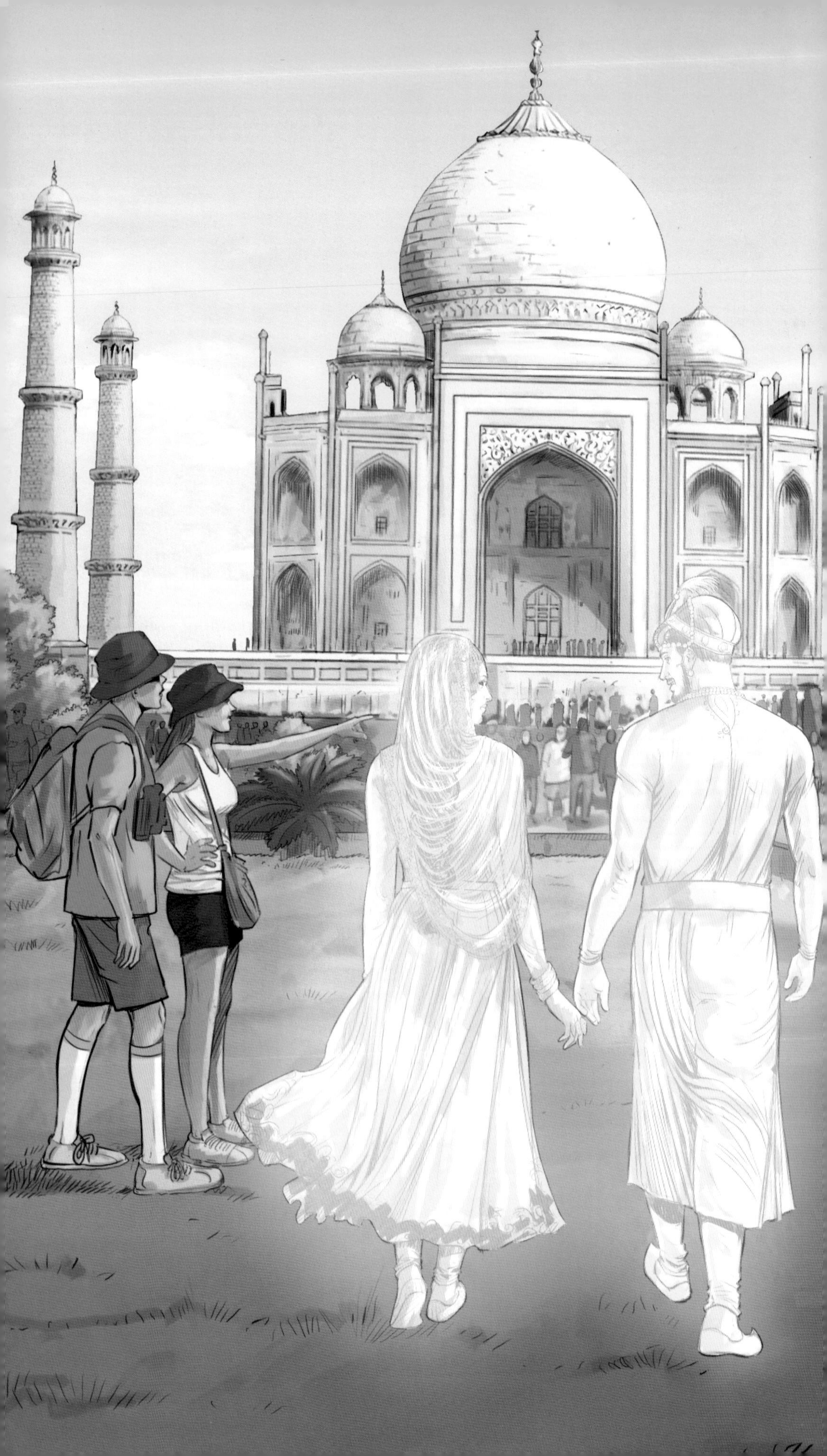

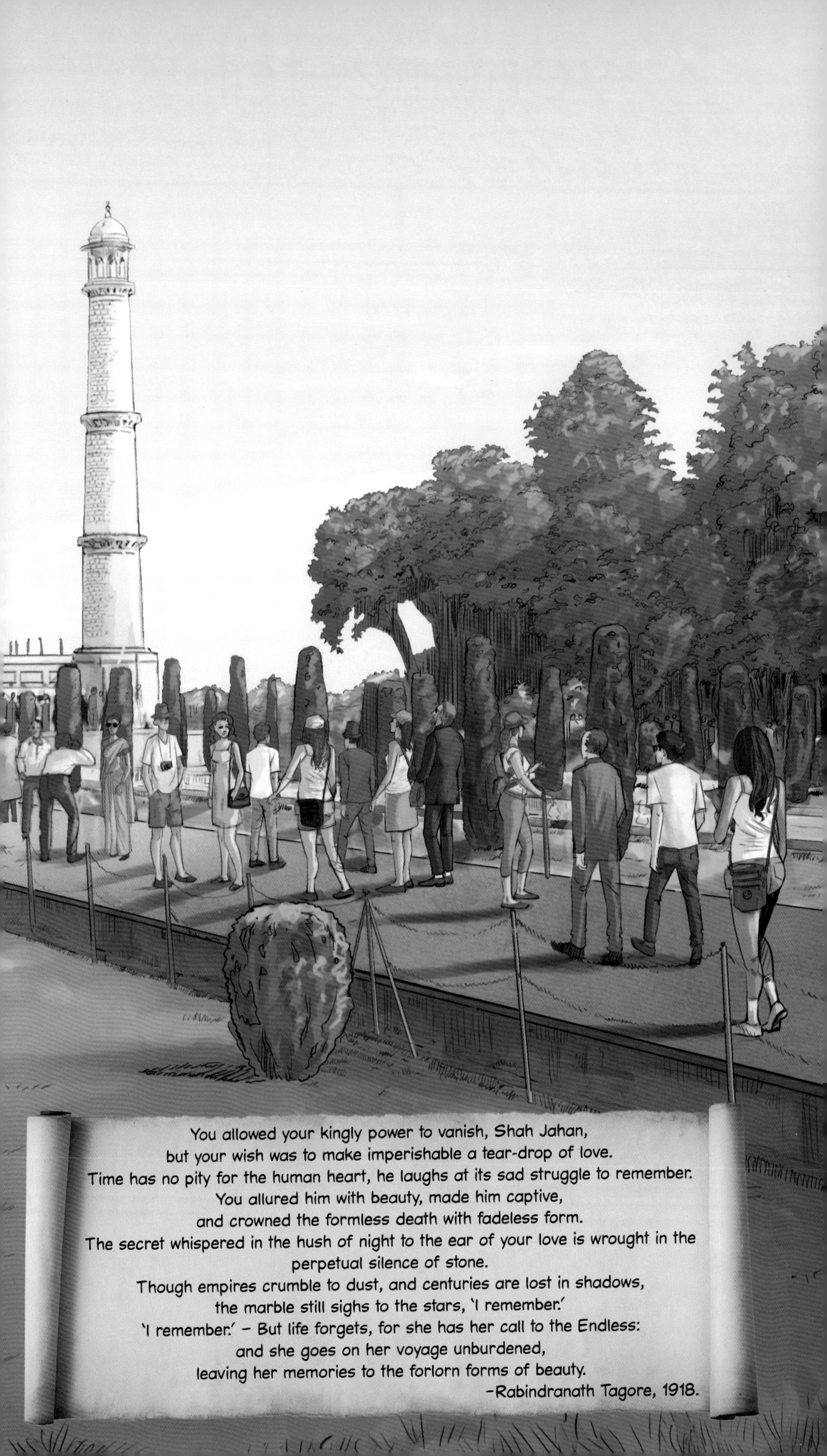
You allowed your kingly power to vanish, Shah Jahan,
but your wish was to make imperishable a tear-drop of love.
Time has no pity for the human heart, he laughs at its sad struggle to remember.
You allured him with beauty, made him captive,
and crowned the formless death with fadeless form.
The secret whispered in the hush of night to the ear of your love is wrought in the
perpetual silence of stone.
Though empires crumble to dust, and centuries are lost in shadows,
the marble still sighs to the stars, 'I remember.'
'I remember.' – But life forgets, for she has her call to the Endless:
and she goes on her voyage unburdened,
leaving her memories to the forlorn forms of beauty.
–Rabindranath Tagore, 1918.

Monumental Matters

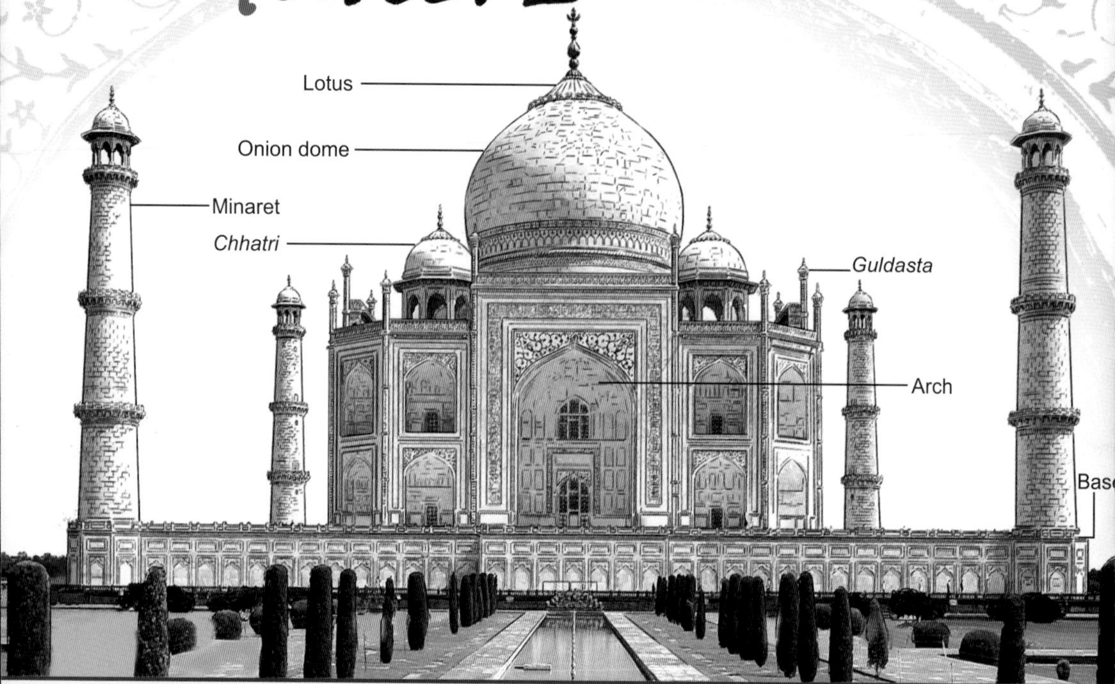

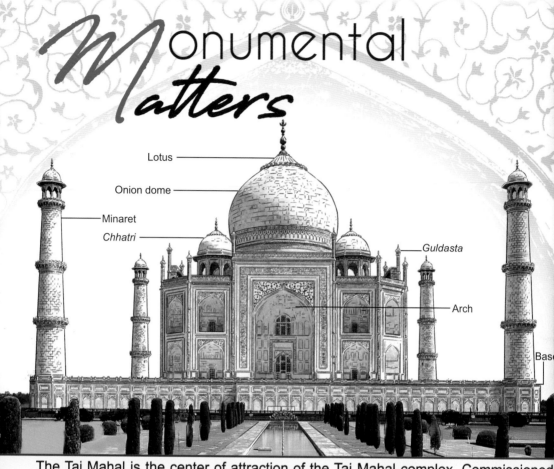

Lotus
Onion dome
Minaret
Chhatri
Guldasta
Arch
Bas

The Taj Mahal is the center of attraction of the Taj Mahal complex. Commissioned in 1632 and completed in 1643, it is the finest example of Indo-Islamic Mughal architecture, and is today a UNESCO protected monument. It is built with white marble situated on a square base and combines elements of Hindu and Persian design. It is topped by a massive onion dome almost 60 meters tall, and four smaller domes in the corners. The smaller domes form the top of four octagonal canopies or *chhatris* and are covered by inverted lotuses. The dome is also surrounded by ornamental spires known as *guldastas*. On each corner of the base of the mausoleum are four minarets, 40 meters tall.

The mausoleum is flanked by two red sandstone buildings identical in design. The one on the west is a mosque while the eastern building may have been used as a guesthouse.

The Taj Mahal is situated at the riverfront edge of a Mughal garden. The Mughals were instrumental in introducing the *charbagh* (four gardens) design that is based on the concept of the four Gardens of Paradise mentioned in the Quran.

Visiting the Taj Mahal

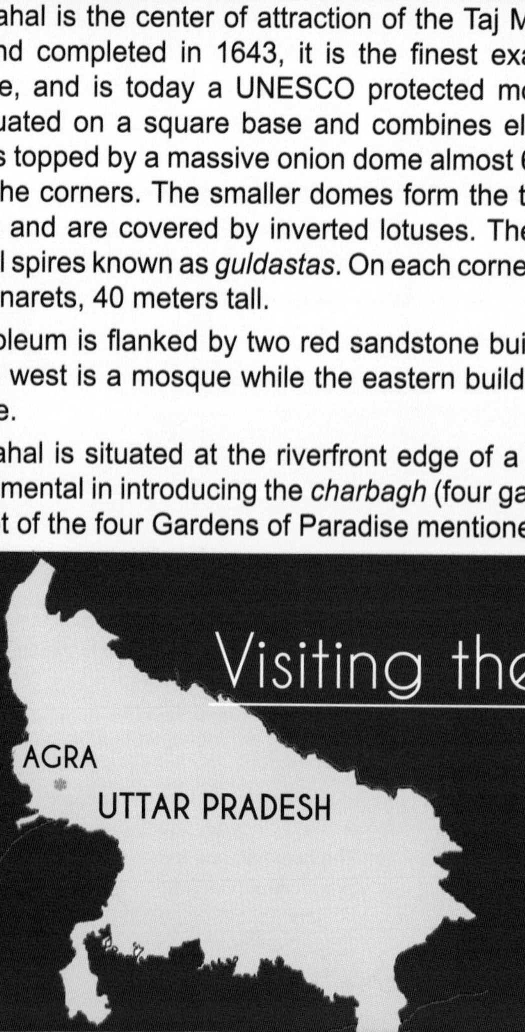

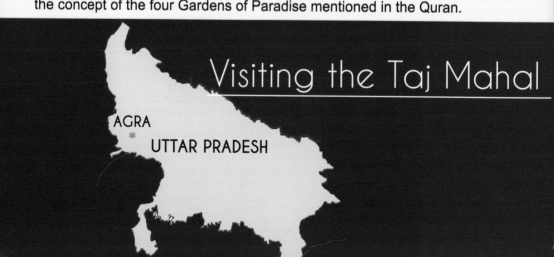

AGRA
UTTAR PRADESH

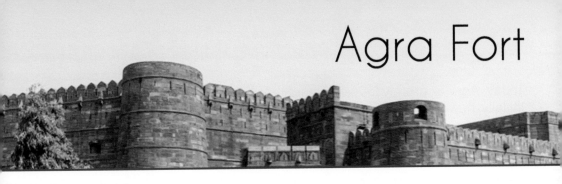

Agra Fort

The Taj Mahal is situated about three kilometers from the Red Fort in Agra. The Agra Fort used to be the principal seat of the Mughal emperors till Shah Jahan moved the capital to Shah Jahanabad (Delhi) in 1648. Agra used to be the capital of the Lodi dynasty that ruled northern India prior to the Mughals. When Babur became the first Mughal emperor by defeating Sultan Ibrahim Lodi in the First Battle of Panipat in 1526, he took over the capital of Agra. It was, however, during the third Mughal Emperor Akbar's reign that extensive constructions were made, as he got the entire fort remodelled with a red sandstone coating. Further changes and additions were made during Shah Jahan's reign, especially with new buildings in marble.

The Musamman Burj, where Shah Jahan spent his last days imprisoned by his son Aurangzeb

The palace area of the fort is still intact today and the main buildings are the Diwan-I-Aam, the Jahangiri Mahal, the Khas Mahal, the Macchhi Mahal, and the Moti Masjid. The fort can be accessed through two massive gates, the Delhi Gate, which is closed to the public, and the Amar Singh Gate. The Musamman Burj is an octagonal tower inside the fort that overlooks the Yamuna river and offers a spectacular view of the Taj Mahal. It was here that Shah Jahan spent the last years of his life after he was imprisoned by his son Aurangzeb.

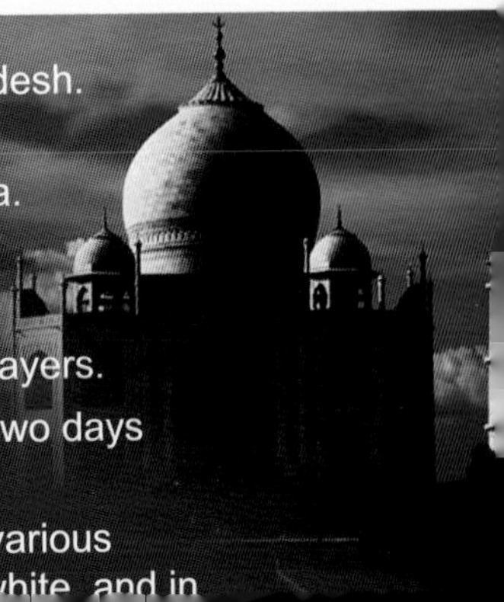

- The Taj Mahal is situated in Agra in the Indian state of Uttar Pradesh. It is about 200 km from Delhi, the capital of India.
- Agra is well connected by road, rail and air to other parts of India.
- The Taj Mahal is open for viewing from Saturday to Thursday, between sunrise and sunset.
- It is closed on Fridays except to those visiting the mosque for prayers.
- The Taj Mahal can also be visited at night during full moon and two days before and after for a spectacular viewing experience.
- The marble of the Taj Mahal reflects light and looks different at various hours of a day—in morning it appears pink, at noon it appears white, and in

Agra: A Riverfront Paradise

Today, Agra is a crowded, bustling city with the Yamuna river running through it. Initially, however, it was conceived as a riverfront garden city. In Shah Jahan's time, both banks of the Yamuna were lined with sprawling havelis and gardens with their pavillions, *chhatris* and other enclosures. Very little of the riverfront gardens and havelis remain today. One of the best preserved is the garden with the **Tomb of Itmad Ud Daulah**, who was the grandfather of Mumtaz Mahal. Another such garden is the **Mehtab Bagh**, situated right opposite the Taj Mahal across the river. According to legend, Shah Jahan had planned to build a black Taj Mahal there for himself but was unable to do so due to his imprisonment by his son Aurangzeb. Most historians think that the legend of the black Taj Mahal is just a myth with no basis in reality.

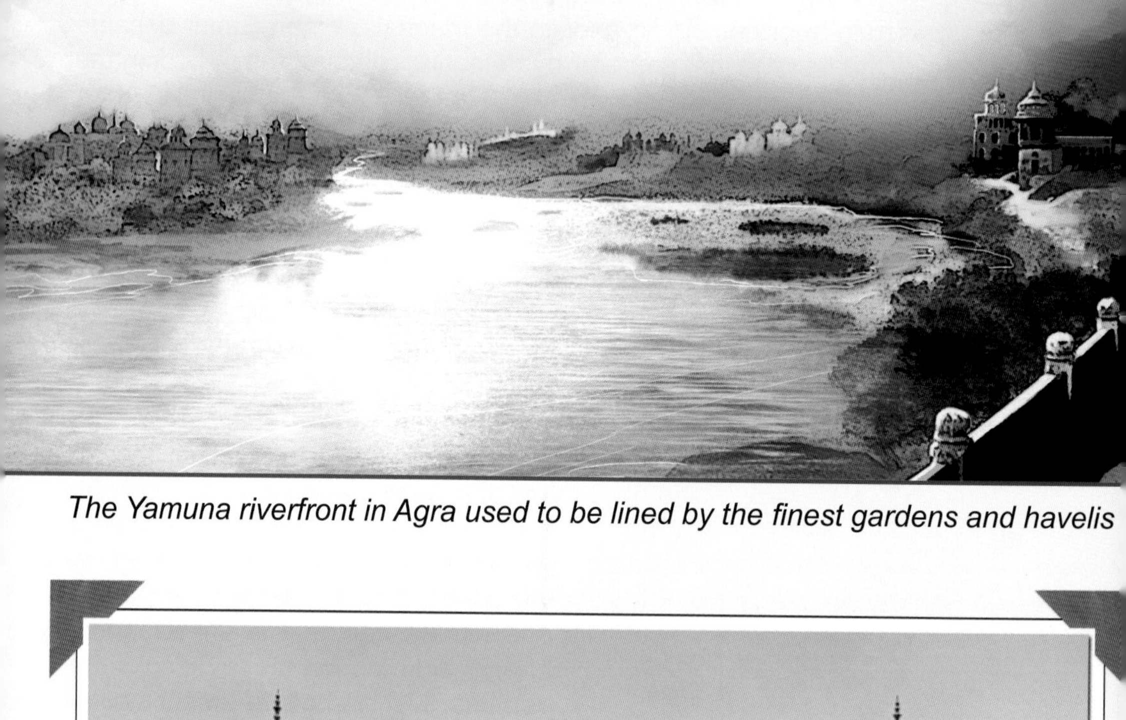

The Yamuna riverfront in Agra used to be lined by the finest gardens and havelis

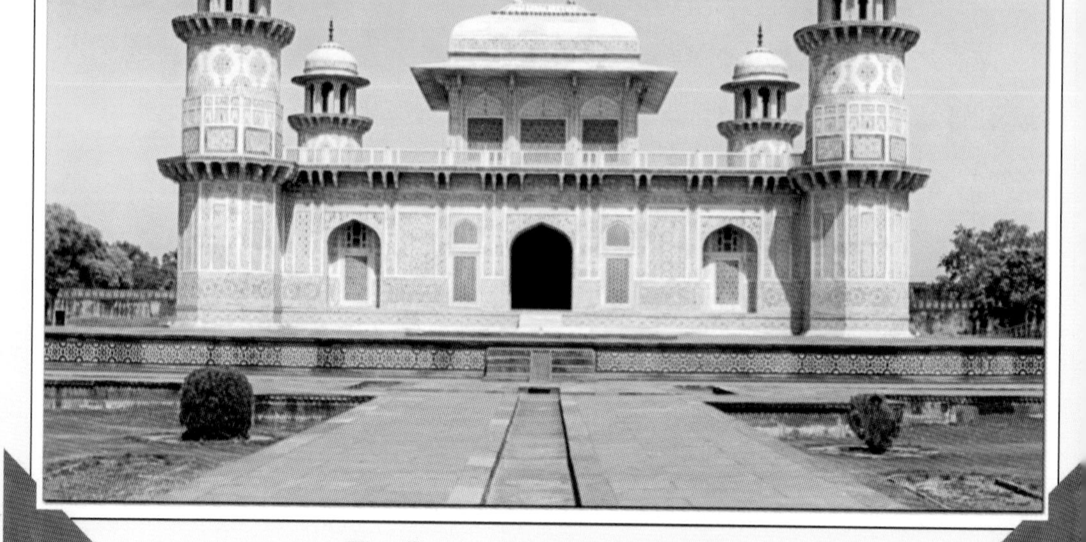

The Tomb of Itmad Ud Daulah

What did Mumtaz Mahal look like?

While many miniature portraits claiming to depict Mumtaz Mahal exist, none of them were painted from life. The most popular such portraits were in fact painted in the eighteenth and nineteenth century by artists influenced by European styles, known as the Company School of painting.

Nineteenth century portraits of Mughal queens, often attributed as depicting Mumtaz Mahal

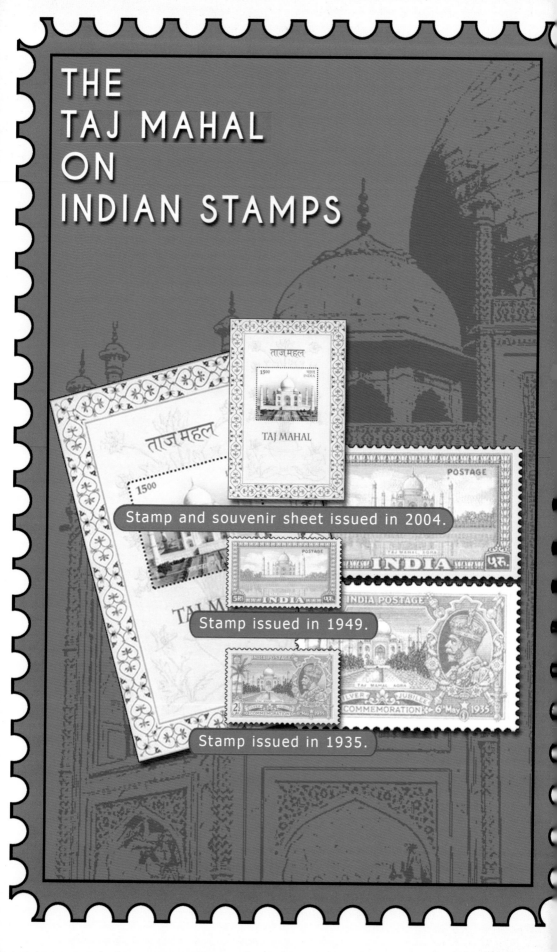

THE TAJ MAHAL ON INDIAN STAMPS

ताजमहल
TAJ MAHAL
POSTAGE
INDIA
INDIA POSTAGE
TAJ MAHAL, AGRA
COMMEMORATION

Stamp and souvenir sheet issued in 2004.

Stamp issued in 1949.

Stamp issued in 1935.

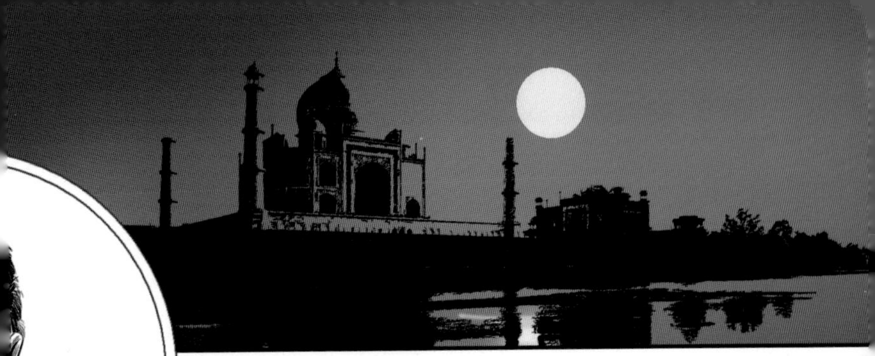

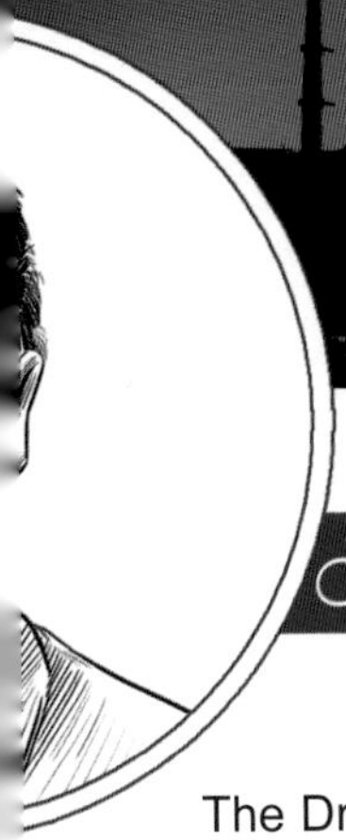

About the Author

The Dragon Award winner 2018 for Best Graphic Novel, Rik Hoskin is a *New York Times* bestselling graphic novelist who has written for various popular series including *Star Wars*, *Superman*, *Doctor Who*, *Shrek* and *Brandon Sanderson's White Sand*. He helped develop and wrote a successful *Spider-Man* series aimed at young readers. He has also written animated stories for BBC Television, and almost thirty novels, many of them under the pen-name James Axler. He has previously written *Karna: Victory in Death* for Campfire.

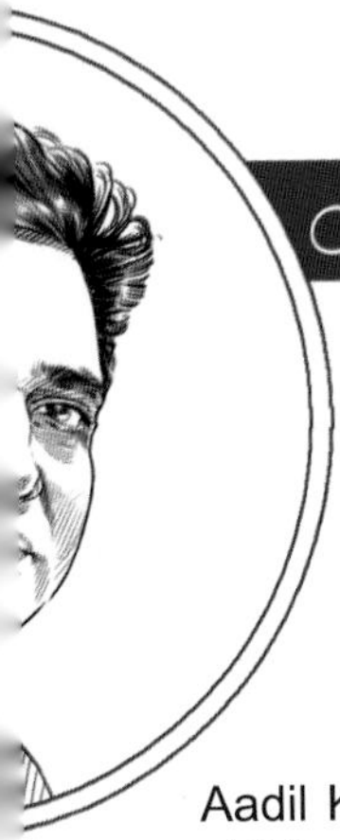

About the Artist

Aadil Khan has been interested in art ever since he was a child, and has a Masters degree in Drawing and Painting from Jiwaji University. Growing up reading comics, he considers Jim Lee, Frank Frazetta and David Finch as his major influences. His clean and dynamic line art and composition liven up the pages of the books that he works on.

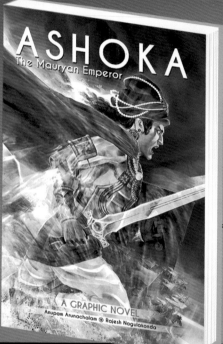

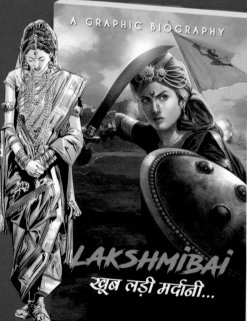